THE GREAT FEAST OF LANGUAGE

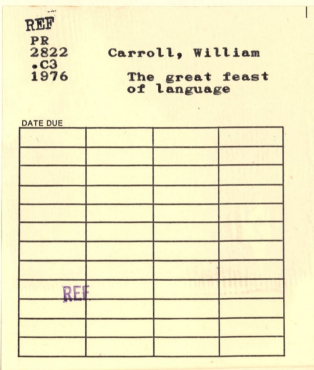

THE
GREAT FEAST
of Language
in *Love's Labour's*
Lost

By

William C. Carroll

PRINCETON UNIVERSITY
PRESS, PRINCETON

Pef
PR
2822
·C 3
1976
Cap. 1

FOR

David Young

Acknowledgments

To acknowledge such pleasant debts as I have incurred is more a privilege than a duty. Richard Ness early interested me in literature, directing my studies with considerable skill and near-heroic patience. Robert Pierce first illuminated many of the strange new worlds of the Renaissance in a course on Milton.

Alvin B. Kernan directed this study as a dissertation at Yale. He proved to be a firm but understanding reader, setting me right when I had gone astray at an early stage. My wife, Carol, provided the sympathy and good sense which kept me and this project going when both needed a lift.

Two long-time friends and colleagues, George Park and Garrett Stewart, read the manuscript in its final stages and gave generously of their best advice and sharpest wit. I have profited greatly over the years simply by reading their own elegant prose, but I am especially grateful for the specific suggestions they made when I was revising. Whatever clarity exists in the book is undoubtedly due to them. A grant-in-aid from the Graduate School of Boston University helped with the preparation of the manuscript by enabling me to enlist the expert typing services of Mrs. E. P. Goodwin.

I owe my greatest debt to David Young, my teacher, colleague, and friend. He read this study in its earliest stages and made valuable suggestions toward revision. More generally, his own books have always been a model of excellence for me. Yet his unfailing sympathy and firm friendship have had the most profound impact on me. Most friendship is feigning, as Amiens says, but not in this case.

Contents

Note on Documentation

All quotations from *Love's Labour's Lost,* unless otherwise noted, are from the New Arden edition, edited by Richard David (London: Methuen, 1956, Fifth Edition), abbreviated in the text as *Arden.* I have followed David's abbreviations for speech-ascriptions. Other works of Shakespeare are quoted from *The Complete Pelican Shakespeare,* ed. Alfred Harbage (Baltimore: Penguin, 1969). Quotations from other Renaissance sources have, when appropriate, been silently modernized.

The editions of works cited in the text, and abbreviations used in citing, are given below.

1. *Var.*: for *A New Variorum Edition of Shakespeare: Love's Labour's Lost,* ed. H. H. Furness (New York: Dover reprint, 1964). First published 1904.

2. *Cam.*: for *Love's Labour's Lost,* ed. John Dover Wilson (Cambridge: Cambridge Univ. Press, 1969). New Cambridge Edition. First published, 1923; Second Edition, 1962.

3. *OED*: for *Oxford English Dictionary.*

4. *Arte*: for George Puttenham, *The Arte of English Poesie,* ed. Gladys D. Willcock and Alice Walker (Cambridge: Cambridge Univ. Press, 1936).

5. Bacon: for Francis Bacon, *Works,* ed. James Spedding, Robert Ellis, Douglas Heath (London: Longmans, 1857–74).

6. Baldwin: for T. W. Baldwin, *William Shakspere's Small Latine & Lesse Greeke* (Urbana, Ill.: Univ. of Illinois Press, 1944).

7. Barber: for C. L. Barber, *Shakespeare's Festive Comedy* (Princeton: Princeton Univ. Press, 1959).

8. Barish: for Jonas Barish, *Ben Jonson and the Language of Prose Comedy* (Cambridge, Mass.: Harvard Univ. Press, 1960).

9. Berry: for Ralph Berry, "The Words of Mercury," *ShS 22* (1969), 69–77.

10. Burton: for Robert Burton, *The Anatomy of Melancholy*, ed. Floyd Dell and Paul Jordan-Smith (New York: Tudor Publishing Co., 1927).

11. Curtius: for Ernst Curtius, *European Literature and The Latin Middle Ages* (New York: Pantheon Books, 1953).

12. Greene: for Robert Greene, *The Life and Complete Works in Prose and Verse of Robert Greene*, ed A. B. Grosart (London: 1881–86).

13. Hoskins: for John Hoskins, *Directions for Speech and Style*, ed. Hoyt H. Hudson (Princeton: Princeton Univ. Press, 1935).

14. Jonson: for Ben Jonson, *Works*, ed. C. H. Herford and Percy Simpson (Oxford: Clarendon Press, 1925–47)

15. Nashe: for Thomas Nashe, *Works*, ed. R. B. McKerrow, rev. F. P. Wilson (Oxford: Basil Blackwell, 1958).

16. Smith: for G. Gregory Smith, ed., *Elizabethan Critical Essays* (Oxford: Oxford Univ. Press, 1904).

THE GREAT FEAST OF LANGUAGE

.

Moth. They have been at a great feast of languages, and stolen the scraps.

Costard. O, they have lived long on the alms-basket of words. I marvel thy master hath not eaten thee for a word; for thou art not so long by the head as *honorificabilitudinitatibus*: thou art easier swallowed than a flapdragon.

Moth. Peace! the peal begins.

(V.i.37–44)

Introduction

Words, words, words. Hamlet's bored reply to Polonius can serve as the artist's perennial rebuke to the critic. Critics, in turn, have leveled the same accusation against *Love's Labour's Lost*, all too often finding it Shakespeare's windiest play. I disagree with that verdict, but in doing so I run the risk of adding more words to the critical debate. Moreover, there exists so great a potential for unintended but self-revealing irony in writing about *Love's Labour's Lost* that one may hesitate even to begin. The imitative fallacy has often proved fatal to critics of the play, but sharing the same profession is still no excuse for sounding like Holofernes. Yet another danger in considering a play as intricate as this one is the tendency to let trivia and background material expand unreasonably. Considering too curiously is the critic's occupational hazard, but it seems particularly tempting, and important to guard against, when analyzing this play.

It is no longer news when a full-length book on a single Shakespearean play appears, and there are already several lengthy studies of *Love's Labour's Lost*.[1] Why, then, another? Because few of the published works have much to do with the play itself. They concern the Earl of Oxford, Lord Strange, John Florio, Gabriel Harvey, Sir Walter Ralegh, the history of the Nine Worthies, contemporary French history, possible early revisions of the play, and the elusive identity of the "Love Labours Wonne" mentioned by Francis Meres in 1598 (Smith, II, 318). But there has been no extended close reading of this difficult play, no full interpretation, to my mind, of the play's language. I believe that such a critical reading is worthwhile to the extent that the play itself examines what is "worthy" in life, love, and art.

Shakespeare's early plays share a liability in their earliness. "Maturity" is not generally allowed to Shakespeare until some indefinite time around *A Midsummer Night's Dream*, and sometimes not even then. To call *Love's Labour's Lost* "apprentice" work, as so many have done, is the critical kiss of death. It and the other early plays deserve to be measured on their own terms. Apprentice he may have been, but the best evidence indicates that Shakespeare was about thirty years old and an experienced playwright when he wrote this play, hardly an untutored youth warbling woodnotes wild. A number of current interpretations of the play, it would appear, derive from this preconception of Shakespeare—as the naive bard of Nature—which dates back to the traditional contrast with Jonson's Art. Shakespeare all too often becomes the simple clown whose "excellencies came and were not sought; / His words like casual atoms made a thought." Like Christopher Sly of *The Taming of the Shrew*, "the drunken tinker in his play, / [Shakespeare] grew a prince and never knew which way. / He did not know what trope or figure meant." This is the simpleton whose art was formed in a perfect vacuum: "Those then that tax his learning are to blame; / He knew the thing, but did not know the name."[2] But Sly was quite incapable of the sophisticated manipulations of "name," of "trope" and "figure," of illusion and reality, which we will find in *Love's Labour's Lost*. I hasten to add that modern criticism of this play has been a good deal more sophisticated and generous than the attitude behind the lines I have just quoted. But simplifications about Shakespeare have a way of turning into oversimplified views of his plays, and it has happened to *Love's Labour's Lost*, in particular, more than once. A. C. Hamilton, on the other hand, has suggested a more useful approach to the early Shakespeare: "Presumably, he was incapable of writing *Lear* in 1590; yet the apparent fact is that he did not try. He seems not to have attempted what he could not succeed in doing. It appears worthwhile, then, to explore the hypothesis that each of the early works is perfect in its kind. I see the early Shakespeare as a sophisticated literary craftsman."[3] "Sophisticated" is the key word here, and it is from a similar assumption that this study proceeds.

4

Love's Labour's Lost has suffered at the hands of its friends as much as of its enemies. The play has always been the darling of the Shakespearean lunatic fringe. Its evident complexities and suggestions of topicality have given carte blanche to a bizarre range of speculation. Most of it centers on the two embassies from France received by the King of Navarre.[4] The first took place in 1578, when the Princess of France, Marguerite de Valois, visited Navarre; the second, in 1586, when Queen Catherine herself arrived. The play is said to have had its nominal source in one or possibly both of these visits, though the play uses little beyond the names of some characters and the fact of the embassy itself. From this modest beginning, elaborate theories, of sometimes greater but more often lesser probability, have been constructed. Given a place to stand, some scholars, like Archimedes, have offered to move the earth. Even Costard's triumphant *"honorificabilitudinitatibus"* has been filched by the Baconians as an anagrammatic windfall. Moreover, a peculiar fascination with topical allegory of all sorts is especially associated with *Love's Labour's Lost.*[5] The wonder, to rephrase Dr. Johnson in another context, is not that such things are done so poorly, but that they are done at all. The durability of the play, however, and its acceptance by audiences who have never heard of John Florio or Gabriel Harvey, testify to sufficient virtues apart from its putative topical satire. It is chiefly with these virtues that this study will be concerned, though I have also made special efforts to trace the topical *literary* allusions related to the play's central debate.

Responsible critics have disagreed often enough about the value of the play. There is a rare first-hand account by Robert Tofte of a performance he attended, published in 1598, but he was too concerned with himself and his uncooperative mistress to record his opinions in any detail (*Var.*, pp. 329–30). We know from the title page of the 1598 Quarto that *Love's Labour's Lost* was performed for Queen Elizabeth "this last Christmas," that is, probably in 1597, and from the title page of the 1631 Quarto that it was acted both "at the Blacke-Friers and the Globe." It was revived for a second royal performance in 1604 for Queen Anne, and reportedly performed at Southampton's. At that time it was described by Burbage, according to Cope, as "an olde one . . . which for wytt & mirthe he says will please her excedingly."[6] From this royal high point, however, the play's reputation began a three-century plunge from which it has only in the last thirty years recovered. The Addisonian disparagement of the pun hastened the decline considerably. Dr. Johnson objected to the play partly on moral grounds, arguing that, though *Love's Labour's Lost* had brilliant flashes in it, as a whole it would not do: "it must be confessed that there are many passages mean, childish, and vulgar; and some which ought not to have been exhibited, as we are told they were, to a maiden queen."[7] Hazlitt began his remarks by saying, "If we were to part with any of the author's comedies, it should be this." But he went on to acquit almost every character in the play, and eventually relented: "we believe we may let the whole play stand as it is" (*Var.*, p. 357). Coleridge, who believed it to be Shakespeare's first play, thought fairly well of it: "Yet if this juvenile drama had been the only one extant of our Shakespeare, and we possessed the tradition only of his riper works, or accounts from writers who had not even mentioned the *Love's Labour's Lost*, how many of Shakespeare's characteristic features might we not discover, tho' as in a portrait taken of him in his boyhood."[8] But Coleridge, like so many others, values the play mostly because of its premonitions of later, "better" works. Yet it is much more, as we shall see, than a dress rehearsal for *Much Ado About Nothing*.

Critics have generally found fault with one of two things in *Love's Labour's Lost*. The first of these is usually its complex language, to which my initial chapter is devoted; the style is felt to be too clever or too convoluted, the linguistic satirist engulfed in and betrayed by his own satire. The second complaint is that the plot of the play is too thin, that Shakespeare, like Armado, "draweth out the thread of his verbosity finer than the staple of his argument." With vary-

6

ing degrees of sophistication, this accusation has been frequently repeated. Rupert Taylor, for example, noted that
the play "really should not be considered a play in the same
sense in which, say Merchant of Venice is to be considered
a play, with a well-connected plot and action. . . . It is really
an Elizabethan equivalent of the modern revue."[9] H. B.
Charlton used the same phrase in a harsher estimate of the
play: it is "more like a modern revue, or a musical comedy
without music, than a play. It is deficient in plot and in char-
acterisation. There is little story in it. Its situations do not
present successive incidents in an ordered plot."[10] But James
L. Calderwood, realizing that the two traditional complaints
are related, looks at the same phenomenon from a far more
interesting and useful point of view: "The evolution of action and plot is reduced to a series of verbal events . . . the
play seems almost an experiment in seeing how well language, spun into intricate, ornate, but static patterns, can
substitute for the kinetic thrust of action in drama."[11]

A number of readers, then, have noted the apparent lack
of a well-ordered plot—the device of the disputed debt is
not, in their eyes, much of an impetus, and Shakespeare does
little with it. All of which is true. Unfortunately, this descriptive statement is usually also a sub rosa prescriptive
statement, and *Love's Labour's Lost* is, once again, condemned for failing to be what it does not even try to be.
This sort of criticism, by readers peering out through exclusively neo-Aristotelian glasses, has belittled rather than
illuminated the play. What is most interesting about *Love's
Labour's Lost*, as Calderwood notes, is precisely that Shakespeare appears to be trying something new.

Yet *Love's Labour's Lost*, to be sure, has not been utterly
friendless. Although Granville-Barker had many reserva-
tions about the play, he did write a preface to it, where he
perceptively noted that "it asks for style in the acting. The
whole play, first and last, demands style."[12] Geoffrey Bullough called it "an intellectual fantasy, the nearest to a play
of ideas that Shakespeare ever wrote, except perhaps *Troilus
and Cressida*."[13] Recent critics, especially since a fine article

on the play by Bobbyann Roesen in 1953,[14] have been more generous and hence more helpful, with C. L. Barber's chapter still the brilliant high point. Traces of the old disdain are still evident, but seen much less frequently now.

In the past, the play was ordinarily subjected to either a microscopic or a telescopic view. Minute inspections of the play's supposed allusions or textual cruces, valuable in themselves, have made no pretense of dealing with the play as a whole. And evolutionary studies of Shakespeare's comedies, running at the rate of one chapter per play, have of necessity subordinated the particularity and subtle nuances of the play to the study of common patterns. It seems to me that a more eclectic and less doctrinaire approach from a kind of middle distance is necessary, a close reading of the entire play with an eye toward the larger patterns developed. The life of *Love's Labour's Lost* centers, beyond all else, in its language, in crackling exchanges of wit and in mindstretching wordplay that must be heard to be believed. To appreciate the play fully, such passages must be experienced and understood in all their energy and, at times, their excess. Shakespeare lavishes his talent here, in even the briefest exchanges, with an enormous prodigality which would have seemed profligate and spendthrift in any other writer. But the well is obviously inexhaustible. In this play, perhaps more than in any other play by Shakespeare, the detail is everything. I have therefore made a special effort to explicate and, I hope, to reanimate as many as possible of the dozens of moments of linguistic genius in *Love's Labour's Lost*.

I believe this play can profitably be read as a debate on the right uses of rhetoric, poetry, and the imagination; extraordinarily self-conscious, the play ultimately exemplifies and embodies, in the final songs, what has only been discussed before. The term "debate" is justified by Shakespeare's use of the medieval *conflictus* between Spring and Winter at the end, but it defines a principle of structure in the play as well. The most typical method of structuring a speech or a scene is through a juxtaposition of opposites, a kind of literary counterpoint, usually in the form of obvious dualisms such as Spring and Winter or Nature and Art. A whole series of such debates take place throughout the play. A related but more complex structural device, however, is the recurring use of "concentric circles of awareness,"[15] seen most clearly in the sonnet-reading scene (IV.iii). There may be three, four, even five different "rings" of character awareness on the stage simultaneously, each more inclusive than the last. The levels modify one another, the complex mixture producing its own unvoiced but felt compromise. We might take this image of concentric circles as yet another controlling metaphor of structure. Like the repeated assertion of antinomies, it grows from the same deep-seated impulse in Shakespeare toward multiplicity—a refusal *not* to look at the other side of the coin, a need, for whatever reason, to see things in their fullest context. Shakespeare seemed constitutionally unable to narrow himself.

In my view, *Love's Labour's Lost* has been oversimplified even by its recent critics, who tend to be dogmatic where Shakespeare is tentative and ambivalent. The standard reading of the play today is that it finally illustrates the rejection of Art for Life, or Nature. I will try to correct this onesided view by leaning the other way: by beginning with the assumption that the play is "sophisticated," that it is largely exploratory, and that it offers multiple viewpoints in order to set them in conflict and create debates. Its strategy is to encourage "dialogue," in all the connotations of that term, and its goal, beyond sheer entertainment, is to reject, not Art, but bad art—something rather different. Ultimately, I think, the various prototypes of style presented and qualified in the course of the play are set aside. Instead, we are given as models of reconciliation and imaginative incarnation the final songs, themselves the emblem of debate.

Each of the six chapters focuses closely on a separate aspect of the play, and at the same time attempts to follow the debate about poetry and the use of imagination which the play conducts. Since *Love's Labour's Lost* is largely concerned with *style* in all its aspects, the first three chapters will examine three kinds of style: prose, theatrical, and then poetic. Chapter One concentrates on the language and prose styles in the play, particularly on that of the six low characters who form a small *commedia dell'arte* troupe. The next chapter discusses the different theatrical styles exemplified in the play, especially in three scenes—the sonnet-reading scene (IV.iii), the Masque of Muscovites (V.ii), and the Pageant of the Nine Worthies (V.ii)—which are plays-within-the-play, metaphors for the play as a whole. The device of concentric circles will be most evident here, where the play is most self-conscious about its own aesthetic principles. The several explicit examples of "poetry," from the archaic style of Armado's bombast to the fashionable fluff of the lords' love sonnets, are the subject of the third chapter.

The fourth and fifth chapters stand further back from the play, considering the larger themes that unify it—transformation, and the paradox of Living Art. I begin the fourth chapter with a look at some of the more spectacularly warped imaginations among the characters, those responsible for the extremes of style previously analyzed. The regnant power in the play is that of transformation, ranging from fantasy and delusion to the impressive verbal creations of Berowne at his best. My fifth chapter examines the structural composition of the play as a whole, in order to confront the traditional Art-Nature dualism. The largest and most important of the many "debates" in the play, its resolution points the way to the final songs.

The sixth chapter concludes with those songs—the dialogue between Spring and Winter. I see them not only as the finest poetry in the play, but as an example of the dialectical blend of Art and Nature which is debated only theoretically elsewhere. They are the ideal toward which the play's dialectic has all along been moving. The debate on the right uses of poetry and the imagination cannot be resolved by logic or theory, just as there cannot be a clear-cut victor in the *conflictus* between Spring and Winter. Rather, the formal debate becomes both exemplum and resolution, and serves as conclusive evidence of Shakespeare's sophistication and craft, even at this fairly early stage of his career.[16]

CHAPTER ONE

The Great Feast

The first thing one notices about *Love's Labour's Lost* is its intense preoccupation with language. Its "great feast" ranges from Dull's spare plate to the verbal gluttony and subsequent indigestion of Armado and Holofernes. In *Much Ado About Nothing*, Benedick tells us that Claudio, in love, has "turned orthography; his words are a very fantastical banquet—just so many strange dishes" (II.iii.20–2). But Claudio's excesses pale before the fantastic appetites indulged by the characters of *Love's Labour's Lost*, many of whom seem to have come from another planet: "A' speaks not like a man of God's making" (V.ii.522) the astounded Princess says of Armado.

It is this cornucopia of excess which most marks the tone and spirit of the play. Yet with all the exotic spices and elaborate side dishes, we may lose sight of the main course of this feast. For *Love's Labour's Lost* is not just a play filled with languages, another comic reminder of the Babylonic dispersal of tongues. It is, rather, a play radically concerned with the very nature of language—with its history, its potential, its proper use by the imagination. *Love's Labour's Lost* offers in its characters a wide range of attitudes toward the power of language, from a skeptical positivism to an almost primitive belief in the inner life of words. It is in the latter that we shall first find traces of the animating force of the imagination, among those for whom the power of names is still semi-magical. For the giving of names, as Emerson argued in his essay "The Poet," is the initial poetic act. I have therefore divided this chapter into two sections: first, a general consideration of the latent energy of words, and then a close look at the style and language of the low characters.

Words and Things: Adam's Legacy

The magical energy of language revealed itself to the Renaissance most clearly in the power of names. The prevailing linguistic theory held that there is an inherent rightness in names, that names are not arbitrary signs but are in some sense themselves the essence of what is named. The name does not symbolically represent the thing named—it *is* the thing. Such a belief is characteristic of what Ernst Cassirer has called "mythic" or "metaphorical thinking," a habit of mind in which "every word is immediately transformed into a concrete mythical figure, a god or a daemon."[1] It may seem a giant step from this to the sophistication of *Love's Labour's Lost*, but Shakespeare's contemporaries, at least, were fully conversant with the theory, and they widely acknowledged its truth.

Two main sources for this belief converged in the Renaissance. The first was Plato's *Cratylus*, in which Cratylus argues that "the power which gave the first names to things is more than human, and therefore the names must necessarily be correct."[2] That Socrates could not fully agree with this theory, and that the dialogue ends inconclusively, are facts that were readily forgotten. What endured was the mysterious power of the "name-maker." But, as Richard Mulcaster argued in his *Elementarie* (1582), "we need not to prove by *Platoes Cratylus*, or *Aristotles* proposition as by best authorities . . . that words be voluntarie, and appointed upon cause, seeing we have better warrant."[3] That better warrant, the second and more important source, derives from Genesis 2:19–20, where God brought the animals before Adam "to see what he would call them: and whatsoever Adam called every living creature, that was the name thereof." Adam is thus the supreme name-maker among men, the first poet.

Knowing the right name confers special powers on the namer. Mulcaster, introducing his own table of words, argues that "God himself, who brought the creatures, which he had made, unto that first man, whom he had also made, that he might name them, according to their properties, doth planelie declare by his so doing, what a cunning thing it is to give right names, and how necessarie it is, to know their forces, which be allredie given, bycause the word being knowen, which implyeth the propertie the thing is half known, whose propertie is emplyed."[4] Mulcaster goes only so far as to claim that the name alone makes a thing "half known"; but other writers went much further. Joshua Sylvester, in his translation of Du Bartas's *La Semaine* (1592-9), waxed ecstatic over the "language all men understood," the "speech / Of God himself: th' old sacred *Idiom* rich, / Rich perfect language, where's no point, nor signe, / But hides some rare deep mystery divine." In those days, "idel, casuall names" were not given to men, "But such as (rich in sense) before the event, / Markt in their lives some speciall accident."[5] Names were therefore prophetic, repositories of the highest knowledge. In his *Dialogues on Rhetoric* (1562), Patrizi would go so far as to argue that knowing the right words once produced "wonders and miracles." By knowing the right names, ancient men "could draw the savage beasts, the dreadful forests, and the massive mountains; they brought the trees to bloom and bear fruit; made the grass grow green or wither in the fields; they produced summer and winter according to their wishes and made the sky cloudy and cleared it at will. They checked the courses of swift rivers and drained them dry; made springs and lakes arise and disappear." And so on, until they reportedly "drew the moon down from the sky and arrested the sun."[6] Such knowledge backfires when given to a creature like Caliban, however. Prospero had taught him "how / To name the bigger light, and how the less, / That burn by day and night" (I.ii.334-6), but he rejects it all with a curse:

> You taught me language, and my profit on't
> Is, I know how to curse. The red plague rid you
> For learning me your language!
>
> (*Tmp*, I.ii.363-5)

It would seem at first glance that *Love's Labour's Lost* records only the aftermath of the Tower of Babel, the confusion of tongues, in which "we can but babble," as Sylvester says, and our search for "knowledge whole / Of Nature's secrets, and of th' *Essence* sole" is hopelessly frustrated. "We tire our minde," he continued, seeming to anticipate Holofernes,

> To vary Verbs, and finest words to finde;
> Our letters and our syllables to weigh:
> At Tutor's lips we hang with heads all gray,
> Who teach us yet to read, and give us (raw)
> An *A.B.C.* for great *Justinian's* law.[7]

In the macaronic gabble of the low characters in *Love's Labour's Lost*—an implausible hash of English, French, Greek, Latin, Italian, Spanish, and creative error—we hear little more than the "Babylonish dialect" of Butler's *Hudibras*, "a parti-coloured dress / Of patched and piebald languages."[8] But there are a number of references in *Love's Labour's Lost* which remind us of the inherent link between names and knowledge.

Navarre's plan for a "little academe" calls for strict rules, and he bids his fellows "subscribe your names" (I.i,19) to the oath. Berowne balks, however, and begins to question the ends of study, which Navarre defines as "that to know which else we should not know." When Berowne asks, "Things hid and barr'd, you mean, from common sense?" Navarre affirms the grandeur of his scheme: "Ay, that is study's god-like recompense." The quest for knowledge is therefore to resurrect that "god-like" wisdom we once possessed, to "repair the ruins of our first parents" as Milton said.[9] The aim of knowledge even for Bacon was a "restitution and reinvesting (in great part) of man to the sovereignty and power (for whensoever he shall be able to call the creatures by their true names he shall again command them) which he had in his first state of creation" (Bacon, III, 222). Berowne, however, comically frames the goal of learning in terms of the original Edenic injunction: "I will swear to study so, / To know the thing I am forbid to know." The "god-like" aspirations of the academics will lead to a fall similar to Adam's, from pride; but the forbidden knowledge in *Love's Labour's Lost* turns out to be self-knowledge.

Berowne then goes on to argue that study already "knows that which yet it doth not know." He attempts a *reductio* of Navarre's position in a brilliantly witty speech which centers on multiple meanings of the word "light," concluding that

> Study is like the heaven's glorious sun,
> That will not be deep-search'd with saucy looks;
> Small have continual plodders ever won,
> Save base authority from others' books.
>
> (I.i.84–7)

In the familiar pun of "sun" and "son," Berowne hints at the religious nature of the lords' quest. But he returns us to earth with the "plodders," several of whom we are about to meet. The First Man was a primary Author, but later generations must look to Authority instead, what has been written in the past.

Berowne next invokes astronomy, a popular subject of the day, to introduce the Adamic notion of names:

> These earthly godfathers of heaven's lights,
> That give a name to every fixed star,
> Have no more profit of their shining nights
> Than those that walk and wot not what they are.
> Too much to know is to know nought but fame;
> And every godfather can give a name.
>
> (I.i.88–93)

Berowne speaks for that "common sense" mentioned earlier (ll. 57, 64), for those who are content merely to see the stars. Few subjects were of greater interest to the Elizabethans than the discoveries of the astronomers—what Donne would later call the "new philosophy." Berowne is arguing sophistically here, as his friends' mocking replies make clear, for the astronomers' quest promised the greatest "god-like recompense" of any discipline. To know too much, on the other hand, is crippling, as Holofernes will soon demonstrate. And the rapid influx of new observations and theories must have seemed confusing, "nought but fame" at first. Shakespeare's audience must have sympathized with Berowne's "common sense," but its more alert members might not have dismissed such knowledge so readily as Berowne does.

One clue to the question lies in the phrase "and wot not what they are" (l. 91). The referent of "they" is "heaven's lights," the stars. "Those" who walk enjoy the stars without knowing the right names. But the grammar leads to an ambiguity, for "they" may also refer to "those"—they do not know the stars' names, nor do they know what they themselves are. A lack of self-knowledge may inhibit the use of acquired knowledge. I believe that the ambiguity is Shakespeare's but not Berowne's, for it cuts against Berowne's argument while alerting the audience to distinctions between the kinds of knowledge. Self-knowledge will continually elude the lords, even at the end of the play.

Berowne's belief that "every godfather can give a name" confidently assumes the arbitrariness of names, a near heretical position which received its major formal exposition in Bacon's *Advancement of Learning* (1605). But the assertion here forms part of a dissuasive pose, a self-conscious argument designed to irk his colleagues. Berowne's formula conveniently conjoins and secularizes the two original name-makers: God, the Author of creation, Who named Adam; and the father of mankind, who named the animals and then Eve. The naming of children, or of stars, is a type of this grander creation. The original name-makers gave the proper names, but those who follow them have considerably more difficulty. Throughout *Love's Labour's Lost*, as I will show, a search for the right names continually informs the dialogue. No one in the play is prepared to go as far as the nant rhetoric of *Love's Labour's Lost*. Two figures of speech receive special emphasis in the play, repeatedly used or abused by virtually every character. The most obvious is synonymy, what Puttenham called "the Figure of store" (*Arte*, p. 214). As its etymology suggests, synonymy is the addition or substitution of "the same name" for the original name. It is the figure most consistently mocked in the play, especially when used by the low characters to prove their learning. The desire for synonymy, for elegant variation, ust have been partly responsible for the increased use of rd words"; as English synonyms were exhausted, other uages were ransacked. The inkhorn ranneth over. Some ricians theorized that synonymy, or an analogous prin- was the origin of our current language. Thomas Wil- his *Arte of Rhetorique* (1553), observing that men ked sufficient words to express their meanings, that they would then remember "thinges of like those whereof they spake: they used suche xpresse their minde, as were most like unto ed to the borrowing of foreign words, among nd eventually to a positive desire for such lated terms: "the likenes of that thynge h in an other worde, muche lighteneth that, e most gladly have perceyved." In *The* (1588), Abraham Fraunce echoed Wil- ropes, or turnings . . . [were] first in- or want of words, but afterwards con- by reason of the delight and pleasant sity is the mother of abuse. imately a metaphor, a "turning." t to the same object, say the moon, mplications of Dictynna, Phoebe, ly. As connotations gradually ert themselves, synonymy is nt, and our awareness of the s. Like a metaphor, a syno- noon is Phoebe. But as the

contemporary astronomers who argued that "no new star could be discovered because there would be no name to call it by."[10] The true energy of words in *Love's Labour's Lost* lies somewhere between this kind of rigidity and Berowne's merely rhetorical skepticism. The audience must already have known this, but Berowne and his friends have yet to discover it. If Berowne dismisses knowledge of the cosmos and, inadvertently, knowledge of the self, he leaves little room in which to learn. No one will reveal less self-knowledge and "common sense," in every meaning of the term, than the four lords who stand debating while their ascetic rules are already being broken offstage.

A concern for correct naming, for wisdom through language, vibrates throughout *Love's Labour's Lost*. When Berowne admits to Navarre that he "for barbarism spoke more / Than for that angel knowledge you can say," he admits also, by way of the etymology of "barbarism," that he has defended "foreign or incorrect speech" against a higher knowledge, this time linked with the angels. The consequences of such barbarism are heard later in the first scene, when the foreign traveller Armado's "high words" buffet our ears, the dead end, within a decade, of Tamburlaine's "high astounding terms." His letter accuses Costard of a liaison with Jaquenetta. Although the facts are clear enough, the incident turns on the question of names. Armado gives Costard names he cannot recognize (Navarre is reading the letter):

> . . . there did I see that low-spirited swain, that base
> minnow of thy mirth,—
> *Cost.* Me?
> *King.* that unlettered small-knowing soul,—
> *Cost.* Me?
> *King.* that shallow vassal,—
> *Cost.* Still me?
> *King.* which, as I remember, hight Costard,—
> *Cost.* O! me.
>
> (I.i.240–8)

17

Like one of Adam's animals (Armado calls him a "rational hind" at I.ii.112), Costard answers to only one, "correct" name. He may be corrupt sexually, but not linguistically. Yet he immediately tries to turn Armado's trick on Navarre, arguing first that Jaquenetta is a "wench," then, in a malapropism, a "demsel," then "virgin" and "maid." Ultimately he punningly admits her to be "mutton" (I.i.274–86). Costard may evade Armado's circumlocutions, but his own fall flat. A rose by any other name would not smell as sweet; it could not even be identified in this play.

Moth and Armado clash over what to call each other. Moth's "young days, which we may nominate tender," as Armado says, produces "tender juvenal," a combination of a common noun—juvenal (i.e., juvenile)—and a proper noun—Juvenal (i.e., a satirist). Moth responds convincingly with "tough Signor, as an appertinent title to your old time, which we may name tough" (I.ii.6–17), combining "signor" and "senior." The Princess must warn Navarre that he wrongs "the reputation of [his] name" in his discourtesy (II.i.155). She will later rebuke his appeal to the "virtue" of her eye: "You nickname virtue; vice you should have spoke" (V.ii.349). Dull is simply confused by the several names for the moon— Dictynna, Phoebe, and Luna (IV.ii.39) —which Nathaniel and Holofernes give him in answer to his riddle, and by the varied names they offer for the pricket shot by the Princess. The pedants, above all, take special pride in nomenclature as a shadowy vestige of knowledge. They go so far as to produce a host of different names for naming. Thus the Spaniard is "intituled, nominated, or called, Don Adriano de Armado" according to Nathaniel (V.i.8), while Holofernes complains that Armado "clepeth a calf, cauf; half, hauf; neighbour *vocatur* nebour" (V.i.23–4). Devising latinate or archaic native names for naming, the pedants hope that some talismanic effect will rub off. Their interest reaches a climax in the Pageant of the Nine Worthies where Judas is "ycleped Maccabaeus" but, as Dumain puns,

"Judas Maccabaeus clipt is plain Judas" (V.ii.591–2). His name suffers further indignities when Boyet bids

. . . adieu, sweet Jude! nay, why dost thou stay?
Dum. For the latter end of his name.
Ber. For the ass to the Jude? give it him:—Jud-as, away!

(V.ii.6

Pompey is inadvertently but aptly "surnam'
(V.ii.545) and "Pompion" ("pumpkin"—V.
Worthies' names are open to such disrespec

The names of the characters in *Love's*
also self-revealing, indicating that Shake
maker who does not fully accept
Some of the names are metonymies
ville's is sundered by Katharine in
Moth's name contains several pu
vant to his functions in the pla
name would violate his essen
two jokes on his own nam
whose nation sent its Arm
generically as "the bra
are told, appropria
(V.ii.667). Holofe
(V.i.13), a bragg
nuchus, the pro
tive of a class.
their uniquer
givers as
suggested
the wo
explo
pos
ir

differences overtake the likenesses, we become aware of new possibilities, new "turnings." The way a character uses synonyms is therefore an index to his inherently "poetic" imagination, since naming is an overt form of metaphoric transformation. Holofernes' sodden lists never catch fire, his alternative names already clichés and stale pedantries, "translations" that are resolutely unmetaphoric. But Berowne's names for Cupid, as I will show in the fourth chapter, are far more successful.

The second major figure of *Love's Labour's Lost* is paronomasia, the pun, whose etymology indicates that it means "to call by a different name, to name besides." No one needs to be convinced that this play lives by the pun. Fatal Cleopatras dance everywhere. The apprehension of two names from the sound of one, or of one from the sound of two, is a variant of synonymy. Coleridge, like Thomas Wilson, saw in this confusion of sounds the origins of our language. "In all societies," he observed, "there exists an instinct of growth, a certain collective, unconscious good sense working progressively to desynonymize those words originally of the same meaning, which the conflux of dialects had supplied to the more homogeneous languages." He continued that "even the mere difference, or corruption, in the *pronunciation* of the same word, if it have become general, will produce a new word with a distinct signification; thus 'property' and 'propriety.' "[14]

The significance for *Love's Labour's Lost* is clear. The more pretentious characters, the pedants especially, attempt to create through synonymic lists; the others, dull and quick alike, manipulate or misconstrue sounds into new words, old names into misnomers. Hoskins observed the popularity of paronomasia, which he called agnomination (the giving of a second or surname), and illustrated it with the kind of wordplay that characterizes *Love's Labour's Lost*: "our paradise is a pair of dice, our almes-deeds are turned into all misdeeds, our praying into playing, our fasting into feasting" (Hoskins, p. 16). Hoskins did not fully approve of this practice, feeling that it was most appropriate for playing with "gentlewomen," and it must be admitted that the urge to pun reaches epidemic proportions in this play.

But *Love's Labour's Lost* risks the dangers of misunderstanding to reveal the marvels of creation. More than any other of Shakespeare's plays, it deliberately explores the nature of language—how language begins with names, as it did in Eden; how language develops by the addition of names and confusion of sounds; how language reveals the imagination, the innate poetic instinct, at work. The play is equally willing to consider both the Adamic or onomatopoetic theory of language and its polar opposite. The final songs are a "dialogue" (V.ii.875) in themselves, but they are also the conclusion to a dialogue that proceeds throughout *Love's Labour's Lost*. The subject of that "dialogue" is the great feast of language.

The fate of language generally may be seen in the single word "fame." The second word in the play, it introduces the major subject of Navarre's orations:

> Let fame, that all hunt after in their lives,
> Live register'd upon our brazen tombs,
> And then grace us in the disgrace of death.
>
> (I.i.1–3)

"Fame" is something noble here, a power which can defeat mutability and produce a kind of immortality. If it is to "live register'd," it can do so only because it consists of written words. Only they can "live" through time. Navarre's speech at first impresses us, but the punning repetition and cross-alliteration of the third line are a bit too glib, too polished and ready-at-hand. The rhetoric anticipates the over-confident plan for the Academy, otherwise a respected institution,[15] which Navarre proceeds to offer. His self-assurance is also brazen, but he will soon learn the caprices of fame himself.

As we learn more about the folly of the lords, and their unrealistic intentions, we notice a trivializing of the concept of fame. We have already heard Berowne's skeptical "too much to know is to know nought but fame" (I.i.92). "Fame" is now more nearly "report" or "rumor." Either they know only what other authorities have said in books, or they know so much that they have achieved a reputation. In any case, the grand "fame" of line one is denigrated. The word tends to slide back from Navarre's elevated sense to something closer to its root meaning of "talk" or "reputation." In Act Two, the Princess inquires after the lords:

> . . . good Boyet,
> You are not ignorant all-telling fame
> Doth noise abroad Navarre hath made a vow.
>
> (II.i.20–2)

Again, "fame" is simply rumor, Dame Gossip making "noise," like the prologue to *II Henry IV*, which is "painted full of tongues." Rosaline uses the same grotesque image when she tells Berowne that "the world's large tongue / Proclaims you for a man replete with mocks" (V.ii.832–3).

Finally, in the fourth act the Princess delivers what seems the antidote to Navarre's opening speech, observing that we often overstep ourselves when, "for fame's sake, for praise, an outward part, / We bend to that the working of the heart" (IV.i.30–3). "Fame" is made to seem tawdry, corrupting our better selves. The meaning of this word follows the course that Coleridge remarked, its original significance broadened by subsequent uses until virtually the opposite meaning is established. The majesty of the written word, graven in brass, which was to overcome "cormorant devouring Time" (l. 4), has instead degenerated into oral ambiguity, and finally into gossip. It is the fate of all language since Babel.

The course of the word "fame"—from written inscription to oral rumor—indicates another aspect of the play's debate about language, the conflict between written and oral language. Terence Hawkes has suggested that in *Love's Labour's Lost* "the oral world of speech is comically opposed to the silent world of books," and that the lords rely too heavily on "penn'd speeches" in the beginning, and must be educated into the social interchange of oral speech, which involves listening and learning as well as talking.[16] This argument has recently been extended by Malcolm Evans, who sees the resort to written speech "a psychic withdrawal," a manifestation of solipsism, and finds that "The words of Mercury are a disruptive force . . . dividing society into literate and illiterate." Evans goes so far, however, as to argue that "the comic ideal of society can only be established with the triumph of the Apollonian medium, speech, and the reformation of the old society according to the innate pattern of 'the converse of breath,' which presupposes a recognition of time, place, and occasion, and of the personality of the interlocutor."[17] The debate between writing and speech is clearly part of the play's background, yet I believe that Evans' argument is too schematic and one-sided. The spontaneous oral speech even of the ladies is not a final model of how to use language; rather (to anticipate my own argument), the model is to be heard in the final songs, the ancient "dialogue" between Spring and Winter, written speech given oral expression. The songs in themselves resolve this debate, as they do the larger debate between the magical and the arbitrary theories of language I am tracing here.

Renaissance rhetoricians believed that Hebrew was the original language, but even the Hebrew then current, they lamented, was corrupt and cloudy. There is no going back, although Holofernes, who puts his faith in Latin, will never give up the battle for the purification of language. Into this fallen world of wanton words, lapsed tongues, scenic ruins, and slippery names steps the poet. His medium is not God's language but man's. The poet learns that "knowledge" comes not simply from attempting to recapture the original names—Holofernes' errant etymologies show us the hopelessness of that—or from listing dictionary equivalents. It comes mainly from a resumption of the original "god-like" gift of *giving* names—what is required is a new name, a "desynonymized" variant, a metaphoric alteration of sound and essence. A new creation. Berowne will achieve this, briefly, when he describes Cupid.

There was no ambiguity in the original language, we are told, but without ambiguity the poet could not now survive. Sidney argued that nature's "world is brasen, the Poets only deliver a golden" (Smith, I, 156). Yet the golden world must be delivered—it can only be delivered—with a fallen but endlessly fertile language, one that can provide a "feast" for high and low alike, invited guests as well as those who depend on the alms-basket of words. To see the "dialogue" of language at work in *Love's Labour's Lost*, we must now look more closely at the styles of the play, and at the variety of attitudes toward language exhibited by the low characters. The special case of Berowne will be studied in chapter four.

Sweet Smoke of Rhetoric

One of the play's strengths is its variety of style. *Love's Labour's Lost* parodies not only euphuism,[18] but also Arcadianism, Petrarchanism, sonneteering, inkhornism, Nashe's idiosyncratic pamphlets, and whatever species of style Gabriel Harvey may be said to have produced. It is truly an embarrassment of riches. Selecting individual styles from such an impressive feast of language is difficult, but I trust it will not seem unusually perverse to direct attention first to the "scraps," to those thriving if seedy linguists in the play who have "lived long on the alms-basket of words." In the midst of such plenitude, even the beggars are choosers.

Style is of such importance in *Love's Labour's Lost* that the characters continually discuss it with one another. The following passage occurs after Dull has entered with Costard, bearing a letter from Armado:

> *King.* A letter from the magnificent Armado.
> *Ber.* How low soever the matter, I hope in God for
>   high words.

Long. A high hope for a low heaven: God grant us
  patience!
Ber. To hear? or forbear hearing?
Long. To hear meekly, sir, and to laugh moderately; or
  to forbear both.
Ber. Well, sir, be it as the style shall give us cause to
  climb in the merriness.
Cost. The matter is to me, sir, as concerning Jaquenetta.
(I.i.189–99)

Later in the play, after the second of Armado's letters has
been read, there is this exchange:

Boyet. I am much deceiv'd but I remember the style.
Prin.   Else your memory is bad, going o'er it erewhile.
(IV.i.95–6)

The pun style=stile (steps for getting over a fence) as
used here is particularly appropriate in describing Armado.[19]
As the first quotation makes clear, the men are expecting linguistic indecorum from Armado's letter—"high words," the
highest style, no matter how "low" the subject "matter."
This is exactly what is heard in both letters, and the ungainly
clash results in laughter. The pun on "stile" makes something
physical of a linguistic structure, something which has to be
scaled or descended, a possible hurdle for the audience. It is
now something to be "gone over," lest we be left behind.
It is a good description of the use of style and language
throughout the play; rampant linguistic excesses may be
barriers to social communication, but looked at from another
point they can also be seen as entrances into the play's remarkable debate on the uses of language. We are given every
extreme: a high style of rhetorical overkill and, conversely,
a strong reductive counter-strain, usually represented by
Costard or the series of "greasy" sexual puns and innuendoes,
which subvert decorum from the other direction (low
words for high matter).

Perhaps the central fact about language in *Love's Labour's*

Lost, whether written or oral, is its radical instability. Words and their usual meanings are separated, transmuted, even totally reversed through puns, wit-play, and simple misunderstandings. The chief means of this exploration and unsettling of norms, of defeating our expectations, are by the dislocation of language and the destruction of decorum. A number of benefits are attendant on this instability. There is a tremendous freedom in creation, to begin with; even the lowest and dullest characters can consider themselves wordsmiths, can coin phrases and riddles. While a Berowne can soar into autonomous realms of invention and association where few can follow, an Armado can produce his own charming if obscure world of language, a private word hoard of romantic archaicism. With so much wit in the air, everyone catches the disease. The result of such freedom in *Love's Labour's Lost* is occasionally the "sweet smoke of rhetoric" (III.i.61) Armado describes, a kind of Dickensian fog which on the one hand disorients and chokes everyone with its thickness, but on the other is nevertheless "sweet" and desirable.

There is a negative corollary to this instability and freedom, which the play does not avoid. It is made clear that linguistic solipsism sometimes defeats communication, and that the social order depends in large part on shared understandings of words. Sigurd Burckhardt notes that "the pun is one . . . way of divesting a word of its meaning. Where writers find so primitive a method especially appealing, we may suspect that they feel the need to create a true medium, and so to rebel against a token language, with particular intensity. . . . The pun gives the word as entity primacy over the word as sign." The pun, therefore, is one way of recapturing at least some of the lost magical power of words. Observing that the pun fell into linguistic disrepute in the eighteenth century, and is still often considered frivolous, Burckhardt speculates that the reason for this aversion may be that the pun "is, by its very directness, revolutionary and anarchic. . . . It denies the meaningfulness of words and so calls into question the genuineness of the linguistic currency on which the social order depends. It makes us aware that words may be counterfeits."[20]

Both an impulse toward verbal liberation and a contrary impulse toward judgment and linguistic decorum are simultaneously and continually present in the play. The standard reading of *Love's Labour's Lost* today tends to emphasize the latter of the two impulses over the former, and to conclude with the darker tones of judgment of the final scene. While conceding the increasingly somber voice of judgment in the play, we must recognize the anarchic spirit of liberation for what it is—the source of the play's vitality, its very heart. This continuous exuberance, especially as it is seen in the play's low characters, defines while exemplifying the power inherent in language available to the inventive, to the true poet as well as to the poetaster. The low characters serve to reflect and parody the linguistic excesses of Berowne and friends, but they have at the same time a life of such irresistible fun that it deserves separate treatment.

It is, to begin with, especially appropriate that the bulk of the linguistic satire in the play emanates from the six low characters who form, in effect, a small *commedia dell'arte* troupe distinct from the courtly figures. Berowne once refers to Boyet as "Some carry-tale, some please-man, some slight zany" (V.ii.463), and Shakespeare shows in several other plays a thorough familiarity with the terms, stock figures, and scenarios of the *commedia*. The key reference in *Love's Labour's Lost* occurs when Berowne lists the familiar stock types (omitting Dull, who has already dropped out of the play): "The pedant, the braggart, the hedge-priest, the fool, and the boy" (V.ii.536–7). It is also of note that the Quarto uses *commedia* "type" names for several of the speech ascriptions: Armado is "Braggart," Moth is "Page" and "Boy," Costard is "Clown," Dull is "Constable," Holofernes is "Pedant," and Nathaniel is "Curate." This may or may not be evidence of revision, but it does suggest one of the probable origins of these characters. A standard feature of *commedia* humor was linguistic satire of all sorts. In a typical company, "Most of the characters were supposed to be natives of a particular city and spoke the local dialect. . . . The babble of dialects only heightened the farcical elements of the play."[21] Verbal *lazzi*, quick-witted pages, slow-witted rustics, *dottores* spouting macaronic Latin in comic dialects: Shakespeare had a ready-made background against which to work with his own little troupe of idiosyncratic voices. This is the troupe that will perform the Pageant of the Nine Worthies later. One of the best and most appropriate puns in the entire play makes them also "The Nine Wordies."[22]

ANTHONY DULL: A CONSTABLE

We may as well begin at the bottom. Like lampblack, Dull absorbs light without reflecting any. None of the verbal ammunition in the play has any effect on him, save when he tries his tired old riddle on Holofernes and Sir Nathaniel: "What was a month old at Cain's birth, that's not five weeks old as yet?" (IV.ii.34–5). Unfamiliar with the string of synonyms offered up by these two ("Dictynna . . . Phoebe . . . Luna"), Dull must have the solution explained to him. For some reason, Armado commends Dull, in still another string of synonyms, as "a man of good repute, carriage, bearing, and estimation" (I.i.257). His main function in the play, however, seems to be to remind us that silence, if not wholly golden, nevertheless has its virtues. He is an unreflecting mirror of the verbal pyrotechnics, a mute in Babel. One imagines him standing with his mouth open through most of the play; he is completely silent through the first 144 lines of V.i., and when Holofernes notices and says, "thou hast spoken no word all this while," Dull answers for many of us, "Nor understood none neither, sir."[23]

Dull's name is, like that of Bottom, self-defining. His share of the linguistic fun is necessarily a small one, for "he hath never fed of the dainties that are bred in a book. / He hath not eat paper" (IV.ii.24–5), as Sir Nathaniel tells us. Aside from his reticence, Dull is most noted for his malapropisms, the first of a series of such Shakespearean characters best exemplified in Dogberry. O. J. Campbell points out that Dull has a prototype in the *commedia*, and that the stupid magistrate was one of Francesco Andreini's favorite roles.[24] Along with the similarly mis-taking Costard, Dull utters a stream of comic howlers. Words are tricky things, after all. Dull has difficulty pronouncing "Armado" at I.i.186, and has "reprehend" for "represent" at I.i.182. In IV.ii, he displays a dogged literal-mindedness, apparently hearing Holofernes' "*haud credo*" as "awd (old) grey doe," (IV.ii.11n.) and insisting throughout the rest of the scene that what was seen was a young buck—a pricket. He is quite correct. Dull's aural error reveals him as one of the very few characters in the play who cannot understand or even conceive of a pun, much less a foreign language. Dull knows only one language: a native Anglo-Saxon. He is occasionally capable of a latinate "commends," but the effort appears to exhaust him. All sounds, in whatever language, are translated into English. The inability to hear puns or to grasp the principle of synonymy, in which there is more than one sound attached to an object, places Dull in a special category—he represents the worst kind of audience, the one which cannot follow "wit" (a word Dull uses only once in the play). His speech represents language at its most primitive, where each object has only one word attached to it, and words can have only that one meaning. Since he is "unlettered" (IV.ii.18), as Holofernes says, Dull's only access to knowledge is through what he hears. But though "A lover's ear will hear the lowest sound" (IV.iii.332), Berowne will tell us later, Dull's hearing on the contrary is irremediably dulled and miscomprehending. Obtuseness is raised to the level of genius.

Because Dull's attitudes are primitive they are not necessarily wrong, however. He is usually correct about the facts involved. It was a pricket, and it was the moon. Perhaps his (unintentionally) wittiest moment comes after he has sprung his riddle, and Holofernes has solved it:

Hol. The moon was a month old when Adam was no
    more;
    And raught not to five weeks when he came to
    five-score.
    The allusion holds in the exchange.
Dull. 'Tis true indeed: the collusion holds in the
    exchange.
Hol. God comfort thy capacity! I say the allusion holds
    in the exchange.
Dull. And I say the pollution holds in the exchange.

                                      (IV.ii.40–6)

Everyone is right. The "pollution" of language remains remarkably constant, and this is one of the best examples of
Dull's transformation of strange sounds. He is, again, unwittingly correct. Holofernes' "allusion" means, broadly, "pun"
or "riddle," and "exchange" refers to the substitution of the
name of Adam for that of Cain. "Collusion," which follows,
is also appropriate; the *OED* defines one meaning as "a trick
or ambiguity, in words or reasoning." There is a "collusion"
between everyone in the play which leads to endless compli-
cations. Literally, then, the semantic "pollution" *has* held in
the "exchange"—the passage is thus also self-referential. This
is the way of language in *Love's Labour's Lost*.

Dull is unaware of all this. Enough for him that it was a
pricket shot by the Princess. In one of our last views of him,
he goes off to dinner with Holofernes and Sir Nathaniel. As
he silently follows the two learned men (having said nothing
during the previous hundred lines of dialogue), he is admon-
ished by Holofernes, in one of the most superfluous commands in all literature, *"pauca verba."* That, after all, is his
very essence.

COSTARD: THE FOOL

Costard is on the stage more than anyone else in the play.
He appears in every scene except II.i, the first encounter of
the men and women of the court. Moreover, in the eight

scenes in which he appears, he enters each well after it has begun. A scene is set, a situation under way, and then Costard enters, almost always with someone else; only twice does he come on the stage alone. What this indicates is that Costard is a "reflective" character and his main business, like Touchstone's in *As You Like It*, is to encounter other people and serve as a contrast. Singly or with others, Costard is shuffled through nearly every possible permutation of encounters. His function in most scenes is reductive: deflating pretensions and pricking hypocrisies. After the foolish plan for the academy has been established in the first scene, for example, the wayward Costard, caught with a "wench," is brought in by Dull, a living refutation of the denial of the flesh just theoretically espoused by the lords. It is also Costard, in the last scene, who reveals that Jaquenetta is pregnant by Armado. In structural terms, Costard balances scenes; one of Shakespeare's favorite methods is to juxtapose opposites, to bring them into dramatic conflict. Costard serves continually, in the midst of sophistication, to remind us of the foibles of the flesh and other inevitable facts about life. We would expect his language to mirror this general function, and it usually does.

Costard is more aware of the possibilities of language than Dull is. He even has some small gift for wordplay. At I.i.202–211, for example, he reaches for verbal elegance in schematically ordering his defense according to the legal phrase, "In manner and form following." In *The Unfortunate Traveller*, Nashe had also mocked the use of this phrase in the welcoming speech of the orator at Wittenberg (Nashe, II, 248). Costard is not adept at such schemes, however, for he must resort to barnyard puns on "manor" and "farm," and the triumphant symmetry of his construction collapses in a tautological heap at the end: "for the form,—in some form." Costard concludes with an oath appropriate to a trial by combat ("God defend the right!"). It has not been an overwhelming performance—the master of this sort of thing is still Armado, as in his letter at IV.i.62–92.

There are many more malapropisms in Costard's mouth than in Dull's. Textual difficulties always leave some ambiguity with respect to errors of usage, but it is probably safe to assume that most of the errors are Costard's rather than the typesetter's. His first words are, after all, an announcement that the "contempts" (I.i.188) of Armado's letter concern him. His rendering of the proverbial phrase *"ad unguem"* is an unfortunate *"ad dunghill"* (V.i.73); he is clearly in over his head here. Costard makes a number of other errors in the play, but one of the most interesting has been altered by all the major editors of the play (and without any comment by the *Arden* editor) to "Such is the simplicity of man to hearken after the flesh" (I.i.215). It has been pointed out, however, that the actual Quarto reading is "sinplicitie," and that a pun may be intended here.[25] Most readers of *Love's Labour's Lost* have praised this gnomic utterance of Costard's as a piece of unalloyed folk wisdom, the voice of "reality" adjusting our response to the variety of foolishness here. But it is quite typical of Costard to make such an error; as we shall see, many if not all of his attempted quotations come out garbled. Moreover, the play on "sin," considering the circumstances of the letter and the actions it describes, is too good to pass up, and preserving it preserves that delightful blend in Costard of insight and ignorance.

Of special interest is Costard's fondness for aphorisms, a habit shared by the rest of the *commedia* figures. The line just mentioned is spoken when the lords receive Armado's letter:

King. Will you hear this letter with attention?
Ber. As we would hear an oracle.
Cost. Such is the sinplicitie of man to hearken after the flesh.

Costard is the comic "oracle," delivering bits of wisdom in mangled words which, like those of the real oracles, must be translated and deciphered by his listeners. In this case, the message of the oracle is double-edged, cutting both hearers and speaker. At the end of the same scene we hear Costard's "and therefore welcome the sour cup of prosperity! Affliction may one day smile again; and till then, sit thee down, sorrow!" (I.i.296–8). This is remembered and mockingly echoed by Berowne: "Well, set thee down, sorrow! for so they say the foola sid" (IV.iii.4–5; the Qto. reads "foole sayd"). Aside from the humor of these tangled aphorisms, the habit itself, Costard's inordinate respect for linguistic and other authorities, is of interest. Even the other characters make fun of it.

A corollary to this simultaneous respect and ineptitude is a literal-mindedness which links him with Dull. All languages are one to Costard. In the third act, he hears and misconstrues the mysterious words "enigma," "riddle," and "l'envoy" (III.i.69). "Enigma," misheard as "egma" (l. 70), is an enigma to Costard; a standard figure of speech, "which for the darknesse, the sense may hardly be gathered,"[26] its power is self-demonstrative here. The usual reading of his misunderstanding is that Costard believes that Armado is offering him "various salves" to heal his broken shin (*Cam.* p. 151). H. A. Ellis, however, has offered a more suggestive reading of the lines in which Costard mistakenly hears the word "enema," then "confuses *salve* 'ointment' with *salve* or *salvo* 'a discharge of firearms'. . . . Perhaps the form of the *envoy* suggested to Costard the dreaded clyster pipe."[27] In any case, a confusion of sounds has led to confusion in meaning, and words, suddenly liberated, begin to take on a wholly different life of their own. A moment later, Costard makes another mistaken connection with "envoy," thinking he hears the word *oie*, French for "goose":[28]

The boy hath sold him a bargain, a goose, that's flat.
Sir [Armado], your pennyworth is good an your goose
    be fat.
To sell a bargain well is as cunning as fast and loose:
Let me see; a fat l'envoy; ay, that's a fat goose.
                                        (III.i.99–102)

After several more lines of elaborate punning, Armado relents of the official punishment of imprisonment: "Sirrah Costard, I will enfranchise thee." But the terrified rustic again hears something else: "O! marry me to one Frances— I smell some l'envoy, some goose in this" (III.i.118–20). The pun on goose (slang for "prostitute") has produced the final term of the equation; "l'envoy," an affected term used by Harvey and ridiculed by Nashe (*Arden* note, III.i.69), has not meant the "epilogue or discourse" (l. 79) Armado intended, but has instead metamorphosed into a goose, and then into a prostitute. It has been a long way around. The whole sequence meets its end, so to speak, with Costard's scatological joke, "now you will be my purgation and let me loose" (ll. 124–5), presumably the very thing he had feared.

Along the way, Costard has also managed to transform the word "enfranchise" (l. 118) into "one Frances," the "goose"/"prostitute" he fears he will be forced to marry. A similar transformation occurs in *Much Ado About Nothing*, when Borachio's question, "seest thou not what a deformed thief this fashion is?" is misheard by the Watch, who assures us, "I remember his name," and an entirely new character, named Deformed, comes into being (III.iii.115–8). The reality of "Deformed" goes unquestioned throughout the play, and by the end Dogberry has given him a complex history and a local habitation: "they say he wears a key in his ear, and a lock hanging by it, and borrows money in God's name, the which he hath used so long and never paid that now men grow hard-hearted and will lend nothing for God's sake" (V.i.295–9). It is a fine irony that "deformed" is the word involved to illustrate the deformation and transformation of language. What the Watch and Costard have both accomplished is a creation *ex nihilo*; each has produced, from the fabric of sounds and words, a character with a name and an identity. The "key" to the reality of Deformed and Frances is, in Dogberry's terms, exactly through the "ear," the very sounds of the words; these characters have no other reality.

Mere speech has been incarnated. The whole process is a parody of the dramatist's art, making people out of words— which is itself a type of the original Creation through the Word. Any rustic godfather can give a name.

One of the most interesting episodes in the play now follows. Armado gives Costard a "remuneration" for delivering a letter, and Costard marvels at it: "Now will I look to his remuneration. Remuneration! O that's the Latin word for three farthings: three farthings, remuneration. 'What's the price of this inkle?' 'One penny': 'No, I'll give you a remuneration': why, it carries it. Remuneration! why it is a fairer name than French crown. I will never buy and sell out of this word" (III.i.134–40). A few moments later, Costard receives a "guerdon" from Berowne for a similar mission: "Gardon, O sweet gardon! better than remuneration; a 'leven-pence farthing better. Most sweet gardon! I will do it, sir, in print. Gardon! Remuneration!" (III.i.166–9). Costard has known the bliss of the lexicographer, the displaced Adamic power of giving names. There could be no clearer picture, as Costard holds the coins in his hand and pronounces the magic sounds associated with them, of the origins of language. The scene suggests the equation, already hinted at before in Costard's various errors, of sound=thing. The strange sound becomes a name, a thing, completely apart from its connection with a coin. As each thick, heavy word rolls off Costard's lips, the sound becomes an independent entity. Like the "fat goose," like "Frances," like "deformed," it magically comes alive, created out of airy nothings. For at least one Elizabethan rhetorician, moreover, a "remuneration" was a figure of speech—"whereby wee give thanks for courtesies, benefites, or good turnes receaved, or care or other liking had or shewen unto us."[29] "Remuneration" is literally verbal coin.

At the opposite pole of linguistic theory, as we have seen, stands the idea of an arbitrary symbolic link between words and things, the sort of thing seen in the Academy of Learning, not of Navarre, but of Swift's Lagado, where "An Expedient was therefore offered, that since Words are only Names for *Things*, it would be more convenient for all Men to carry about them such *Things* as were necessary to express the particular Business they are to discourse on. . . . for short Conversations a Man may carry Implements in his Pockets and under his Arms, enough to supply him, and in his House he cannot be at a Loss."[30] The requisite proximity to the object is similar, but Costard shows that, unlike Swift's theoreticians, he values the sound of the word in itself nearly as much as the coin. In both cases, the heavier the better. Best and heaviest of all is Costard's production of "*honorificabilitudinitatibus*," supposedly the longest word known (V.i.42n.). It is sound as pure incantation; merely pronouncing it supplants any need for interpreting its meaning.

SIR NATHANIEL: THE HEDGE-PRIEST

Nathaniel fancies himself an authority on the church fathers and a polished raconteur. Yet he knows when he has met his match, and stands in great awe of Holofernes. In a play about affected fashions, Nathaniel is the most slavish of the imitators, with, inevitably, the worst results. He attaches himself so carefully to the great scholar that there is little doubt of Nathaniel's ancestor, the classical parasite; Campbell finds a clear connection with the *commedia* as well, with "the *affamato*, who only in the *Commedia dell'Arte* is attached to the Pedant."[31]

Nathaniel's prose style reflects his folly all too clearly. He has a great fondness, for example, for that spurious oratorical profundity associated with politicians and divines. As he enters the play in IV.ii, saying, "Very reverend sport, truly: and done in the testimony of a good conscience," we may catch a proleptic whiff of Ben Jonson's Zeal-of-the-Land Busy (cf. Barish, pp. 197–204). There is a pun in "reverend" —referring both to the sport in itself (as worthy of honor) and as "a sport in which a reverend gentleman might participate with a good conscience" (Baldwin, II, 627)—and also a self-satisfied allusion to a well-known Biblical text (2 Corinthians 1:12). It is a typical performance.

Foremost among Nathaniel's stylistic enthusiasms is his use of parataxis. Here is his description of Dull:

> Sir, he hath never fed of the dainties that are bred in a book.
> He hath not eat paper, as it were; he hath not drunk ink: his intellect is not replenished; he is only an animal, only sensible in the duller parts;
> And such barren plants are set before us, that we thankful should be,
> Which we of taste and feeling are, for those parts that do fructify in us more than he;
> For as it would ill become me to be vain, indiscreet, or a fool,
> So were there a patch set on learning, to see him in a school.
>
> (IV.ii.24–31)

A strange melange: the second half of a couplet in irregular sixteeners, three lines of paratactic prose, then two more couplets in sixteeners, in relentless pursuit of the central metaphor from "fed" to "eat" to "drunk," "replenished," a kind of literary Eucharist,[32] then up the chain of being from "animal" to "plant," and finally to a human being, just barely. The effect of this is a zany sententiousness, a lunatic determination to impress with erudition, no matter the effort or chaos.

The best example of Nathaniel's paratactic efforts comes in V.i, as the little group returns from an offstage dinner: "I praise God for you, sir: your reasons at dinner have been sharp and sententious; pleasant without scurrility, witty without affection, audacious without impudency, learned without opinion, and strange without heresy" (V.i.2–6). No one could believe Nathaniel's description of Holofernes' speaking ability, to be sure, but it sounds impressive, and is

itself an almost perfect specimen of parisonic prose. Dr.
Johnson's comment on this passage is especially interesting:
"I know not well what degree of respect *Shakespeare* intends
to obtain for this vicar, but he has here put into his mouth a
finished representation of colloquial excellence. It is very difficult to add any thing to this character of the schoolmaster's
table-talk, and perhaps all the precepts of *Castiglione* will
scarcely be found to comprehend a rule for conversation so
justly delineated, so widely dilated, and so nicely limited."[33]
Johnson gives himself away by echoing, in his final sentence,
the very qualities for which he is commending the prose of
Nathaniel: a happy irony. Johnson also appears to beg the
question of context, professing not to know the "degree of
respect" to be given to Nathaniel, a character who is steeped
in folly throughout the play. The passage is simply compli-
mented in itself. Shakespeare's audience would have heard an
echo of Sidney, Lyly, and most of all Harvey in it (*Arden*,
p. 117). But it is significant that Johnson's comments did not
apparently apply to Nathaniel's entire speech, which continues, "I did converse this quondam day with a companion of
the king's, who is intituled, nominated, or called, Don
Adriana de Armado" (V.i.6–9). Suddenly the "elegance"
collapses under the weight of foppish affectation ("quondam") and a "sweetly varied" string of synonyms, two latinate for the one more than adequate native word. In a play
filled with erratic styles, Nathaniel practices his own special
blend. When we hear him trying to match Holofernes' lat-
inisms, "*Perge*, good Master Holofernes, *perge*; so it shall
please you to abrogate scurrility" (IV.ii.53–4), we know he
is beyond help.

Costard's bungled aphorisms find a more elevated parallel
in Nathaniel's speeches. If the rest of the characters are devoted in various ways to the primacy of words, Nathaniel
is devoted to the primacy of The Word, as expressed in the
words of Holy Writ and the writings of the Church Fathers.
Virtually everything he says has a Biblical or patristic allusion lurking near the surface (cf. Baldwin, II, 627–43). The

idea of authority is important everywhere in the play, but it is nowhere better exemplified than in Nathaniel, who scarcely breathes without uttering "as a certain father saith" or "saith the text." The text and the fathers are equivalent to Holofernes' rhetoric books, Costard's folk sources, or Armado's chivalric and military heroes. But as we see in Nathaniel, man's link to the Word has been sundered; the magic power of words is only fitfully evident, for everything here has been trivialized. The Word becomes only another collection of quotable words, the *Logos* is evident mainly as logorrhea. Berowne's "base authority" reigns supreme.

HOLOFERNES: THE PEDANT

Holofernes is Nathaniel's master, the comic pedant of the *commedia dell'arte*, the *dottore* whose erudition masks his ignorance of life, whose style obscures rather than clarifies. His antecedents are everywhere: in the *commedia*, in Rhombus of Sidney's *Lady of May*, in *Pedantius*, in Rabelais' Holofernes. Shakespeare's Holofernes represents the dead end of one of the great humanist ideals, the life-blood of Erasmus and Ascham. Samuel Daniel, perhaps anachronistically, expressed the traditional view in his *Musophilus* (1599):[34]

> Powre above powre, O heavenly Eloquence,
> That with the strong reine of commanding words,
> Dost manage, guide, and master th'eminence
> Of mens affections, more then all their swords.

"O heavenly Eloquence." A long and noble tradition of education through the study of rhetoric is summed up in that phrase. If the power inherent in language, and in particular the "eloquence" cultivated by the study of rhetoric, could be so overwhelming for Daniel and others, then it is a measure of the distance from that ideal when we can find the abuse of it so ludicrous in Holofernes. His "wisdom" is nothing but folly speaking copiously. The immense power inherent in language is not being mocked, but the traditional means of access, through the rhetorical training of the schools, is. It is hopeless to try to discuss everything that Holofernes says. It can be taken on faith that virtually every "vice" of language listed by the rhetoricians may be found illustrated somewhere by Holofernes: "soraismus," "cacemphaton," "pleonasmus," "bomphiologia," "solecismus," "cacozelia." The more pretentious the pedant becomes, the more grotesque and erroneous his language.

Like everyone else in *Love's Labour's Lost*, Holofernes floods us with aphorisms and sententiae. *Sufflaminandus erat*, as Ben Jonson said of Shakespeare: "His wit was in his owne power; would the rule of it had been so too." Holofernes makes a revealing error in one of his aphorisms: *"Facile precor gelida quando pecus omne sub umbra Ruminat*, and so forth" (IV.ii.92–3). As many editors have pointed out, the correct first word is *"Fauste,"* and this is a quotation every schoolboy would know by heart, one very recently bandied back and forth by Nashe and Harvey (*Arden*, p. 85); Holofernes' slip makes nonsense of the passage. But it also suggests how Holofernes is obsessed with the idea of "facility," a term meaning fluency in the production of rhetorical figures, an ease of copious invention. He mentions the word twice again in the play. In promising to "affect the letter," he praises alliteration because "it argues facility" (IV.ii.55–6), and Berowne's sonnet is criticized because it lacks, among other things, this same "facility" (IV.ii.121).

Aphorisms derive from authorities, and Holofernes, like the others, has his own little pantheon of "Worthies" on whom to base all action and thought. "Good old Mantuan" (IV.ii.93); Lyly's Latin Grammar; "Priscian" (V.i.29); "Horace" (IV.ii.100); we can be certain of Quintilian though he is not mentioned by name; and above all "Ovidius Naso" (IV.ii.122). These figures are all important to his theories of poetry as well. A large number of other authorities, mostly traditionalist rhetoricians, stand behind Holofernes' judgments on etymology and pronunciation. By the early 1590s they are largely out of date, as we might expect, and the battles Holofernes maniacally fights were long since lost. Nevertheless, he sticks to his authorities, to what he has read and himself been taught, rather than to what people are saying. That Shakespeare did not is also evident.

As Ben Jonson noted, "*Language* most shewes a man. . . . It springs out of the most retired, and inmost parts of us, and is the Image of the Parent of it, the mind. No glasse renders a mans forme, or likenesse, so true as his speech" (Jonson, VIII, 625). The mind behind Holofernes' language is sterile and pedantic, and therefore comic, because of its pretenses of fertility. Holofernes conceives of language as fixed and static; his devotion to Latin and his use of words in their original meanings suggests a suffocating imaginative stagnation. He would transfer dead writing to live speech. His language is studded with technical and rhetorical jargon and bits of famous quotations, scraps from other great feasts that promise much but nourish little. His theories of pronunciation, already obsolete, show him in his most rigid stance. Every letter which is written down must be pronounced, no fashionable variations are allowed, no common-sense simplifications tolerated, every hieroglyphic is sacred. Words are to be pronounced so as to emphasize their Latin origin, even if they don't have any; thus "abhominable" from "*ab homine*" (an incorrect though common derivation—V.i.25n.). That almost everyone in England already said "det" for "debt" does not deter his zeal.[35] Practice and custom mean nothing; "authority from others' books," as Berowne warned in the first act, everything.

Holofernes' ideas about language are admittedly not an isolated aberration, nor are they confined only to pedants through the ages. A desire to fix the language is a recurring phenomenon, as in France today. Swift's *Proposal for Correcting the English Tongue* argued, typically, that "after such Alterations are made in it as shall be thought requisite," the language should be fixed forever, "for I am of Opinion, it is better a Language should not be wholly perfect, than that it should be perpetually changing."[36] Holofernes possesses none of Swift's reasonableness, however, simply insisting that there be no deviation from the original source. It is a pedantic and sycophantic position so extreme that deviation in others, he confesses, "insinuateth" him of "insanie."

Predictably, Holofernes' favorite device of style is synonymy. He considers it to be the highest mark of wit and inventiveness to give the greatest possible number of synonyms for a simple word, preferably in more than one language. Thus:

coelo, the sky, the welkin, the heaven (IV.ii.5);

terra, the soil, the land, the earth (IV.ii.6–7);

Let me hear a staff, a stanze, a verse (IV.ii.103);

He is too picked, too spruce, too affected, too odd, as it were, too peregrinate, as I may call it (V.i.13–15);

The posterior of the day . . . is liable, congruent, and measurable for the afternoon (V.i.86–7);

he was a babe, a child, a shrimp (V.ii.583).

And so on. Nathaniel is always impressed by the pedant's facility: "Truly, Master Holofernes, the epithets [synonyms] are sweetly varied, like a scholar at the least" (IV.ii.8–9). And after one of Holofernes' most extravagant lists of synonyms, Nathaniel copies one of them ("peregrinate") in his commonplace book with the commendation, "A most singular and choice epithet" (V.i.16). It is truly "copious invention" to a fault. The disease of synonymy was apparently highly infectious at the time; Hoskins, writing in 1599, uses the schoolmaster as a stock example of the abuse of "accumulation," the "heaping up of many terms . . . like a schoolmaster foaming out synonymies" (Hoskins, p. 24).

The effect of these lists, this great "store" of nouns and adjectives, is anaesthetic for the reader and narcotic for the speaker. Compiling such lists demands a minimum of wit, a modicum of cleverness, and a large vocabulary of latinate and Latin words—in short, erudition devoid of wisdom, the special province of the pedant. The beauty of the method is that, though it is not truly imaginative, it is usually impressive to those who have smaller vocabularies. The lulling rhythm of such lists, the aggregation of words, the steady and pleasing drone of one's own voice placing sounds next to one another, are an agreeable substitute for thought. If for Costard words are physically attached to things, very nearly identified with them, then we see the opposite condition in Holofernes. He comes closest to existing in a totally solipsistic world; the fact that most of his words do have recognizable referents links him but tenuously with the rest of us.

Holofernes also considers himself an expert philologist. Etymologizing evidently became something of a national sport during the great Inkhorn controversies, and a lively interest was taken in all strange words. In all fairness, Holofernes' derivations have some initial plausibility; but like his epitaph on the pricket, they are pursued to a fault. Virtually every speech of his depends upon a thorough knowledge of Latin roots, as in this example: "Most barbarous intimation! yet a kind of insinuation, as it were *in via*, in way of explication; *facere*, as it were replication, or, rather, *ostentare*, to show, as it were, his inclination,—after his undressed, unpolished, uneducated, unpruned, untrained, or rather unlettered, or ratherest, unconfirmed fashion—to insert again my *haud credo* for a deer" (IV.ii.13–20). "Intimation"="thrusting inwards"; "insinuation"="insertion"; "explication"= "explanation"; "replication"="reply."[37] The frozen syntax of this passage (through a series of seven "un-" synonyms and an "or rather . . . or ratherest" construction) serves as a handy frame on which to hang such unwieldy words.

Like most of Holofernes' speeches, this one is chopped up into a number of short phrases—endless repetitions, qualifications, refinements. His mind moves by fits and starts, stumbling through a darkened warehouse filled with trivia and choking dust. He finds and produces many items, but they all turn out to be the same thing. There are few sentences in which Holofernes is able to string together more than six or seven words without a qualification or interruption of some kind. He works by rote association alone; as one item is mentioned, a string of synonymic relatives is produced. In the passage quoted above, no phrase or clause contains more than five words except the final main verb clause. The six lines before it form one gigantic noun phrase and, as Francis Christensen notes, "The very hallmark of jargon is the long noun phrase."[38] The whole passage is held together by schematic formulae and fillers: "as it were" (three times—the Latin *quasi* is used at IV.ii.82), "or rather," and the mindless continuity of the "un-" adjectives. Holofernes also has a habit, common now among politicians and technocrats, of turning verbs into nouns, thus freezing language even more. A word-count of Holofernes' speeches shows an unusually high percentage of words ending in "-tion." The fondness for synonymy thus produces still another odd effect: the language of such speakers is by necessity heavily freighted with nouns and adjectives, and there is a corresponding scarcity of verbs of any kind. The speeches produced are thus heavy, static, and clotted, a precise correspondence with Holofernes' philological conservatism.

Predictably, Holofernes displays little "wit" in the sense of punning word-play. He is skilled in manipulating syntactical constructs, even better at devising lists of synonyms; he considers himself a highly qualified judge of other people's rhetoric and poetry. But his attitude toward language appears to have stifled his ability to pun, for a pun, as we have seen, is anarchic, a subversive threat to the kind of order and fixed meanings he seeks. In a pun, etymologies mean nothing, meanings are deliberately scrambled, and (worse) pronunciations are changed or forced for the sake of spurious identification. If anything is certain about a pun, it is that the words which make it up have not remained fixed and stable.

The exception to this, which proves the rule, is Holofernes' miserable attempt in his "extemporal epitaph" on the death of a deer:

> The preyful princess pierc'd and prick'd a pretty
>   pleasing pricket;
> Some say a sore; but not a sore, till now made sore with
>   shooting.
> The dogs did yell; put 'ell to sore, then sorel jumps from
>   thicket;
> Or pricket sore, or else sore'll the people fall a-hooting.
> If sore be sore, then 'ell to sore makes fifty sores—
>   O—sorel!
> Of one sore I an hundred make, by adding but one
>   more l.
>
> (IV.ii.57–62)

It is ingenious, and it can all be worked out to mean something, if we try hard enough. But who will? It depends on a punning combination of sounds; there is even, in Nathaniel's terms, an unabrogated "scurrility" present, mindlessly emphasized by the staccato alliteration (almost "illiteration") and the heavy-handed use of "pricket."[39] But the whole thing is sterile, lifeless. Far from arguing "facility," the epitaph is a purely mechanical exercise. There are puns, but they do not liberate the language, they suffocate it. Holofernes' attitude towards language and its uses stands as a barrier against the free play of the imagination. Costard turns words like "enfranchise" into people; Holofernes has the opposite tendency, turning people back into words and categories of grammar. Jaquenetta, for example, is described as "a soul feminine" (IV.ii.80) and Moth is derisively called a "consonant" (V.i.51), since there is very little of him. This process is the very reverse of the playwright's creation, reductive rather than expansive, limiting rather than enlarging.

46

Armado: The Braggart

We are told that Armado is "a refined traveller of Spain" (I.i.162), and his suggestive name aids the identification, but it appears that a few detours have been taken along the way. Armado must be a successful character, since no one has ever managed to specify a single source for him. Sir Thopas from Lyly's *Endimion*, Capitano Spavento from the *commedia*, the *miles gloriosus* of Plautine comedy: all are obvious possibilities, not to mention Gabriel Harvey, Sir Walter Ralegh, or even Don John of Austria, the allegorists' nominees. What is beyond doubt is the strangeness, in every sense of the term, of Armado.

Comic expectations about Armado are aroused from the beginning, for it is from him that a "high" style for low matter is anticipated. He is a more elegant and "refined" ancestor of scruffy Pistol, in whom the world of romance and bombast has fallen on harder times. In Armado, Shakespeare seems to have found the perfect representative of a bygone era of knights, chivalric romances, and flamboyant grandiloquence. He is a man "in all the world's new fashion planted," full of "complements," a comic soldier and energetic linguist. The young men have imported him for a special reason: "Costard the swain, and he, shall be our sport, / And so to study three years is but short" (I.i.178-9). He is supposedly a fabulist, a teller of old stories, "in high-born words." "I will use him for my minstrelsy," the King affirms. Given this kind of background and buildup, Armado's linguistic excesses are almost predictable: an overblown high style, self-inflating rhetorical posturing, stilted invocations, fashionable words and phrases, an excessively latinate diction, scraps of old legends and romances, and above all a great deal of what was known as "fancy." Even those near him catch the disease, and we have already heard the King and Berowne using archaisms like "hight" and "wight."

Armado's two letters (to Navarre at I.i.216-64, and to

47

Jaquenetta at IV.i.62–92) reveal him in his most formal and most copious style. In addition to synonymy, he specializes in the figure of periphrasis, in bulky circumlocutions that obliterate rather than amplify their subject. Like synonymy, periphrasis takes us further and further away from the proper name. Not necessarily a bad thing, but in Armado's hands strange things happen. He begins his first letter, for example, with five high epithets for Navarre: "Great deputy, the welkin's viceregent, and sole dominator of Navarre, my soul's earth's God, and body's fostering patron" (I.i.216–8). This is known as covering all the angles. He explains to Navarre the event "that draweth from my snow-white pen the ebon-coloured ink, which here thou viewest, beholdest, surveyest, or seest" (I.i.236–8). Jaquenetta is "a child of our grandmother Eve, a female" (I.i.253). Amused by Costard, Armado tells Moth that "the heaving of my lungs provokes me to ridiculous smiling" (III.i.74), a speech that produces what it describes. This figure of rhetoric was identified by Hoskins with Sidney especially. Noting with wonder that "common English words" may be combined in the unlikeliest periphrases, Hoskins observed that "though all the words of it, by themselves, are most known and familiar, yet the bringing-in and fetch of it is strange and admirable to the ignorant" (Hoskins, p. 47). As if to prove the point, Armado refers to "the posteriors of this day, which the rude multitude call the afternoon" (V.i.84). The construction is "strange and admirable" to Holofernes alone.

Armado's first letter betrays as well his most typical mannerism—an expandable but basically rigid syntactic structure, often modeled on some structure of logic which would have been familiar to courtly readers of the past twenty or thirty years: "the time when? About the sixth hour; when beasts most graze, birds best peck, and men sit down to that nourishment which is called supper: so much for the time when. Now for the ground which? which, I mean, I walked upon: it is ycleped thy park. Then for the place where?" (I.i.230–5). The who-what-where approach, as has been pointed out by several editors and critics, was recommended by Wilson's *Art of Rhetorique* (1553), and used again and again by Harvey and others. If it is appropriate to the particular situation, it is no less typical of Armado's usual method of thought. The habit is shown in an even more extreme form in his second letter, to Jaquenetta, as he spins out the permutations of *"veni, vidi, vici"* in illustration of the old ballad of King Cophetua (himself) and the beggar Zenelephon (Jaquenetta): "he came, one; saw, two; overcame, three. Who came? the king: why did he come? to see: why did he see? to overcome. To whom came he? to the beggar: what saw he? the beggar: who overcame he? the beggar" (IV.i.70–4). By the time we learn what has occurred, we no longer care.

Armado's passion for such logical and schematic construction continues throughout the play. He also fancies the figure auxesis, or "the Avancer,"[40] as Puttenham has it: "I do affect the very ground, which is base, where her shoe, which is baser, guided by her foot, which is basest, doth tread" (I.ii.157–9). A few lines later we see him locked into another associative progression (a false syllogism, incidentally): "Love is a familiar; Love is a devil; there is no evil angel but Love" (I.ii.162–3). In his first encounter with Holofernes, Armado sews his narration together with a string of four strategically placed "let it pass" constructions (V.i.90–112). Richard David (V.i.95n.) calls this a "common colloquialism," but it is undoubtedly also a parody of the rhetorical figure paralipsis,[41] and hence an attempt at elevation by Armado, who is trying to convince Holofernes of his intimacy with Navarre. Indeed, Armado elevates himself so far that he begins speaking of himself in the third person (l. 102), a habit shared with self-important public figures of all kinds.

Armado also has a fondness for elaborate invocations, for "poetic" apostrophe, a hangover from whatever chivalric romance or sonnet-sequence he has just come from. We have already heard his address to Navarre in the first letter. In III.i, after Moth leaves, he says, "By thy favour, sweet

49

welkin, I must sigh in thy face" (III.i.65). And when he succumbs to "ridiculous smiling" a moment later, he begs, "O, pardon me, my stars!" (III.i.74–6). The habit is so pronounced that Moth parodies it, as he does most of Armado's tics: "My father's wit and my mother's tongue assist me!" Missing the irony, Armado praises this as a "Sweet invocation of a child; most pretty and pathetical!" (I.ii.90–1). Like the creaking syntax, such attempts at elegance remind us continually of an older era and an older literature. Armado is a walking anachronism. More precisely, his prose recalls for us an older group of courtly writers: Harvey, Lyly, and especially, in the apostrophes, Sidney. Echoes of each of them are strewn throughout the play, but they are probably most concentrated in Armado's second letter. It is all familiar, or would have been to a sophisticated audience, from the casual "Arcadianism" (IV.i.69n.) of "which to annothanize in the vulgar (O base and obscure vulgar!)" to the question-and-answer internal dialogue used by Harvey, to the whole series of echoes of plays and novels by Lyly. The letter to Jaquenetta smacks of Lyly in particular, especially in the latinate diction and the pleonastic pairs ("magnanimous and most illustrate," "pernicious and indubitate").

Like everyone else, Armado is obsessed with the idea of authority, and he too has his own pantheon of worthies—in his case, the real Worthies. His first words in the play suggest his interest in the past: "Boy, what sign is it when a man of great spirit grows melancholy?" (I.ii.1–2). He habitually looks for a "sign" from the past, and goes on to link himself, ludicrously, with the great heroes of antiquity, other warriors who have fallen in love: "Comfort me, boy. What great men have been in love?" (I.ii.61–2). He cries to Moth for "more authority, dear boy, name more." He will have the old ballad of the King and the Beggar "newly writ o'er, that I may example my digression by some mighty precedent" (I.ii.109–10). Armado looks to the past, here, for examples and "names" to rationalize and excuse his violation of the oath of the Academy. His search for authority occurs not before but only after the fact, trying to justify spontaneity through precedent.

At his most typical, at his most extravagant, Armado's speech and letters reveal him as stylistically distinct from Holofernes. In contrast to the staccato phrases and usually shapeless copiousness of the pedant, the automatic heaping on of synonyms, Armado's prose is more notable for a schematic and rigid formalism, an intricate but completely predictable set of patterns. The elaborate rhetorical figures employed by Armado serve as the bones and connective tendons of a rigid exoskeleton; in the spaces between the joints, one can perhaps invent a few synonyms, insert an apostrophe to the stars, or make an aside. But it is the immutable form which counts. It is, again, an easy substitute for more rigorous or creative thought. Once one of the series is started, as in base-baser-basest, everyone, but especially the speaker, knows where it will end up, and there is a security in that.

We may leave Armado for the moment by recalling an earlier comment on him by Navarre. Armado was, he said, "a refined traveller of Spain," stuffed with the latest fashions, chosen as a court minstrel, one

> That hath a mint of phrases in his brain;
> One who the music of his own vain tongue
> Doth ravish like enchanting harmony.
>
> (I.i.164–6)

In this casual allusion to the Orpheus legend there is delicious irony, as we realize once we have actually met Armado; for he is, at best, only a solipsistic Orpheus. He ravishes only himself, not wild beasts or savage hearts, with his own "vain" tongue. As such, he is an extreme version of the solipsistic tendencies of the other men, high and low, in the play. His prose is an accurate reflection of his narcissism, for nothing seems so admirable to him as the drone and surge of his own voice.

MOTH: THE BOY

Moth is wit. He is the personification of a quality of mind much discussed but too rarely heard. Like Ariel, he is all fire and air. Even his name is a witty pun—several of them, in fact. The obvious play is on *mote*, by analogy to the pun on note-ing in the title of *Much Ado About Nothing*.[42] Moth is first of all like the winged insect, flitting around various sources of "light," darting in and out of their haloes; he is a kind of pest, as Armado finds out. Moth is also a mote. He is extremely small, a particle; he is presumably the only one of the *commedia* group to have been played by a boy actor. There are several comic references in the play to his size, and it is he who is selected to portray the mighty Hercules "in minority" in the Pageant of the Nine Worthies. Moth is also the mote in the mind's eye of Matthew vii.3 and Luke vi.41. Berowne makes a similar allusion when he gloats over his colleagues revealed in love: "You found his mote; the king your mote did see; / But I a beam do find in each of three" (IV.iii.159–60). Pricking with ease the illusions cherished by Armado and Holofernes, Moth reminds us, if not them, of their folly. The page is always "quick in answers" (another pun, with "quick" as "alive" or "pregnant" as well as "swift").

This irritation corresponds with Moth's reductive functions in the play, for he is there partly to show up pretensions and to cut through the fogs of rhetorical posturing. The metaphor of incision is deliberately chosen, for his wit is variously described as "sharpe," "acute," or piercing. After Moth has made a fool of Holofernes, for example, Armado congratulates him: "Now, by the salt wave of the Mediterraneum, a sweet touch, a quick venue of wit! snip, snap, quick and home! it rejoiceth my intellect; true wit!" (V.i.56–8). The language of fencing is to be expected from Armado, with his fashionable "Spaniard's rapier," but it is also a good description of the way Moth usually works. There is yet another pun on "Moth," and that is *mot*,

French (and English) for "word."[43] It is an appropriate pun, given Moth's character and the fact that this is a "French" play for a courtly (French-speaking?) audience. Like the other possible meanings, "word" fits Moth's role in the play —he is a quip, a reply, turning the words of others around with his own. In reference to his size and name Costard says, "I marvel thy master hath not eaten thee for a word" (V.i.40–1).

Moth's prose style reflects the various connotations of his name. It is quick, witty, and lively. He speaks in short syntactic bursts of cleverness, usually spinning off what someone else has said:

Arm. What wilt thou prove?

Moth. A man, if I live; and this, by, in, and without, upon the instant: by heart you love her, because your heart cannot come by her; in heart you love her, because your heart is in love with her; and out of heart you love her, being out of heart that you cannot enjoy her.

(III.i.39–44)

It is an extremely clever reply to Armado's gullible question, and seems even more clever when we learn, as T. W. Baldwin tells us, that Moth is making a "punning division upon the signs of the ablative case, by, in, and without," as in the school-grammars of the time (Baldwin, 1, 570). This is exactly what Costard was trying to do with "manner" and "form" and what Armado did poorly in his who-what-where structures; we see in Moth's playful superiority of invention that he is both more skilled and less foolish—a rare combination in this play—than his companions. He works the joke out as he goes, inventing the details as he needs them—all this after he has twisted the meaning of "prove." The speech occurs in short spurts, with the clauses gradually lengthening until the final one, the longest, which rounds off the "set."

More typically, however, Moth's speeches are even shorter, one- or two-line replies. He too is a reflecting character, since he depends on the speech of others to set up his best witticisms. He is particularly fond of what Puttenham called "*Antanaclasis*, or the Rebounde": "Ye have another figure which by his nature we may call the *Rebound*, alluding to the tennis ball which being smitten with the racket reboundes backe againe, and where the last figure before played with two wordes somewhat alike, this playeth with one word written all alike but carrying divers sences" (p. 207). Moth's skill at such exchanges was evident in the speech just read. Puttenham's use of the analogy with tennis is suggestive, for *Love's Labour's Lost* abounds with allusions to games and play, as C. L. Barber has shown (Barber, pp. 100–102). At one point, after a great contest of wit, the Princess commends Rosaline and Katharine, "Well bandied both; a set of wit well play'd" (V.ii.29). This is Moth's game, and he is probably the best in the play at it. Self-conscious virtuosity is standard for him, and his supposed "master" (whom, in a total reversal, he calls his "negligent student"— III.i.34) provides a continually gullible audience, a parody (or reflection?) of our own attempts to follow Moth. Moth is simply too "quick" for him, and Armado sighs in helpless admiration at the latest linguistic sleight-of-hand, "A most fine figure!" (I.ii.52). Since he is not afflicted with vanity or self-delusion, Moth is available as an instrument against those who are. Armado's puffery is punctured again and again.

Much bawdiness lurks behind Moth's oh-so-innocent puns, and he seems fully aware of the "sinplicitie" of man. Moreover, Moth is the only one of the low characters, indeed of all the characters except Berowne, who has a special relationship with the audience. He is privileged to make asides to us, letting us hear his punch lines, and he invites us to laugh with him at Armado. He addresses us directly: "These are complements, these are humours, these betray nice wenches, that would be betrayed without these; and make them men of note (do you note, men?) that most are affected to these" (III.i.20–4). Moth's question, in the form of a clever chiasmus, will keep us alert, and insure a large measure of sympathy with him. Berowne and Moth, the two acknowledged, self-conscious "satirists" of the play, are thus set on a level with the audience, which theoretically shares their larger and more ironic vision of the folly of love.

There remains to be considered the putative identification of Moth with Thomas Nashe, known at the time as "Young Iuvenall, that byting Satyrist" (Greene, XII, 143). This is one case where historical allegory seems most plausible, but the external evidence for such an identification is inconclusive. Moth's usual style, moreover, is unlike Nashe's most typical expression—the quick rejoinders, the turning of phrases, the economy of language, are all different from Nashe's often frenetic expansiveness. Nashe was just as "quick," but more "voluble," and much more copious.[44] When Nashe's voice *is* heard in the play, as it once very clearly is, it is unmistakable. Moth tells Armado the meaning of "French brawl" (a dance): "No, my complete master; but to jig off a tune at the tongue's end, canary to it with your feet, humour it with turning up your eyelids, sigh a note and sing a note, sometime through the throat as if you swallowed love with singing love, sometime through the nose, as if you snuffed up love by smelling love; with your hat penthouse-like o'er the shop of your eyes; with your arms crossed on your thin-belly doublet like a rabbit on a spit; or your hands in your pocket, like a man after the old painting; and keep not too long in one tune, but a snip and away" (III.i.9–20). This passage, however, is not typical of Moth; in fact, it is his only speech of such length in the entire play. It is syntactically quite different from his other speeches, a different brand of wit from the "quick venue" so often heard elsewhere, and thus an exception.

A bewildering range of linguistic satire presents itself in *Love's Labour's Lost*. No doubt every sixteenth-century "vice" of language is represented somewhere in the babble.

It is hard to see how the clowns, Costard and Dull, "emerge unscathed from the play," as one critic believes (Berry, p. 75), or how anyone else, for that matter, can be singled out for unqualified approval as a linguistic model. Of the six *commedia* figures, all but Moth exemplify false wit and folly in various degrees. Costard is down-to-earth, but it is not immediately obvious that his linguistic habits and attitudes represent any norm. His is one use of language among several possibilities. We can say with the certainty of experience that every line spoken by Armado or Holofernes is pompous and foolish, and that Nathaniel's sycophantic imitations mark him as equally hopeless. But Moth's language escapes the general condemnation. Elements of real wit animate his speeches, a wit which is lively, quick, not motivated by vanity or folly, a wit which occasionally transforms rather than deforms language. His wit is usually parasitic, and it tends to be mostly witticism, but it is still the closest among that of the low characters to the real thing.

It is more difficult, with the court figures, to distinguish true from false wit or, from another angle, Shakespeare from his own parody. There are obvious enough cases of false wit and over-cleverness. Berowne's speech at I.i.72–93 ringing the changes on "light" is a set piece, and the other men comment on its cleverness. Boyet soars to strange heights of linguistic playfulness in a remarkable speech at II.i.234–49, and the ladies comment that he "is disposed" and "speak'st skillfully" (II.i.250–4). In V.ii, however, Rosaline and the Princess have this exchange, referring to the noblemen:

> *Ros.* Well-liking wits they have; gross, gross; fat, fat.
> *Prin.* O poverty in wit, kingly-poor flout!
>
> (V.ii.268–9)

Here the "li-king" pun, which Rosaline might accentuate in performance, is rapidly picked up, judged, and placed into an even wittier line by the Princess; the two lines manage to be self-referential comments on the nature of wit at the same time. Whether this exchange goes too far is debatable. Few in the audience could be expected to follow such twisting puns, rebounds, and lightning-quick associations; we feel like Berowne when he says, after another such exchange, "Speak for yourselves: my wit is at an end" (V.ii.430). Such passages are found everywhere in *Love's Labour's Lost*. My point is that the self-conscious cleverness of the characters, their (often punning) confessions of having gone too far, are vitally important to the dialectic of the play's debate on wit, and Shakespeare goes out of his way to call our attention to it. Energy often excuses the excesses.

If we are Baconians or positivists, we will naturally condemn such wit and wordplay as nonsense; if we are verbally licentious—poets—we might revel in it. If, however, we are a sympathetic and sophisticated audience, somewhere in between, we probably will experience both impulses at once, since the play offers them simultaneously. Even in cases of obviously false wit, in Armado's letters or Berowne's deliberately blatant sophistries, although we may condemn them on moral or social grounds, the sheer fun of it all, the exuberance and unleashed intellectual energy, takes us along with it in spite of ourselves. And in the best moments of Berowne's Promethean Fire speech in IV.iii, as we shall see, we listen in full admiration. Any wit, good or bad, is better than none, for the presence of wit signals the presence of the active imagination. Without its shaping pressure, nothing will be created.

The play continually forces us to make distinctions, however, to judge wit and to discriminate between the genuine and the spurious. Shakespeare offers us a full spectrum of wit, ranging from the most elementary malapropisms to the subtlest paronomasia. The kind of wit, as we have seen, depends on the attitudes toward language. Although the satiric focus is wide, it does appear that elaborate *schemes* are consistently mocked; *tropes* of language are less often subjects of scorn. This assumes the traditional distinction between tropes, which involve a change of meaning in a word (as by a metaphor), and schemes, which include the external manipulation of language (as in the patterning of sentences or whole paragraphs). *Love's Labour's Lost* has the most fun with elaborate and archaic schemes. Such devices, as used by Harvey, Sidney, or Lyly, for example, would be easily recognized by the audience in their extreme form here. If *Love's Labour's Lost* was written for a courtly audience, as seems likely, an arena in which Lyly and Sidney had made the greatest impression, then the delight in recognition would be all the greater.

Consider, for example, the use of chiasmus in the play, which the Elizabethans usually called "antimetabole." Puttenham termed it "the Counterchange" (p. 208), while Hoskins defined it as "a sentence inversed or turned back." By 1598, it is a figure of speech already outmoded, too "artificial" in the worst sense. Hoskins mocked its abuse in his famous "Fustian *Answer made to a* Tufftaffata *Speech*" (c. 1597–8): "For even as a Mill-horse is not a Horse-mill; nor Drink ere you go, is not Go ere you drink; even so Orator Best, is not the best Orator" (Hoskins, p. 112). In *Twelfth Night*, the disguised Viola and Feste self-consciously bounce this figure back and forth:

> *Feste.* I do live by the church; for I do live at my house, and my house doth stand by the church.
> *Viola.* So thou mayst say, the king lies by a beggar, if a beggar dwell near him; or, the church stands by thy tabor, if thy tabor stand by the church.

Feste replies mockingly with a good definition of the figure: "You have said, sir. To see this age! A sentence is but a chev'ril glove to a good wit. How quickly the wrong side may be turned outward!" (III.i.5–13). The wits of *Love's Labour's Lost* likewise turn the wrong side out again and again in order to demonstrate their cleverness. Boyet shows us the way in his first speech to the Princess:

Be now as prodigal of all dear grace
As Nature was in making graces dear
When she did starve the general world beside,
And prodigally gave them all to you.
(II.i.9–12)

To show us that she is made of sterner stuff than other
women are, the Princess launches into a seven-line denunciation of Boyet's language, calling his praise a "painted flourish" of style (l. 14). A few moments later, Navarre himself
makes an appeal to the Princess regarding her father's claim:

Dear princess, were not his requests so far
From reason's yielding, your fair self should make
A yielding 'gainst some reason in my breast,
And go well satisfied to France again.
(II.i.150–3)

Although the Princess does not comment directly on Navarre's style, she is not pleased with him; the tinkling echo of
Boyet's "painted flourish," reverberating again in the "reason" / "yielding" chiasmus, must have irritated her. But even
the ladies are not immune to the rhetorical plague: Maria's
"The only soil of his fair virtue's gloss, / If virtue's gloss will
stain with any soil" is echoed a few lines later by Katharine's
"He hath wit to make an ill shape good, / And shape to win
grace though he had no wit" (II.i.47–8, 59–60). The figure
runs throughout the play, and is usually associated with a
self-conscious cleverness.

The use of chiasmus is but the most glaring example of a
habit of thought that governs the speeches of all the characters—an instinctive resort to antithetical structures of all
sorts. We have already heard Navarre's cross-alliteration in
"grace us in the disgrace of death." In the final moments of
Berowne's Promethean Fire speech the reliance on such constructs becomes compulsive:

Let us once lose our oaths to find ourselves,
Or else we lose ourselves to keep our oaths.
It is religion to be thus forsworn;
For charity itself fulfils the law;
And who can sever love from charity?

(IV.iii.358–62)

Everything must be balanced, opposed, turned back by these characters. If Rosaline asks "What's your dark meaning, mouse, of this light word?" Katharine must answer "A light condition in a beauty dark" (V.ii.19–20). This habit characterizes what Jonas Barish has called Shakespeare's "logicality," the most important feature of which is "the habit of proceeding disjunctively, of splitting every idea into its component elements and then symmetrizing the elements so as to sharpen the sense of division between them" (Barish, p. 23). Barish connects this trait ultimately with euphuism, as we would expect. In *Love's Labour's Lost*, the most obvious vestiges of euphuism are clearly parodied, but the disjunctive impulse informs almost everything else in the play as well.

It would seem that parody of schemes such as chiasmus occurs in part for purely theatrical reasons. Such schemes are easy to hear, and they are if anything more obvious when spoken aloud than when they are simply read. A pun, involving a play on meaning, is harder to follow, and a really difficult pun, playing on three or four different meanings, may go unappreciated altogether. Elaborate schemes are heard immediately and are comic in themselves even if we don't know what exactly is being parodied. They involve a manipulation of sound ("pretty pleasing pricket") or compositional unit ("In manner and form following") that is unmistakable. Elaborate tropes and far-fetched metaphors are by no means accepted *en bloc* in the play—especially the clichéd Petrarchan imagery of the lords' sonnets—but the schemes are given a rougher time. The play appears to work toward a distinction between simple manipulation and genuine transformation.

The predominant styles being parodied are *prose* styles, those of Harvey, Lyly, Sidney, perhaps the earlier Greene, and at one point Nashe. Thus the traditional social association of prose with the "low" characters is enhanced in *Love's Labour's Lost* since these characters are the major vehicles for parodying courtly linguistic fashion. Arthur H. King has described the transition in style during the 1590s as one from "copie" to "sentence," or from schemes to tropes.[45] "Copie" is the aim and result of inventive uses of schemes such as periphrasis or synonymy, and *Love's Labour's Lost* seems situated squarely in the middle of this transition, however oversimplified King's description of it is. For the play, while continually mocking the old schemes, also searches for sounder models and examples, and it finds many of the more fashionable Petrarchan tropes and conceits equally lacking.

Beneath the games of wit and the parodies of style lie conflicting fundamental assumptions about language and what should be done with it. To say, as Ralph Berry does, that the play finally asserts the validity of the concept of words as "symbols of reality," or "symbols for things," or as "counters," is to oversimplify. Berry does allow, in Holofernes alone (who, he says, "has his passion for words under control"), that the idea of "words as things in themselves" is allowed by the play to stand (Berry, p. 76). This is backwards: the play stands on the idea. The test of language for Berry, nevertheless, is still its relation to "reality" or "things," and if there is no clearly perceived relationship, then it is condemned, supposedly by the play as a whole, as frivolous, escapist, self-deceiving.

This is essentially a Baconian position, and though there is a grain of truth in it, it rests on a questionable distinction between matter and words, *res* and *verba*.[46] It makes style into mere ornament—the very vice it attacks. The *locus classicus* of this concept is Bacon's statement of the first

distemper of learning: "when men study words and not matter . . . Pygmalion's frenzy is a good emblem or portraiture
of this vanity: for words are but the images of matter; and
except they have life of reason and invention, to fall in love
with them is all one as to fall in love with a picture" (Bacon,
III, 284). The trouble is, people *do* fall in love with pictures,
they do fall in love with language; it is just as unreasonable,
and just as much fun, as falling in love with people. Pygmalion's frenzy is an occupational hazard with poets. We can
imagine Bacon's reaction to a performance of *Love's Labour's Lost*, full of sound and fury and not signifying
enough. A suspicion lingers that Bacon was thinking of this
very play when he observed that "the conditions of life of
Pedantes [Holofernes?] have been scorned upon theatres"
(Bacon, III, 276).

It is tempting to conclude, as we now generally share
Bacon's materialism, that at the end of *Love's Labour's Lost*
Shakespeare, with Berowne, forswears "taffeta phrases" and
"silken terms." That this is simply not so is evident in the
continuing use of such phrases in the rest of the play—indeed, in the rest of his plays. And we should recall the impressive range of possible attitudes toward language, no one
of which is wholly sufficient in itself. The ideal Bacon aims
toward is a perspicuous, presumably transparent language,
one with no ambiguities. Swift's parody of the Academy
theory had many real-life counterparts, as R. F. Jones has
shown, culminating in the seventeenth century in the bathos
of John Wilkins' *Essay towards a Real Character and a
Philosophical Language* (1668) in which, Jones notes, Wilkins "attempted to classify everything in the universe, and
then by a combination of straight lines, curves, hooks, loops,
and dots, to devise for each thing a symbol which would
denote its genus and species. For those creations of the
imagination, such as fairies, which lie beyond the realm of
nature, he frankly made no provision, claiming that since
they did not exist, they should not be represented in language."[47] In the chilly company of Hobbes, Wilkins, and

the Royal Society extremists, in a wholly referential language—one that approaches the status of symbolic logic—there is no room for ambiguity, for the play of imagination, for the liberty of language. This is a possibility barely conceived of in *Love's Labour's Lost*, much less affirmed.

At the other end of the continuum, there is Costard tossing his "remuneration" in the air, very nearly a total identification between name and thing, in the impressive sound of the word; the two seem inherently connected, in an Adamic sense. The punsters and malaprops treat words as autonomous entities, rhyming and twisting them, jostling them next to one another, taking them apart and reassembling them in intricate patterns. The most important result is the "dislocation" Burckhardt mentions, the creation of that nagging and fruitful ambiguity so necessary to the poet. Words are slippery things, as Bacon well knew: "Yet even definitions cannot cure this evil in dealing with natural and material things; since the definitions themselves consist of words, and those words beget others" (Bacon, IV, 61). Or as Feste ironically complains, "words are grown so false I am loath to prove reason with them" (*TN*, III.i.23–4). A vicious circle in which scientists squirm and poets thrive; the mystery of words, the uncanny energy which seems to issue from within them, which causes one word to "beget" another, always in transformation, never remaining still, never fixed—if the play asserts anything, it is just this power.

The energy of language in *Love's Labour's Lost* reminds us that poetry is almost always language used for its own sake as well as language used referentially; not an absolute polarity, but a kind of double exposure. The antinomies mentioned earlier—of play and judgment, of solipsism and society, of words as things and words as signs—constitute a dialectic, a "dialogue," in the play's own terms. The play is a "great feast of languages" in the sense that it gives us everything at once—appetizers and dessert, the "scraps" and the main dish. What the men come to learn, in their little "academe," is not simply that words must be used as symbols of things, since words are always more than that, nor simply that speech is better than writing, but that there is a time and a place in which different attitudes are required or sanctioned. What the men and the audience "learn," therefore, is the principle of decorum, the way to use words in a variety of situations, in whatever "manner" and "form" the imagination decrees.

CHAPTER TWO

Theatricality

Theatrical styles are no less important in *Love's Labour's Lost* than verbal ones are, and the play provides us with an equally broad range of models and parodies of both actors and audiences. There is nothing new in saying that a Shakespearean play is concerned with its own theatricality, and there are other plays, like *Hamlet* and *A Midsummer Night's Dream*, with compelling plays-within-the-play. Few of the other early plays, however, are as insistent about exploring their own roots, or as self-consciously "artificial" and "theatrical" as this one. In addition to the usual brief allusions to the stage, *Love's Labour's Lost* contains three sections so clearly set off and emphasized that each of them may be termed a play-within-the-play: the sonnet-reading scene (IV.iii), the Masque of Muscovites (V.ii), and the Pageant of the Nine Worthies (V.ii).

The reason for this variety is clear enough. *Love's Labour's Lost* is an exploratory play. In the first chapter, we saw that the play examined the widest range of linguistic attitudes and responses, and was at times openly self-referential. The same qualities recur in the use of theatrical metaphors and inset theatrical scenes. Each of these three sections is not simply an emblem of the play as a whole, a mirroring that both distorts and clarifies. The sections also shape the course of the play's debate and guide the audience's responses to the play as a whole. The interrelationships among the sections are complex, not simple, and the best description of them may be "synergetic," the effect of the whole being greater than the sum of its parts. The audience's probable responses are transformed with each succeeding scene, and we find ourselves being moved between "engage-ment" and "detachment" throughout the play.[1] It is the careful modulation of this theatrical image, paralleling the subtle interplay of linguistic styles, which makes *Love's Labour's Lost* so impressive an accomplishment, and which distinguishes it from the three comedies preceding it.

THE SONNET-READING SCENE (IV.iii)

This scene (from ll. 1–210) provides us with the clearest possible image of multiple audiences. Berowne begins the scene, reading from a sonnet he is writing for Rosaline. A moment later the King enters with his sonnet, and Berowne steps aside—or rather, as the speeches seem to indicate, he climbs into a tree, from which he watches the rest of the scene.[2] Longaville then enters "with several papers," and the King also steps to the side. The "mess" ("a party of four at table") is completed when Dumain enters, also reading a poem, and Longaville finds a hiding place. There are at this point three hidden audiences watching Dumain—or four, counting the real audience—and each man is unaware that he too is being observed. The ultimate audience in the play is now Berowne, who is conscious of his special position: "Like a demi-god here sit I in the sky, / And wretched fools' secrets heedfully o'er-eye" (IV.iii.77–8). If, as seems likely, Berowne is literally clinging to a tree on the stage, then his "demi-god" situation is physically ludicrous. But his knowl-edge is nearly coincidental with ours, because our awareness in the play is also that of a "demi-god," privileged but not absolute.

An elegant formalism governs this scene, and its schematic pattern is not concealed, but intensified. If verisimilitude is destroyed with this improbable succession of audiences, we are compensated for it by the sudden focusing of critical aesthetic issues. In this case Shakespeare is doing nothing less than exploring the nature of a play's relationship with its own audience. The exaggeration of the scene increases our detachment from it and invites us to consider some of its implications. One conclusion is that a multiple awareness of different "planes of reality" can be easily and carefully controlled. A good example of this occurs at line 187 of this scene, just as we are beginning to warm up to Berowne's exposé of his comrades' folly. If we have been attentive, we will remember throughout IV.iii that Costard and Jaquenetta are on their way with Berowne's misdelivered sonnet (from IV.ii.145). Still, as we are drawn into the sonnet-reading scene, artificial as it is, and into Berowne's denunciation of his fallen colleagues, we tend to forget what has happened before. As Berowne winds himself up, the rhetoric of his mock-blazon becomes more and more feverish: "When shall you hear that I / Will praise a hand, a foot, a face, an eye, / A gait, a state, a brow, a breast, a waist, / A leg, a limb—?" (IV.iii.181–4).

Suddenly Costard and Jaquenetta enter with his poem. Berowne is deflated, and a rhetorical and dramatic balance is restored. The effect is like that of a governor on a steam engine—when it reaches too great a speed from too much hot air, and threatens to explode, a countervailing force automatically engages and everything slows down and begins to change direction. The absurdities and folly of each "actor" are qualified by the comments of the immediate unknown "audience," which are in turn qualified by the next audience. A similar effect is produced in *A Midsummer Night's Dream*, but it is nowhere more overtly and schematically emphasized than in *Love's Labour's Lost*.[3]

One of the conclusions implicit in the sonnet-reading scene is that the effect of such a multiple awareness is almost inevitably *reductive*—illusions and rhetoric which are active on one level are dissolved and rearranged in the next as awareness is forcibly expanded. The process begins with Dumain at the center, but it quickly widens to include the others. Longaville steps forth in a moment and comments on Dumain's hypocrisy and sentiment. Then comes the King, who chides them both for their behavior and their language, and quotes their extravagant, Petrarchan gestures back at them: "I heard your guilty rhymes, observed your fashion, / Saw sighs reek from you, noted well your passion . . ." (IV.iii.137–8). Berowne reveals himself next, or perhaps drops from the tree, mocking the King's hypocrisy and, with sarcastic echoes, his verses as well: "Good heart! what grace hast thou, thus to reprove / These worms for loving, that art most in love?" (IV.iii.151–2). But with Costard's entrance, Berowne's facade collapses. (Holofernes' judgment of Berowne's poem, for what it's worth, has been given at IV.ii.118–26.) Again Costard, one of the least sophisticated characters in the play, reveals the folly of the most sophisticated of the men. The "reductionism" thus works in every direction; both "low" and "high" circles of awareness may qualify one another.

It is important, too, to note the close connection of this technique with the rhetorical excesses seen in the first chapter. Something like counterpoint is created by the multiple levels of the sonnet-reading scene. Consider the following passage, in which Berowne's asides punctuate and puncture Dumain's romantic folly—clearly a matter of diction as well as perception—and turn each Petrarchan cliché on its head:

Dum. O most divine Kate!
Ber. O most profane coxcomb!
Dum. By heaven, the wonder in a mortal eye!
Ber. By earth, she is not, corporal; there you lie.
Dum. Her amber hairs for foul have amber quoted.
Ber. An amber-coloured raven was well noted.
Dum. As upright as the cedar.
Ber.   Stoop, I say;
      Her shoulder is with child.
Dum.   As fair as day.
Ber. Ay, as some days; but then no sun must shine.
                                              (IV.iii.81–9)

In the next few lines each of the four levels is expressed and then undercut in succession:

Dum. O! that I had my wish.
Long.   And I had mine!
King. And I mine too, good Lord!
Ber.   Amen, so I had mine. Is not that a good word?

Berowne's final aside to the audience emphasizes the artifice of the situation. This kind of linguistic and dramatic counterpoint occurs throughout the play, most notably in Moth's puns and asides, in Berowne's mocking, and especially in Costard's malapropisms and mangled aphorisms. We have already heard how Costard responds to Armado's elaborate circumlocutions with the simplest of personal pronouns (I.i.240–54).

The sonnet-reading scene indicates how in passages like these the linguistic dimension of the play finds an exact counterpart in the dramatic structure: counterpointed levels of diction imply contending levels of awareness. When there is irony at work—when low uses high diction or high uses low diction—the linguistic levels become a vicious circle and the multiple structural levels dissolve and crystallize in a new form. Perceptively distinguishing between "dry" and "sly" humor, Maynard Mack reminds us that the pun "is a voluntary effect with language, as malapropism is involuntary. Instead of single-mindedness, pun presupposes multiple-mindedness; instead of preoccupation with one's present self and purposes, an alert glance before and after; and instead of loss of intellectual and emotional maneuverability, a gain, for language creatively used is freedom."[4] In structure as well as language, then, *Love's Labour's Lost* continually leads us from the narrow to the broader, from the single to the multiple, from folly to clarification. Solos always become a chorus.

We are carefully guided through IV.iii partly by the formal structure of gradual revelation, but also by a handy commentator, Berowne. As noted in the previous chapter, Berowne has a special, privileged relationship with the audience. This relationship is partly responsible for the ap-

69

parent "contradictions" in his behavior noted by those critics who insist on a psychological consistency. In the first scene of the play, for example, Berowne lucidly criticizes the proposed "academe" and points out the absurdity of the ascetic oath, then suddenly drops his arguments and signs the oath himself. One non-psychological explanation for this can be made in terms of structural function: Berowne must be both *detached* commentator and *engaged* participant at the same time, he must mock folly and yet partake of it, be simultaneously wise and foolish, in order for the play to work the way it does. We can never be sure when Berowne is merely Byronic, aware of his own shortcomings and self-contradictions, and when he actually believes in the folly he is committing. The tension in his character becomes the audience's.

The tension in Berowne between engagement and detachment is especially evident in the sonnet-reading scene. He enters, as do his three comrades later, reading from a love-sonnet: "The king he is hunting the deer; I am coursing myself" (IV.iii.1–2). A comic interior monologue now follows ("I am toiling in a pitch,—pitch that defiles: defile! a foul word"), and we soon realize, if we haven't already, that Berowne is "defiled" with and to the same pitch that everyone else is: "By heaven, I do love, and it hath taught me to rhyme, and to be melancholy" (ll. 12–3). Worse, Berowne's speech is beginning to take on the stilted and affected quality of Armado's: "Well, she hath one o' my sonnets already: the clown bore it, the fool sent it, and the lady hath it: sweet clown, sweeter fool, sweetest lady!" (IV.iii.15–7). The use of the comparative progression is a familiar trick, and we have noted its abuse several times already. Berowne's sonnet to Rosaline, read at IV.ii.104–17, is swollen with the same hyperbolic diction and forced comparisons as those of the other infatuated noblemen, who have also been listening to Armado. An inflated parody of the courtly lovers generally, but especially of Berowne, Armado is a foppish instance of what they are all becoming under the influence of what they call "love."

If Berowne is deeply "engaged" in IV.iii—if he acts and even sounds like Armado—it does not last long. It is the other Berowne, the "detached" one, who later mocks the lords and says, "Tush! none but minstrels like of sonneting" (IV.iii.156). He is the instrument of linguistic and dramatic counterpoint, the master of low diction (who has himself abused high diction): "Proceed, sweet Cupid: thou hast thumped him with thy bird-bolt under the left pap" (IV.iii.22–4). This is the same Berowne who exposes Longaville's sentimentality with a punning obscenity: "O! rhymes are guards on wanton Cupid's hose: / Disfigure not his shop" (IV.iii.58–9). Once again, an ethereal notion is brought to earth linguistically, through the bawdiness of "shop" as phallus or codpiece. The "critic" (III.i.173) Berowne is our commentator-guide for the rest of this section, a "demi-god" suddenly aware of theatrical artifice and folly (he has, he says, witnessed a "scene of foolery"—IV.iii.161). "Are we betray'd thus to thy over-view?" (IV.iii.173) the King asks later.

If Berowne is a "demi-god" at line 77, he appears at line 149 as a medieval morality figure, Plain-Speaking, or Honesty, come in moral self-righteousness to expose vanity and deceit: "Now step I forth to whip hypocrisy."[5] His homiletic moralizing continues at an irritating intensity ("Too bitter is thy jest," says Navarre), until he has "whipped" himself instead into a comic frenzy, and has transformed himself into the same state of hypocrisy which he pretends to scourge:

> I, that am honest; I, that hold it sin
> To break the vow I am engaged in;
> I am betray'd, by keeping company
> With moon-like men, men of inconstancy.
> When shall you see me write a thing in rhyme?
> Or groan for Joan? or spend a minute's time
> In pruning me?
>
> (IV.iii.175–81)

The posture of detachment has led Berowne, through a familiar circular route, back into total "engagement," total
folly. His is the greatest, the most comic "inconstancy." A
final tipoff to the paradox of his character comes in the
couplet above where, with both end and internal rhyme, he
asks when he has ever written anything in rhyme. His
"hypocrisy" is blatant, for Plain-Speaking is a cover for Dis-
sembling. Berowne's very language here is an unwitting self-
"pruning" ("preening"). The high and the low, the mighty
and the humble, are bent around to a common meetingpoint
in folly.

Throughout this scene we have heard two voices, which
have been emphasized both structurally and linguistically;
one leads us toward participation and the other toward judgment. They are the same as the impulses toward and away
from verbal licentiousness described in the first chapter. The
effect, in both cases, is of a sustaining tension, of a dualism
no sooner asserted than denied. In IV.iii Shakespeare for a
moment telescopes the problem of audience response—with
three audiences on-stage—and provides us with an emblem
of balanced and modified responses; it seems clear that we
are supposed to remember, in the rest of the play, what we
have seen here. The dramatist does the work for us now, in
the most schematic way, with the implication that we should
do it for ourselves elsewhere.

The Masque of Muscovites (V.ii)

The Masque of Muscovites is less schematic than the sonnet-
reading scene, but ultimately no less formal and stylized,
with the same self-conscious artificiality guiding our responses to it. More overtly than IV.iii, the Masque contains
all the requirements of "drama": actors are given parts to
memorize, rehearsals are held, audiences are either hidden,
in the case of Boyet, or open but still unsympathetic, as with
the ladies, and an array of masks and disguises is worn.

With Moth as their herald, the lords intend to play the part of "Muscovites" before the ladies, as the final stage of their wooing campaign. But there has been a prior, unseen audience at their rehearsals; Boyet reports to the ladies that he has

> overheard what you shall overhear:
> That, by and by, disguis'd they will be here.
> Their herald is a pretty knavish page,
> That well by heart hath conn'd his embassage:
> Action and accent did they teach him there;
> "Thus must thou speak, and thus thy body bear."
> (V.ii.95–100)

Consequently, there is considerable dramatic irony when the lords actually enter, and all the acting lessons go for naught. Different levels of awareness are again at work onstage, with predictably comic results. The unsympathetic audience in IV.iii (Berowne) finds a parallel here in the ladies, who plan to destroy the intended masque, refusing to participate in the dramatic illusion by withholding the imaginative sympathy necessary to sustain the idea of a "role":

Prin. Nor to their penn'd speech render we no grace;
But while 'tis spoke each turn away her face.
Boyet. Why, that contempt will kill the speaker's heart,
And quite divorce his memory from his part.
Prin. Therefore I do it; and I make no doubt
The rest will ne'er come in, if he be out.
There's no such sport as sport by sport
o'erthrown,
To make theirs ours and ours none but our own.

But later, during the Pageant of the Nine Worthies, there will be no such prepared retaliation by the ladies, and the Princess will in fact counter the King's testy rejection of the intended pageant in language that echoes but reverses her earlier speech:

Nay, my good lord, let me o'er-rule you now.
That sport best pleases that doth least know how.
Where zeal strives to content, and the contents
Dies in the zeal of that which it presents;
Their form confounded makes most form in mirth,
When great things labouring perish in their birth.

(V.ii.511–16)[6]

The ladies have clearly changed their tune again, confounding form as they like it; they are scornful and unresponsive in the masque, but they represent a better audience for the Pageant.

Concealed, sharp-eyed audiences seem the rule rather than the exception in *Love's Labour's Lost*. The profusion of receding circles of awareness suggests that it may be ill-advised to take a condescending attitude towards "naive" art, since there may be someone looking over your shoulder. Berowne at least recognizes the uncomfortable parallel between the masque and the pageant when, following the Princess's speech to the King quoted above, he says, "A right description of our sport, my lord" (V.ii.517), referring to their masque. Berowne's advice to Navarre—that he see the Pageant of the Nine Worthies—is shrewd: " 'tis some policy / To have one show worse than the king's and his company" (V.ii.509). But he overlooks the possibility that the audience may see a greater resemblance than difference between the two productions.

In a court masque the participants wore masks and other disguises, and in V.ii virtually everyone assumes a disguise of some sort. The ladies don masks and exchange "favours," deliberately confusing their outward identities. The men are coming as "Muscovites, or Russians," a disguise which probably suggested to Shakespeare's audience little more than the exotic or strange.[7] Their reception is befittingly cold:

> *Prin.*   . . . ladies, we will every one be mask'd,
> And not a man of them shall have the grace,
> Despite of suit, to see a lady's face.

(V.ii.127–9)

"Grace" (l. 128) is exactly what will also be denied to the
lords' "penn'd speech" (l. 147), and what the men in turn
deny later to the Worthies. Only Boyet, who is detached
from the action and whose identity is not in question, goes
without a mask.

With all eight lords and ladies on stage in visors and exotic
costumes, this section (ll. 158–265) is extraordinarily suggestive, and can hardly fail to be visually effective in production. Because there has been little but confusion and decep-
tion among the four couples all along, it is only fitting that
all faces should now be covered. This use of masks conveniently epitomizes the problematical relationship between
appearance and reality. Berowne, for one, comes to realize
this later, when it dawns on him how their Masque was
anticipated:

> . . . our intents . . . once disclos'd,
> The ladies did change favours, and then we,
> Following the signs, woo'd but the sign of she.
> (V.ii.467–9)

The audience has known all along that the men have been
wooing little more than the "sign" of the women, paying
homage to a false and outmoded image of the nature of
woman, a case of "pure, pure idolatry" of the most self-
deceiving kind. They have misunderstood and underesti-
mated the women from the very beginning, and we are privy
to a strong dramatic irony which opens up the play—the
men unaware of the distinction between sign and thing sig-
nified, between appearance and reality, and the women manipulating the distinction to their own advantage.[8]

The confusion over "signs" and their referents moves us
in at least two directions. The first is epistemological, and
ultimately moral; we see here how much the lords have yet
to learn, and how the women will eventually manage to
teach them. The second direction is linguistic, and ultimately
aesthetic; the confusion in this scene offers an exact parallel
to the lords' linguistic abuses, naive and otherwise, and we

are again given an indication how the ladies will manipulate the lords' words against them. This kind of irony brings us again to the familiar tension of opposites held temporarily in balance. The conflict over the meaning of "sign" and "referent" leads inevitably to distinctions in the kind and quality of art such people can produce. The lords, at this moment, are naive, hardly superior to the low characters who will soon produce the Pageant of the Nine Worthies, and in some ways inferior to them, because they do not yet perceive the contradiction between their apparent sophistication and their actual ignorance. The ladies' cool control augurs better "art" in the broadest sense of the term.

The lords cannot "see," stricken with metaphorical blindness, and this defective vision naturally engenders corresponding linguistic deficiencies. We find an ironic measure of the extent of the lords' darkness (*Feste*: "there is no darkness but ignorance"—*TN*, IV.ii.42) in the frequency with which they employ weary Petrarchan conceits about "eyes" and "light." Berowne's witty and paradoxical "light" speech to Navarre earlier in the play gradually becomes a self-betraying prophecy:

> Light seeking light doth light of light beguile:
> So, ere you find where light in darkness lies,
> Your light grows dark by losing of your eyes.
>
> (I.i.77–9)

The theme of light and vision receives a final twist in one of Berowne's fashionable similes and the replies to it:

> *Ber.* Vouchsafe to show the sunshine of your face,
> That we, like savages, may worship it.
> *Ros.* My face is but a moon, and clouded too.
> *King.* Blessed are clouds, to do as such clouds do!
> Vouchsafe, bright moon, and these thy stars, to shine,
> Those clouds remov'd, upon our watery eyne.
>
> (V.ii.201–6)

76

The metaphor of "cloud" as "mask" is especially apt, because it suggests how a dazzling light beneath the surface is hidden from the men. Later, before the lords return without their disguises, Boyet tells the ladies to change favors back again and un-mask:

> Fair ladies, mask'd, are roses in their bud:
> Dismask'd, their damask sweet commixture shown,
> Are angels vailing clouds, or roses blown.
>
> (V.ii.295–7)

As roses are about to bloom and angels about to let their cloud-cover drop, so the ladies are preparing a revelation of their own. The damsels' masks conceal damask (blush-colored) complexions. The mask and the face beneath are identified by the same word; "damask," in fact, is itself a sweet verbal "commixture," a telescoping of its two referents, "damsel" and "mask." Berowne and the King beg, in fashionable terms, for an unveiling of the ladies' faces, for a literal revealing of "light" and identity. They actually need, and will get, a much more general and far-reaching revelation.

The men have been playing hackneyed roles throughout the play, and the Masque represents only the most literal example of it, a specifically theatrical occasion with rehearsals and costumes. Taking the part of the lovesick Petrarchan wooer afflicted with melancholy and heart-burn requires a certain rhetoric and vocabulary, as we have seen. In one dazzling passage in the Masque, Shakespeare neatly summarizes the problem:

> *Kath.* What! was your visor made without a tongue?
> *Long.* I know the reason, lady, why you ask.
> *Kath.* O! for your reason; quickly, sir; I long.
> *Long.* You have a double tongue within your mask,
>   And would afford my speechless visor half.
> *Kath.* Veal, quoth the Dutchman. Is not veal a calf?
> *Long.* A calf, fair lady!
> *Kath.*   No, a fair lord calf.

Long. Let's part the word.
Kath.   No, I'll not be your half.
                                             (V.ii.242–9)

This is as complicated as anything in the play. Longaville
has remained silent so far, and Katharine asks if his "visor" or
face can speak. He replies briefly, and she asks his reason.
He refers to her mask. The *Arden* note explains that such a
mask, which they are all wearing at this moment, was made
of black velvet (said to be of "taffeta" at l. 159), which
"covered the entire features and was kept in place by a
tongue, or interior projection, held in the mouth"
(V.ii.245n.). The "double tongue" of Longaville's comment
thus has a literal reference, as well as the self-demonstrative
figurative sense of "ambiguous" or "quibbling." Katharine is
in the process of demonstrating this very ability to quibble:
one of her lines ended with the word "long" and her next
one began with "Veal," thus making the identification "long-
veal" or Longaville. In addition, "veal" (the "Dutchman's"
pronunciation of "well") puns on "viel"—Dutch for
"plenty" (in response to Longaville's "half"); on "veal"—
"calf" or fool; and on "veil"—i.e., mask. Longaville responds
by asking to part the word "calf," and "ca-" equals *K*ath-
arine. She refuses to be his " 'alf," or wife. And so it goes.

The point of this passage, which continues through several
further permutations of "calf" to "ox" to the inevitable tired
old joke about a cuckold's "horns," is that it is all set up by
the allusion to the mask's construction. Katharine and Longaville's language confirms the interpretation of "double" as
"quibbling," making the entire set-piece, as so often happens
in the play, self-conscious. Moreover, the mask has its own
"tongue," and anyone wearing one has a "double tongue."
The broader implications of this conceit are interesting. As
the mask has its own physical tongue, so (in the analogy)
does the role played by the wearer of the mask, the actor,
have its accompanying "tongue," in the sense of a rhetoric

78

implied by the role. The lords have just shifted from portraying academics to the more fashionable role of the melancholy poet-lover, and as an inevitable result have fallen into a syrupy combination of elevated diction and hyperbolic conceit, the usual dregs of the sonneteering tradition. Everyone else in the play, similarly, is afflicted with some other rhetoric associated with his role, and the implication is that to play a role, to wear a mask literal or figurative, is necessarily to adopt another language at the same time. The connection with my earlier discussion of linguistic style is apparent. Each of the traditional *commedia dell'arte* types (known, coincidentally, as "masks," or stock types) had a particular dialect or linguistic habit associated with it, and the six low figures in *Love's Labour's Lost*, we saw, are carefully distinguished by verbal idiosyncrasy. The mask-tongue metaphor links the high and the low figures even more closely, and suggests again how the outlandish idiom of the lower group is only a more extreme version of the glib wit of the lords.

Ample justification exists, finally, for having the low figures wear the traditional *commedia* masks in production. The link with the high characters would be all the more apparent—no one can "see"—and the "double tongue" reference not as isolated as it may seem. The ubiquity of the mask-role conceit would be further emphasized, and the visual effect of seeing, at one time or another, fourteen of the seventeen principal characters in the play wearing some sort of mask would be an emphatic reminder of the theatricality of *Love's Labour's Lost*. The end of the play would then show a widespread literal as well as figurative discovery on several levels, when the masks are removed once and for all.

Boyet functions throughout this scene as an ironic Presenter of the Masque, a potential guide, like Berowne earlier, to our responses. He has been an unseen audience to the boyish preparations of the lords, offers during the Masque

79

itself a series of mocking observations, and single-handedly
puts Moth out of his part. At one point he sums up, like a
chorus, what we have seen:

> The tongues of mocking wenches are as keen
>   As is the razor's edge invisible,
> Cutting a smaller hair than may be seen;
>   Above the sense of sense; so sensible
> Seemeth their conference; their conceits have wings
> Fleeter than arrows, bullets, wind, thought, swifter
>   things.
>   (V.ii.256–61)

Boyet is a different kind of commentator from Berowne in
IV.iii, however, because he remains completely apart from
the action. The foppish lord, who is called "wit's pedlar"
(V.ii.317), wears no mask and is sexually uninvolved with
the ladies, however "greasy" his puns, because he cannot, as
Rosaline so unkindly puts it, "hit it" (IV.i.125).

The movement initiated by the masque is finally completed
in a kind of instant replay, when the lords return without
their disguises and the ladies have dropped their masks
(ll. 310–483). The dramatic irony remains strong, for each
lord thinks that the "sign" and his "she" now correspond.
There has been an uncovering but no discovery. Before the
lords return, the ladies joke about it:

> *Prin.* Will they not, think you, hang themselves
>   to-night?
>   Or ever, but in visors, show their faces?
>   This pert Berowne was out of countenance quite.
> *Ros.* O, they were all in lamentable cases!
>   (V.ii.270–3)

"Out of countenance," like "cases," means both "situation"
and "mask" (from "face"). In this second part of the
Masque, both aspects of the lords remain lamentable. As the
men become increasingly confused, in spite of the removal
of masks, Rosaline finally reveals the ladies' game:

Ros. Which of the visors was it that you wore?
Ber. Where? when? what visor? why demand you this?
Ros. There, then, that visor; that superfluous case
That hid the worse and show'd the better face.

(V.ii.385–8)

Rosaline's clever reversal implies that the outer, "super-fluous" face was preferable to the one Berowne wears now. "Superfluous" means primarily "on the surface," but also "unnecessary." Berowne is playing almost as elaborate and exotic a role now as when he was a "Russian," but Rosaline has seen through both of them.

The Masque of Muscovites, like much of the rest of *Love's Labour's Lost*, is marked by thwarted expectations, by "form confounded" as the Princess says—symmetry and structure are asserted only to break down time and again. The traditional harmonious fusion of actors and audience fails to occur at the end of the masque just as, at the end of the play, the traditional comic conclusion fails to come about. In both cases, common expectations of dramatic structure are aroused but not satisfied, and the innovative dramatist goes on to give a different shape and form to his material. In the masque, for example, Rosaline plays with the men's and the audience's assumptions of convention, disrupting the usual concord:

Play, music, then! nay, you must do it soon.
Not yet?—no dance: —thus change I like the moon.
. . . . . .
Since you are strangers, and come here by chance,
We'll not be nice: take hands: —we will not dance.

(V.ii.211–2, 218–9)

But, as C. L. Barber perceptively notes of this passage, "In breaking off the dance before it begins, Rosaline makes a sort of dance on her own terms, sudden and capricious; and clearly the other ladies, in response to her nodded signals—'Curtsy, sweet hearts'—are doing the same pirouette at the

same time" (Barber, p. 94). The same impulse toward disso-
lution and re-formation governs the language of the play as
well; words, too, change like the moon.

Berowne's famous forswearing of "taffeta phrases" (to be
discussed in detail later) concludes the pretension of the
masque, and the lords recognize, and admit, how they were
betrayed. Berowne preserves the theatrical metaphor:

> I see the trick on't: here was a consent,
> Knowing aforehand of our merriment,
> To dash it like a Christmas comedy.
>
> (V.ii.460–2)

He sadly admits that they all "are again forsworn, in will and
error" (l. 471). In the next moment Costard enters to an-
nounce the Pageant of the Nine Worthies, as if, in reply to
the lords' failure, to offer a model of those who once were
truly "worthy."

Including its sequel, the Masque of Muscovites covers over
300 lines of V.ii, and its length and complexity suggest its
importance in *Love's Labour's Lost*. It continues and ex-
pands the theatrical concerns established in the sonnet-reading scene and leads thematically into the pageant. The mask,
in particular, is used as an emblem of disguise and discovery,
of self-deception and self-knowledge; and when in the next
moment we see the Worthies, dressed in "ancient" costumes
and quite possibly wearing masks themselves, we find the
connection between the two sections all the more compelling.

The Pageant of the Nine Worthies (V.ii)

The Pageant of the Nine Worthies is the third of the large
"theatrical" sections, and the most important of them. As a
dramatic offering, it is no more successful than the masque,
however, and would have seemed much less fashionable to
Shakespeare's audience. The pageant is the brainchild of
Holofernes, and an unhappy birth it is. The tradition of the
Nine Worthies shows that they were associated with fame,

with feats of heroism so exemplary that their legends defeated time, surviving into Shakespeare's day on conduits
painted for royal entrances, in figured tapestries, in Lord
Mayors' Shows, and in the popular literature of the time.
But there was, almost inevitably, a simultaneous comic debasement of the Worthies, as more and more local favorites
became a ninth or tenth Worthy, usually substituted for
Godfrey of Bouillon. For a sophisticated audience in the
1590's, such a pageant, however it was performed, would
have been something of a joke.[9] As Holofernes' linguistic
theories are dated, so is his choice of dramatic subject. The
audience would have thought of it as an "old" subject, like
the play of Pyramus and Thisby in *A Midsummer Night's
Dream*,[10] one of those moldy old tales Shakespeare so often
resuscitated. Our suspicions of aesthetic disaster are soon
confirmed in performance.

From the start, Holofernes has difficulty in casting the
pageant. All the characters are obsessed with the question of
decorum. The diminutive Moth, played by a boy actor, is
chosen for the role of Hercules, traditionally one of the
"Giants" in pageants, though there is no evidence that Hercules was ever one of the Nine Worthies. The others realize
that Moth is too small for the part, so he is to portray Hercules "in minority," strangling a snake, complete with ex-
planatory apology. Armado's objection to Moth, "Pardon,
sir; error: he is not quantity enough for that Worthy's
thumb: he is not so big as the end of his club" (V.i.126–8),
reminds us of the dogged literal-mindedness with respect to
language seen in the first chapter. The decorum the actors
are concerned with here is a sheerly physical one, for they
are determined to present a literal imitation of the Worthies.
Costard is selected to play Pompey the Great because of his
"great limb or joint," whatever anatomical curiosity that
may be. Sir Nathaniel is put out of his part as Alexander the
Great when Boyet tells him his nose is "too right," alluding
to Alexander's legendary manner of holding his head
twisted to the side (V.ii.56on.), and Armado-Hector is dis-

concerted by mockery about his "leg" and "calf"(=fool) being the wrong size.

The narrator in Nabokov's *Bend Sinister* makes the snide observation that "devices which in some curious new way imitate nature are attractive to simple minds," and that same fascination is evident in the preparations for the Pageant of the Worthies, as it is in *A Midsummer Night's Dream* when Bottom suggests opening the window to let the moon into their play, only to be countered by Quince's suggestion that someone be chosen "to disfigure, or to present, the person of Moonshine" (*MND*, III.i.52–3). The least important sense of decorum, as both plays demonstrate, is the urge to physical realism. The directors of these plays-within-the-play assume that the failure of their imaginations to overcome certain physical obstacles proves a similar inability in the audience. The first chapter ended with the suggestion that what the lords in *Love's Labour's Lost* learn most of all is a sense of decorum in style; the pageant brings the subject literally to center stage, more overtly posing the question of artistic intention and effect.

Costard is the only actor in the pageant who understands the difference between his role and himself. When Nathaniel asks the loaded question, "Where will you find men worthy enough to present them?" (V.i.120–1), Holofernes and Armado are not bashful in offering themselves. Each will play several of the Worthies, and Moth exclaims sardonically of Holofernes, "Thrice-worthy gentleman!" (l. 138). During the pageant itself, most of the actors take themselves, and their roles, too seriously and too literally and are thus easily flustered by the mockery—an obvious parallel to the lords' Masque. Costard, on the other hand, knows that he is only to "parfect one man in one poor man, Pompion [Pumpkin] the Great" (ll. 499–500). He carefully distinguishes himself from his role: "It pleased them to think me worthy of Pompey the Great: for mine own part, I know not the degree of the Worthy, but I am to stand for him" (ll. 502–4). Costard also inadvertently suggests

84

that his "great limb or joint," his "own part" which will
"stand" for Pompey, is his phallus, the same weapon which
first got him into trouble with Jaquenetta. At the end of his
speech, Costard replies to the Princess' praise, " 'Tis not so
much worth; but I hope I was perfect. I made a little fault
in 'Great' " (ll. 554–5). Such an awareness of his assumed
role and of his own "worth" is virtually unique in *Love's
Labour's Lost*, and Berowne is correct that in one sense, at
least, "Pompey proves the best Worthy" (l. 556). The lords
in the Masque of Muscovites, by contrast, overvalue their
own "worth" and are unaware of the foolish roles they are
portraying.

The Pageant of the Nine Worthies never has a chance to
get started. Just as the women earlier refused to encourage
the masque, so the lords now are not disposed to be properly
sympathetic as an audience. As each of the pageant figures
steps forth, he is ragged unmercifully and forced to retreat.
As in the masque, the dramatic effort fails because of a mis-
judgment of the audience and, in addition, because of misconceptions about the requisite "verisimilitude" of the theater. Costard berates Nathaniel for his failure as Alexander:
"O! sir, you have overthrown Alisander the conqueror. You
will be scraped out of the painted cloth for this: your lion,
that holds his poll-axe sitting on a close-stool, will be given to
Ajax: he will be the ninth Worthy" (ll. 568–72). After
Nathaniel has departed in disgrace, Costard must assure us
that, like his other *commedia* friends, Nathaniel is a good
neighbor and "a very good bowler," but he is, alas, "a little
o'erparted" (ll. 576–8). We may wonder if Costard—who
so frequently refers to his own "great limb" and is apparently
"o'erparted" himself—is thinking specifically of Nathaniel's
"poll-axe" here.[11] It seems that there is a continuing phallic
joke about the Worthies. In *Much Ado About Nothing*,
Borachio refers to "the shaven Hercules in the smirched
worm-eaten tapestry, where his codpiece seems as massy as
his club" (*Ado*, III.iii.126–8). In a figurative sense, at any
rate, all the pageant actors are "o'erparted" in their heroic

roles and so, by implication, are the lords, who have through-out the play been confusing role and self.

The four lords mock the Worthies' performance unchar-itably, considering that they were themselves the victims of a similar scourging in the Masque of Muscovites. Berowne, we saw, made a clear parallel between the two performances (V.ii.517), and Dumain says "Though my mocks come home by me, I will now be merry" (l. 625). Dumain seems to say that though the folly of the pageant reminds us of the lords' folly in the masque—and so his mockery of the pageant will be in a sense self-reflexive—nevertheless he intends to take part in the fun, although not as the Worthies would like. After the ladies had mocked Moth out of his part in the masque, Navarre had complained, "A blister on his sweet tongue, with my heart, / That put Armado's page out of his part!" (V.ii.335–6). Moth has no lines in the pageant, but Navarre's condemnation still reflects on the lords, who here disrupt every actor's part. Extensive parallels between the two sections are thus at work: in the masque, Moth was mocked out of his prologue by Boyet, just as the pageant figures are discountenanced by Boyet and the lords. In both cases, the intended audience refuses to sympathize properly, and the planned effects go awry—the women won't dance, the Worthies aren't allowed to finish their speeches. In each instance, a more sophisticated and knowledgeable—but un-sympathetic—audience looks down on the amateurish theat-rical effort offered it.

If we have learned anything from the sonnet-reading scene and the Masque of Muscovites—from the vertiginous spiral of expanding circles of awareness, of concealed and succes-sively more knowledgeable audiences—it is that the audience must respond with a certain charity or sympathy if dramatic illusion is to be effective. The power of the audience's imag-ination must, it is shown, be nearly as large and as generous as the dramatist's. Though there is no overt appeal in *Love's Labour's Lost*, as in the choruses to *Henry V*—"let us. . . On your imaginary forces work" (Pro.); "eke out our per-

formance with your mind" (III, Cho.)—still the structure of
the plays-within-the-play indicates that a similar effort is required here. At the least we should have learned that dogmatic inflexibility, on the stage or in the audience, will sooner
or later be shattered. In contrast to the sonnet-reading scene
or the Masque of Muscovites, the Pageant of the Nine
Worthies offers no authorial-commentator as a guide through
the scene—that role has been bequeathed by implication to
the actual audience. We should have been "educated" by
now, even if no one in the play has been. Holofernes' lament in the midst of the pageant—"This is not generous, not
gentle, not humble" (l. 621)—rings true and serves to check
our spontaneous responses to the mockery, even though his
moving plea, predictably, collapses the next instant in a
Chaplinesque pratfall as he stumbles in the growing darkness. Each theatrical section teaches us that audiences must
be responsible and sympathetic.

The same attitude applies, by analogy, to verbal style.
Love's Labour's Lost uses the wittiest, most "conceited" and
up-to-date language to mock and qualify the older and less
fashionable rhetoric of the low characters, which reverberates with echoes of Sidney, Harvey, and Lyly. Now, in the
pageant, we hear the most archaic idiom yet, the stilted sing-
song of fourteeners. It too seems to have been scraped off a
worm-eaten "painted cloth":

> When in the world I liv'd, I was the world's
>   commander;
> By east, west, north, and south, I spread my conquering
>   might.
>
> (ll. 557–8)

Checked by an awareness that our knowledge, our judgment, has been disconcerted more than once before, we
should caution ourselves against dismissing this older style
too easily. Whether the courtly audience of 1597–98 reacted
in this way is a matter of speculation, but the structure of
the play demands it of us. Imagination, sympathy, patience:

87

the requisite virtues of the audience are also those of the playwright. Our responses to the plays-within-the-play have a way of becoming angles of vision on ourselves. One of the strategies of the play is to lead us as an audience into a response to the pageant similar to that of the lords', with only the briefest reminders, apart from what we have learned in the course of the play, to suggest that this is an inadequate response to the play as a whole. It is a built-in warning for all future audiences—that the play should be judged for itself, not its antiqueness; for its own style, not the styles it displays.

PRAISE AND WORTH

Granted certain differences, there are strong similarities among the three theatrical sections; most obviously, the continuing concern for the relationship between author and audience, audience and actor, actor and role. Each of the three sections is also thematically concerned in some way with the question of "praise" and "worth," two terms usually linked together in this play. Nathaniel's simple-minded question, "Where will you find men worthy enough to present them?" turns out to be one of the most important in the play. Most of the characters have a false sense of their own worth and are poor judges of others'. Each of the lords' sonnets, for example, suffers from hyperbole and clichéd diction. Early in the play, the Princess had rebuked Boyet's over-clever and sophistical praise of her, using these terms:

> Good Lord Boyet, my beauty, though but mean,
> Needs not the *painted flourish* of your *praise*:
> Beauty is bought by judgment of the eye,
> Not utter'd by base sale of chapmen's tongues.
> I am less proud to hear you tell my *worth*
> Than you much willing to be counted wise
> In spending your wit in the *praise* of mine.
>
> (II.i.13–19; my emphasis)

88

Yet Berowne's sonnet embodies exactly what the Princess cautioned against:

> Thy eye Jove's lightning bears, thy voice his dreadful
>   thunder,
> Which, not to anger bent, is music and sweet fire.
> Celestial as thou art, O! pardon love this wrong,
> That sings heaven's praise with such an earthly tongue.
>
> (IV.ii.114–7)

The romantic hyperbole of the sonnet-reading scene is punctuated by the reductive puns of one Berowne, the critic, while the other Berowne again takes flight defending his mistress, in a witty and paradoxical speech as extravagant as any in the play:

> O! but for my love, day would turn to night.
> Of all complexions the cull'd sovereignty
> Do meet, as at a fair, in her fair cheek;
> Where several *worthies* make one dignity,
> Where nothing wants that want itself doth seek.
> Lend me the *flourish* of all gentle tongues,—
> Fie, *painted* rhetoric! O! she needs it not:
> To things of sale a seller's *praise* belongs;
> She passes *praise*; then *praise* too short doth blot.
>
> (IV.iii.230–8; my emphasis)

These lines provide a number of parallels with the Princess's speech to Boyet, even down to the same terms: "painted," "flourish," "worth," "praise." And Berowne's elaborate eschewal of "painted rhetoric" is, paradoxically, the same kind of "painted flourish" that the Princess rejected in Boyet. The "worthies" in her cheek, still another kind of "painted flourish"—of cosmetics—suggest a further reflection of the pageant itself.

The Masque of Muscovites is prepared for by a literary discussion. The ladies criticize the men's sonnets, in particular their tendency towards false praise and false evaluations of worth. Berowne's verses are typical:

Ros. The numbers true; and, were the numbering too,
   I were the fairest goddess on the ground:
   I am compar'd to twenty thousand fairs.
   O! he hath drawn my picture in his letter.
Prin. Anything like?
Ros. Much in the letters, nothing in the praise.

(V.ii.35–40)

Katharine and Maria make similar complaints about Dumain and Longaville's efforts. Boyet reports that the men have encouraged Moth, "making the bold wag by their praises bolder" (V.ii.108). In the masque itself, the ladies rebuff all the traditional gambits of wooing, including Moth's salutation, "All hail, the richest beauties on the earth!" This address is countered by Boyet, "Beauties no richer than rich taffeta," in reference to the masks they are wearing (V.ii.158–9).

The women go on to chide the men even more thoroughly. Rosaline says that the Princess, in complimenting the mysterious "Russians," gives "undeserving praise," because the Russians are in fact fools (V.ii.366). In the rest of this part of the masque, the women one by one report the sweet nothings the lords have uttered (to the wrong ladies), and the men are confounded once again. At one time the Princess apparently believed in the idea of "worthiness," as is suggested when she tells Boyet at II.i.28 that she was "bold of your worthiness" to be her solicitor. But in the final act, Maria sums up what the lords have become—men whose "wit doth dote," spending all their powers of wit "to prove, by wit, worth in simplicity" (V.ii.78). If this had been Costard's "sinplicitie," it would have been worth the effort, perhaps; but "simplicity" here means plain "foolishness." Once Marcade enters, the Princess's tone may be ironic: "Farewell, worthy lord!" she tells Navarre (V.ii.726). But when the men persist in their wooing efforts, she must tell them, once and for all, that she and the other ladies have already "rated" or evaluated the lords' letters and favors as "bombast and as lining to the time" (V.ii.769–71). In short, they have found them unworthy.

The clearest statement of the women's view occurs in what is practically a fourth "theatrical" scene, the gathering of the women, Boyet, and the Forester for the deer-shoot (IV.i). The artifice of the scene is emphasized from the beginning, through language of the theater: the Princess asks the Forester "where is the bush / That we must stand and play the murderer in?" (IV.i.7–8), and she apparently enters a specially constructed hunting "stand" (l. 10), which suggests still another theater. The Princess begins to banter with the confused Forester, twisting his words with playful irony, turning his compliments to insults: "What, what? first *praise* me, and again say no? / . . . Nay, never *paint* me now: / Where fair is not, *praise* cannot mend the brow?" (ll. 14–6; my emphasis). She concludes with paradox: "A giving hand, though foul, shall have fair praise" (l. 23). Continuing to speak in increasingly meditative terms, she considers how some hunters will deliberately only wound an animal, "more for praise than purpose meant to kill." This leads to what is an almost choric commentary on the theme of fame, praise, and worth, and amounts to a dialectical reply to Navarre's opening speech:

> And out of question so it is sometimes,
> Glory grows guilty of detested crimes,
> When, for fame's sake, for praise, an outward part,
> We bend to that the working of the heart;
> As I for praise alone now seek to spill
> The poor deer's blood, that my heart means no ill.
>
> (IV.i.30–5)

The very idea of the quest for praise, for the "fame" that will "live register'd" upon men's tombs, as Navarre said, now seems tawdry, demeaning, itself "guilty." The connection between Navarre's quest and the Princess's deer-hunt is evident in the King's belief that all men "hunt" after fame during their lives (I.i.1). The Princess's reply has directly confronted the issue of how best to defeat time, how best to achieve fame, how to tell what is and is not "worthy" in human behavior. The tone brightens quickly, however, as Boyet follows up with banter about "curst wives," which the Princess answers light-heartedly: "praise we may afford / To any lady that subdues a lord" (IV.i.39–40). At this moment Costard enters, as opportunely as ever, bearing Armado's ridiculous love-letter to Jaquenetta, full of the hyperbolic "praise" and "bombast" just condemned: "By heaven, that thou art fair, is most infallible; true, that thou art beauteous; truth itself, that thou art lovely. More fairer than fair, beautiful than beauteous, truer than truth itself" (IV.i.62–5). This ironic juxtaposition would not have gone unnoticed by the audience; and Berowne's sonnet will be heard in the very next scene.

The Nine Worthies themselves are similarly identified with the idea of false praise. Through a gradual vulgarization, they appear to have become emblems of exaggerated or spurious praise, venerated relics from the past that are misused in the diminished present.[12] They have declined so far that Doll Tearsheet can console an exhausted Falstaff, who has vanquished the likes of Pistol, in their name: "Ah, rogue! i'faith, I love thee. Thou art as valorous as Hector of Troy, worth five of Agamemnon, and ten times better than the Nine Worthies. Ah, villain!" (*2H4*,II.iv.202–5). One of the last definitions of "worthy" in the *OED* is that it may be "applied colloquially or facetiously to any person, esp. one having a marked personality." The fall from military hero of epic legend to local eccentric is quite a drop. *Love's Labour's Lost* stands near the midpoint of that descent, and takes note of the phenomenon at the same time that it encourages it. When the diminutive Moth is chosen for the role of Hercules, parody can reach no further. Hercules' diminution is all the more appropriate when we recall that he was thought of not only as a strong-man but also as a type of the orator, a warrior in words.[13] When Bottom wants to "play Ercles rarely," the audience knows what to expect from "Ercles' vein, a tyrant's vein." The stage-role of Hercules is "a part to tear a cat in, to make all split," full of rant and inflated bombast (*MND*, I.ii.24–35). In the pageant, however, Hercules-Moth is happily silent, deprived of his traditional gift of language; the other "warriors" are continually defeated by their own words.

Everyone in the play offers or claims "praise" of some sort. Armado is tripped up by it, as usual:

> *Moth.* Speak you this in my praise, master?
> *Arm.* In thy condign praise.
> *Moth.* I will praise an eel with the same praise.
> *Arm.* What! that an eel is ingenious?
> *Moth.* That an eel is quick.
>
> (I.ii.24–8)

So is Moth "quick." Berowne later explains how women with "red" or natural complexions, "that would avoid dispraise"—the ultimate sin, apparently—are now darkening their brows, "painting" them (IV.iii.261). Rosaline relates how her "Russian" in the masque held her "dear / As precious eyesight, and did value me / Above this world" (V.ii.444–6). But in the pageant, the Worthy's traditional "praise" for the sovereign onlooker declines to this:

> And travelling along this coast, I here am come by
>   chance
> And lay my arms before the legs of this sweet lass of
>   France.
>
> (V.ii.549–50)

And in the final moments of the play, Armado asks the King, "will you hear the dialogue that the two learned men have compiled in praise of the owl and the cuckoo?" (V.ii.875–7). What we find there, however, as we shall discover later, is something quite different from what we would have expected —a "praise" not false or awkward or hyperbolic but exactly right, a "praise" startlingly different from the misguided examples in the rest of the play. Moreover, we should note that the traditional vehicle for praising "worth" is poetry (hence all the sonnets exalting the lover). As Donne said at the end of "The First Anniversary,"

> Verse hath a middle nature: heaven keepes soules,
> The grave keepes bodies, verse the fame enroules.[14]

Given the extensive parallels between the treatment of style and the performance of the Pageant, it would seem that the use of extravagant rhetorical hyperbole is like casting Moth as Hercules, or having the local yokels put on the Pageant of the Nine Worthies at all. *Love's Labour's Lost* works toward a redefinition of style in all its aspects: in life, in love, in art, in every direction.

One of the sources of unity in the play, especially among the three theatrical sections, is therefore to be found in this concern for praise, particularly in its connection with the theme of "worthiness." We have seen that most of the characters have their own versions of "authority," of the qualities worthy of respect and emulation. Moreover, they each worship a different kind of worthy, from the church fathers to Horace, Priscian, and Ovid. The play also alludes to a large number of other legendary heroes: Caesar, Joshua, and Achilles (all three among the traditional Nine Worthies), Solomon, Nestor, Timon, Hannibal, Ajax ("a-jakes"; called the "ninth Worthy," V.ii.572), not to mention Saint George. More powerful than any other figure in the play, Cupid is virtually a tenth worthy himself. Asked by the lovesick Armado to name other "great men" who have been in love, Moth mentions only Hercules and Samson (I.ii.63,67), but the list could go on.

In II.i, the Princess protests Boyet's praise of her "worth" (II.i.17), and Katharine reports of Dumain, "much too little of that good I saw / Is my report to his great worthiness" (II.i.62–3). In this same scene, the question of the debt between the Princess's father and Navarre is raised, and the King says that his part of Aquitaine is "not valued to the

94

money's worth" (II.i.137). A moment later, he bids the Princess, "receive such welcome at my hand / As honour, without breach of honour, may / Make tender of to thy true worthiness" (II.i.169–71). At the end of this scene, Boyet tells the Princess that Navarre revealed his love for her in his very eyes:

Methought all his senses were lock'd in his eye,
As jewels in crystal for some prince to buy;
Who, tend'ring their own worth from where they were
    glass'd,
Did point you to buy them, along as you pass'd.

(II.i.242–5)

So the word skips through the play, from the "several worthies" in Rosaline's cheek (IV.iii.233), to Nathaniel's query about "men worthy enough," to the most famous single word in this entire logorrhetic play, "*honorificabilitudinitatibus*" (V.i.42); Dover Wilson translates it as "the state of being loaded with honours," or, more or less, "worthy." Among other things the play is thus an exploration of what is and is not "worthy" in rhetoric, drama, and human behavior. The question is examined from every conceivable point of view. The appearance of the actual Worthies on stage in the final scene is a foregone conclusion—for they have long since been called into life metaphorically. Personifying the Worthies at the end of the play is comparable to conjuring up a "Frances" earlier. Both are acts of poetic creation, incarnating verbal allusions in dramatic characters. But the success of this final characterization is wholly ironic.

The audience has learned a good deal about dramatic creation along the way. Circles of awareness have expanded gradually through the three plays-within-the-play until the real audience must finally examine its own responses. It must judge itself by the lessons it has learned and the other audiences it has overheard. The rhythm of expansion and contraction has not continued at the same rate. Rather, it has widened to become more and more inclusive, until the au-

95

dience must consider its own "worthiness." The very structure of the play therefore provokes new discoveries about the nature of the theatrical experience. "Form" is defined only to be "confounded" and redefined at every turn. None of the plays-within-the-play ends in the manner expected— Berowne is exposed, the lords are laughed away, Marcade intervenes before two of the Worthies can join battle.

Love's Labour's Lost itself ends unconventionally. The audience has seen the expected form frustrated three times as "naive" art built houses of cards. In Marcade's entrance in the final scene, at the outermost circle of apprehension, the audience encounters "form confounded" in the play at large. The confidence we have placed in the plot of comedy, its traditional and inevitable outcome, is abruptly betrayed. Our education is being put to a test. If the audience has learned something about language, poetry, and theatrical representation, it will be able to distinguish the naive from the sophisticated. Its awareness will be large enough to take in something new, something daring. Berowne complains that "our wooing doth not end like an old play" (V.ii.864), but no one in the audience should make a similar complaint, for though the form of the "old play" is shattered, something entirely new, both strange and admirable, has come to life.

In a way, then, Berowne *is* like Shakespeare—not in the biographical sense, but in his attitudes toward human and theatrical ideals. The division in Berowne between detachment and engagement reflects Shakespeare's own practice as he sets events in motion only to pull back and watch them go wrong. It is, as Berowne says, the viewpoint of a "demigod": elevated but earthly, fitfully omniscient, just but sympathetic. The view is, finally, experimental.

CHAPTER THREE

Poets

Ber. Necessity will make us all forsworn
  Three thousand times within these three years'
    space;
  For every man with his affects is born,
  Not by might master'd, but by special grace.

(I.i.148–51)

Berowne articulates what the audience already knows—that every man is, more often than not, ruled by his "affects," his "affections" or passions, rather than by his reason. Whether "grace" is capitalized or not, these "affects" amount to a kind of original sin that man cannot overrule by his own will. Navarre had earlier in the same scene described the lords' proposed asceticism in similar terms:

> Therefore, brave conquerors—for so you are,
> That war against your own affections
> And the huge army of the world's desires—
> Our late edict shall strongly stand in force:
> Navarre shall be the wonder of the world;
> Our court shall be a little academe,
> Still and contemplative in living art.

(I.i.8–14)

When Navarre predicts a civil "war" within each man—will and reason against "affections"—we know that the "huge army" will inevitably triumph since, as Berowne puts it, only a special grace can conquer it, and no one in *Love's Labour's Lost* is so blessed. The King's confident tone—he uses "shall" three times, as if simply to declare a desire is to fulfill it—and his glib use of alliteration in lines 11–14 suggest that he is not fully aware of the difficulty of what he proposes. The inevitable outcome of the lords' "war" is anticipated immediately in Costard's confession of love for Jaquenetta, in his declaration that the "sinplicitie" of man is to hearken after the flesh. Indeed it is. In the next scene, the "soldier" Armado, a hero in other wars, confesses that he too has lost the skirmish with his own affections and desires. Continuing the metaphor of warfare, Armado couches his admission in medieval and courtly terms: "I will hereupon confess I am in love; and as it is base for a soldier to love, so am I in love with a base wench. If drawing my sword against the humour of affection would deliver me from the reprobate thought of it, I would take Desire prisoner, and ransom him to any French courtier for a new-devised courtesy" (I.ii.54–60). Armado's is a futile "if," to be sure, since all the men in *Love's Labour's Lost* are ruled by the "humour of affection," by their natural condition as fleshly beings, and by their particular passions. Desire has taken them all prisoner.

Because the word "affection" and its variations recur throughout the play, it will reward us to give some attention to the term. In the second scene of the play, for example, Armado says of Samson's love, "He surely affected her for her wit" (I.ii.84). And a moment later, in soliloquy, he confesses his love for Jaquenetta, "I do affect the very ground, which is base, where her shoe . . . doth tread" (I.ii.157–9). In the next scene, Boyet tells the Princess that Navarre is "infected," as if by disease, "With that which we lovers entitle affected" (II.i.230–2). Later, Moth tells Armado how those men may become "men of note" who "most are affected" to his advice (III.i.23). In another passage which implies that the individual has control over his desires, Holofernes declares that he chooses to "affect the letter" (IV.ii.55), or alliterate, as if he could do anything else. In the fifth act, Armado tells Holofernes, "Sir, it is the king's most sweet pleasure and affection to congratulate the princess at her pavilion" (V.i.82–3). And Berowne begins his

Promethean Fire speech with this call: "Have at you then, affection's men-at-arms" (IV.iii.286–7).

There is considerable irony, by this time, in Berowne's use of the word. The characters in the play have assumed a variety of definitions for "affection," ranging from the irrational forces ruling all men, and the power of love specifically, to the supposedly rational choice of alliteration. At the beginning of the play, the men were at war with their affections, locked in the combat of a civil war; by IV.iii, they are "men-at-arms," working in consort with their passions. This is a good sign in itself, for the noblemen had been seriously deluding themselves in thinking that they could resist their own natures. The Renaissance recognized a dangerous, dark side to the affections, vividly described by the Friar in Chapman's *Bussy d'Ambois*: "You know besides, that our affections' storm, / Rais'd in our blood, no Reason can reform."[1] Bacon echoes this distrust of the irrational: "Numberless in short are the ways, and sometimes imperceptible, in which the affections colour and infect the understanding" (Bacon, IV,58). Note again the conjunction with "infect," as if the affections were in themselves evil, a disease. Cicero had defined *affectio* as "an unstable condition, literally a sudden change in mind or body owing to some cause . . . such as joy, desire, fear, annoyance, illness, weakness."[2] In a darker world, it is but a short step to Leontes' confused anguish:

> Affection, thy intention stabs the center!
> Thou dost make possible things not so held,
> Communicat'st with dreams—how can this be?
> With what's unreal thou coactive art,
> And fellow'st nothing. Then 'tis very credent
> Thou may'st co-join with something; and thou dost,
> And that beyond commission, and I find it,
> And that to the infection of my brains
> And hard'ning of my brows.
>
> (WT, I.ii.138–46)

In addition to the range of meanings already defined, "affection" is here clearly linked with, and very nearly a synonym for, the imagination.[3] It is associated with "dreams," with the "unreal," with "nothing"—all those forces which Theseus so confidently dismisses in *A Midsummer Night's Dream*. And again there is the familiar conjunction with "infection."

Renaissance critics, applying analogies to formal rhetoric, often described the special function of poetry as working on the affections of men, of "moving" them. The poet's words, said Peacham, were supposed to "pearce into [man's] inward partes."[4] We recall Samuel Daniel's assertion that "heavenly Eloquence," simply through "commanding words," could "manage, guide, and master th'eminence / Of mens affections, more then all their swords." For Sidney, "mooving is of a higher degree then teaching" (Smith, I,171). This sort of power alarmed Puritan critics like Gosson, who remarked that poets "by the privy entries of the eare sappe downe into the heart, and with gunshotte of affection gaule the minde, where reason and vertue shoulde rule the roste."[5] This assault is what has happened to the jealous Leontes, with tragic consequences; when the reason is overcome by the affections, the unfettered imagination runs wild.

This discussion of "affection" is meant to demonstrate, in the terms provided by *Love's Labour's Lost*, the truth of Theseus' famous pronouncement:

> Lovers and madmen have such seething brains,
> Such shaping fantasies, that apprehend
> More than cool reason ever comprehends.
> The lunatic, the lover, and the poet
> Are of imagination all compact.
>
> (*MND*, V.i.4–8)

The noblemen in *Love's Labour's Lost* are poets, of course, and each grinds out a traditional love sonnet. But the variety of connotations in "affection" enables us to draw even closer parallels between the bearing of the noblemen—their dress, their style of speech, their intellect—and the poetry they produce. We begin to see that the way in which one deals with one's affections is roughly analogous to the way in which one writes poetry; disorder or foppery in one is reflected in the other.[6] This connection is made more explicit in *Twelfth Night*, when the love-sick Orsino boasts, "So full of shapes is fancy / That it alone is high fantastical" (I.i.14–5). "Fancy" itself meant both "imagination" and, as here, "love."

We can approach the male characters from another direction when we realize that the word "affection," not surprisingly, is also a pun. "Affection" is a contracted form of "affectation," and "affect," as either a verb or a noun, could also mean affectation. The point is that, as Fielding argues in his Preface to *Joseph Andrews*, the only source of the true Ridiculous is affectation. In *Love's Labour's Lost*, all the male characters are ruled by their affections, by their passions and natural inclinations, or, as Fielding would have it, by their vanity or hypocrisy. When Berowne describes his colleagues as "affection's men-at-arms," the irony works in both directions.

In his carefully balanced and highly affected speech in V.i, Nathaniel praises Holofernes' dinner speech as being "witty without affection" (V.i.4), a judgment we know to be ludicrously inaccurate. We are proven correct when Holofernes replies in the next instant, by picking up Nathaniel's very words. Armado's behavior, he says, is "vain, ridiculous, and thrasonical. He is too picked, too spruce, too affected, too odd, as it were, too peregrinate, as I may call it" (V.i.13–5). Holofernes is correct, but he also unwittingly describes his own language. Berowne later echoes Holofernes' phraseology when, in his famous renunciation speech, he forswears

> Taffeta phrases, silken terms precise,
> Three-pil'd hyperboles, spruce affection,
> Figures pedantical. . . .

> (V.ii.406–8)

But "spruce affection" is itself spruce affection. Nathaniel, Holofernes, Armado, and the four noblemen are guilty of affectation throughout the play—in their immature love, childish behavior, and foppish style. Only at the end do the lords begin to mature. By way of a pun, the idea of affectation thus indicates another sense in which the lunatics, the lovers, and the poets are parallel, and provides moreover another principle of unity in the play. The power of "affection" (passions, love) released too far will lead inevitably to "affection" (affectation) in behavior. Affectation in love can lead to folly and self-deception, and eventually to bad poetry, which means in turn bad sonnets, over-elaborate invention, and pretty pleasing prickets. *Love's Labour's Lost* anticipates Theseus by repeatedly marking that loving and writing poetry are kindred acts of the imagination.

That lovers are poets is no news. What is interesting in this play is the way in which the various parallels between high and low characters, between the lovers and the lunatics, continually confound geometry by intersecting. This interaction indicates that there is a complex thematic equivalent to that structural neo-Aristotelian logic and unity which, critics forever tell us, are so lacking in the play. If *Love's Labour's Lost* is a play primarily concerned with poetry and the imagination, with its own processes and structures, as I believe it is, then it should prove useful to examine in some detail those lunatics and lovers in the play who are also professed poets.

The probable date of *Love's Labour's Lost*, c. 1593–97, coincides with the height and waning of the Elizabethan craze for "Petrarchan" sonnets and sonnet sequences. If the qualitative high point of this movement had come, in 1591, with the publication of Sidney's *Astrophel and Stella*, which was then already several years old, that did not prevent would-be poets from continuing to write similar sonnets. As J. W. Lever notes, "During the four years that followed the appearance of *Astrophel and Stella* in 1591, more sonnets saw the light than in all the decades since Wyatt made his first renderings from Petrarch."[7] Shakespeare, too, was probably beginning to write his own sonnets at this time. There were dozens of nutshell-kings of the finite space of fourteen lines.

Dissenting voices were also heard, however. Donne, also probably beginning his *Songs and Sonets* at this time, wrote no regular sonnets among his often shocking anti-Petrarchan lyrics. Ben Jonson was to write only one regular sonnet, and made a joke about it at that:

> I that have beene a lover, and could shew it,
>   Though not in these, in rithmes not wholly dumbe,
>   Since I exscribe your Sonnets, am become
> A better lover, and much better Poet.
>
> (Jonson, VIII,182)

Jonson further complained to Drummond that sonnets "were like that Tirrants bed, wher some who were too short were racked, others too long cut short" (I, 134). The most discerning poets, Lever concludes, would learn that "Sidney's achievement was in essence a culmination, not, as they thought, a fresh start."[8] The noblemen of *Love's Labour's Lost*, devout followers of fashion, are gallant young sonneteers in the general sense of the term—only two of their four poems are regular sonnets, and Berowne's is in alexandrines. Three of the four sonnets were later collected in *The Passionate Pilgrim* (1599) and Dumain's was also included in the nostalgic pastoral collection, *England's Helicon* (1600), an indication that the audience would not have considered them in any way avant-garde.[9] But it is past time to turn to the "poets" of the play and examine their songs and sonnets, one by one, beginning with the young sonneteers and ending with the grotesque exotica of Holofernes.

BEROWNE

"Tush! none but minstrels like of sonneting" (IV.iii.156). Berowne's easy condemnation of the literary efforts of his fellow academics is also a judgment on his own literary taste. His love sonnet, which is read aloud in IV.ii by Nathaniel, will be brought into the sonnet-reading scene by Costard and ridiculed:

> If love make me forsworn, how shall I swear to love?
>   Ah! never faith could hold, if not to beauty vow'd;
> Though to myself forsworn, to thee I'll faithful prove:
>   Those thoughts to me were oaks, to thee like osiers
>   bow'd.
> Study his bias leaves and makes his book thine eyes,
>   Where all those pleasures live that art would
>   comprehend.
> If knowledge be the mark, to know thee shall suffice;
>   Well learned is that tongue that well can thee
>   commend;
> All ignorant that soul that sees thee without wonder;
>   Which is to me some praise that I thy parts admire.
> Thy eye Jove's lightning bears, thy voice his dreadful
>   thunder,
>   Which, not to anger bent, is music and sweet fire.
> Celestial as thou art, O! pardon love this wrong,
> That sings heaven's praise with such an earthly tongue.
>
> (IV.ii.104–17)

Berowne's sonnet anticipates many of the ideas and images of the Promethean Fire speech he will deliver in the next scene. The opposition of "study" and "eyes" and the familiar paradox of "forsworn" yet "faithful" will soon be amplified at length. But the primary purpose here is to "praise" the mistress, a theme whose widespread use we have seen elsewhere in the play. This is the traditional function of love sonnets; thus Margaret asks Benedick "Will you then write me a sonnet in praise of my beauty?" to which he replies with a familiar double-entendre, "In so high a style, Margaret, that no man living shall come over it" (*Ado*,V.ii.3–6). Berowne's sonnet is also in a "high" style. His praise, moreover, is self-congratulatory ("Which is to me some praise") simply because he recognizes Rosaline's beauty.

Two of Berowne's metaphors need some explanation: "Study his bias leaves and makes his book thine eyes, / Where all those pleasures live that art would comprehend." "Bias" is derived from the game of bowls, and describes the oblique curving path of the weighted ball. Berowne's figurative sense is that Study will leave its indirect path to wisdom and pursue another one—presumably a straight line—to the mistress's "eyes." But "bias" also had the sense of "natural tendency or leaning"; and so there is an implication that by making "his book thine eyes," Study is indulging an "unnatural" tendency. The metaphor is ambiguous, just as the lords are ambivalent about their course of action at this point in the play. They will soon throw caution to the winds, but until the multiple recognitions of IV.iii none of the lords will whole-heartedly declare himself.

The second interesting metaphor is that of making the "book" the "eyes" of the mistress, turning from the literal to the figurative "text," where one "reads" true wisdom. This is a variant on the well-worn trope of "the book of the face";[10] an elaborate exposition of the theme occurs in *Romeo and Juliet*, when Lady Capulet persuades Juliet of Paris's virtues:

> Read o'er the volume of young Paris' face,
> And find delight writ there with beauty's pen;
> Examine every married lineament,
> And see how one another lends content;
> And what obscured in this fair volume lies
> Find written in the margent of his eyes.
> This precious book of love, this unbound lover,
> To beautify him only lacks a cover.
>
> (I.iii.81–8)

The dandies of *Love's Labour's Lost* are exceptionally fond of this conceit. Observing marks of love in Navarre, Boyet tells the Princess that "His face's own margent did quote such amazes, / That all eyes saw his eyes enchanted with gazes" (II.i.246–7). The ladies have little difficulty in "reading" the lords. But the lords, of course, are equally enamored of and confused by both kinds of books. The frequency with which the metaphor appears in the play is significant, for its very bookishness and artificiality constitutes its chief attraction to these students. In another parody of the affectation of the lords, Nathaniel uses the trope far too literally when he explains Dull's ignorance to Holofernes, the other of the two "book-men":

> Sir, he hath never fed of the dainties that are bred in a book. He hath not eat paper, as it were; he hath not drunk ink: his intellect is not replenished.
>
> (IV.ii.24–6)

By forcing the metaphor to a *reductio ad absurdum*—you are what you eat—Nathaniel prepares us to be somewhat skeptical of the ringing affirmations in Berowne's Promethean Fire speech in the next scene, where he will invoke the same terms in grand style:

> O! we have made a vow to study, lords,
> And in that vow we have forsworn our books:
> . . . . .
> From women's eyes this doctrine I derive:
> They sparkle still the right Promethean fire;
> They are the books, the arts, the academes,
> That show, contain, and nourish all the world.
>
> (IV.iii.315–6; 347–50)

And Berowne goes on to affirm that men are "the authors of these women" (IV.iii.356), thereby comically usurping still another godlike function.

It is plainly too much. Berowne's sonnet, we recall, had said that in the book of the lady's eyes "all those pleasures live that art would comprehend." Theseus, in his famous speech, had been careful to distinguish two mental activities;

lovers, madmen, and poets "apprehend," whereas "cool reason . . . comprehends." Berowne's use of the word "art" has more the sense of diligence or craft than imagination; he is still trying to "comprehend" books whether literal or figurative. The play argues that a more imaginative sympathy is necessary, a "special grace" that still eludes the lords.

The usual Petrarchan clichés glue Berowne's poem together: a fascination with the lady's "eyes," a respect for her imperious nature (the "dreadful thunder" of her voice), a description that makes her "celestial" and links her with "heaven." As Bacon remarked in his essay "Of Love," "It is a strange thing to note the excess of this passion, and how it braves the nature and value of things, by this; that the speaking in a perpetuall hyperbole is comely in nothing but in love" (Bacon, VI, 397). Hyperbole is certainly at the heart of the Petrarchan conceit, at least as Berowne uses it. As Bacon says, it "braves" the value of things; it pumps up a false praise, which leads ultimately to a false or unperceptive poetry. It is specifically this habit of hyperbole which the women object to, as we saw in the previous chapter. Rosaline's comment on Berowne's poetry is forthright:

> *Ros.* Nay, I have verses too, I thank Berowne:
> The numbers true; and, were the numbering too,
> I were the fairest goddess on the ground:
> I am compar'd to twenty thousand fairs.
> O! he hath drawn my picture in his letter.
> *Prin.* Anything like?
> *Ros.* Much in the letters, nothing in the praise.
> (V.ii.34–40)

The reference to "fairs" suggests she has seen a different poem from the one quoted above, but they were surely similar. The meter ("numbers") is correct, but nothing else— the idealized deification is rejected, for the "numbering" or reckoning (judgment) is false.

Holofernes' comments on Berowne's sonnet echo Rosaline's: "Here are only numbers ratified; but, for the elegancy, facility, and golden cadence of poesy, *caret*. . . . I will prove those verses to be very unlearned, neither savouring of poetry, wit, nor invention" (IV.ii.119–21, 156–8). Holofernes agrees with Rosaline that the poem is metrically correct, that the lines have "a correct *ratio* of feet and syllables" (Baldwin, II, 392). This in spite of the fact that Nathaniel hasn't read the poem properly, according to Holofernes.[11] Most seriously, however, he feels the poem lacks "elegancy," with which we can all agree, and especially that it lacks "facility" (or "invention"). We saw in the first chapter Holofernes' idea of "facility": great heaps of synonyms. He goes on to a more interesting criticism when he says that the poem is merely an imitation (I will return to this later). It is apparent that Holofernes finds nothing "original" in the poem.

Berowne disparages his own poetry at the start of the great sonnet-reading scene. He enters reading a paper, apparently his next sonnet (the one Rosaline comments on?) and, with his usual blend of hearty participation and witty detachment, declares himself a conventional lover: "By heaven, I do love, and it hath taught me to rhyme, and to be melancholy; and here is part of my rhyme, and here my melancholy. Well, she hath one o' my sonnets already: the clown bore it, the fool sent it, and the lady hath it: sweet clown, sweeter fool, sweetest lady!" (IV.iii.12–7). We never see much of his melancholy, but his one example of rhyme, like his countless examples of "wit," can lead us to only one conclusion—that Berowne is fashionable and clever, that he excels in paradoxes, but that he is not a sonneteer of any distinction. Berowne's saving grace as a character, the quality in him that wins us over to his side, is that he at least knows when his forces are losing the war, and when to retreat before, or surrender to, the "huge army" mustered by Desire.

Navarre

The King needs a reminder of his mediocrity, however. He enters IV.iii reading, with a sigh, his own sixteen-line sonnet:

So sweet a kiss the golden sun gives not
    To those fresh morning drops upon the rose,
As thy eye-beams when their fresh rays have smote
    The night of dew that on my cheeks down flows:
Nor shines the silver moon one half so bright
    Through the transparent bosom of the deep,
As doth thy face through tears of mine give light[.]
    Thou shin'st in every tear that I do weep:
No drop but as a coach doth carry thee;
    So ridest thou triumphing in my woe.
Do but behold the tears that swell in me,
    And they thy glory through my grief will show:
But do not love thyself; then thou will keep
My tears for glasses, and still make me weep.
O queen of queens! how far dost thou excel,
No thought can think, nor tongue of mortal tell.
                   (IV.iii.25–40)

    This is the only one of the four sonnets in the play not col-
lected elsewhere; if it is inferior to the others, it is merely a
matter of degree. Although Navarre's poem relies on hyperbole ("queen of queens," "nor tongue of mortal"), its main
feature is the extended conceit of the "tears," which faintly
resembles Donne's image in "A Valediction: Of Weeping."
The differences are instructive. The compression and complexity of Donne's language and imagery, a quality often
attained in Shakespeare's own sonnets, are not present in
Navarre's poem. We have instead a flaccid syntactical structure which leisurely presents parallel similes: "so-as"; "nor-
so-as"; "no-so." The mistress' image reflected in a tear
rides "triumphing in my woe," as "a coach" would carry
her.
    Navarre's appeal against vanity is interesting. He suggests
that if she doesn't reciprocate his love, his tears will be
"glasses" or mirrors for her, and she will only gaze vainly at
her own image. But if the love is reciprocated, her "glory"
will show "through" his grief—the tears will reflect her
image but will also reveal his love. It is a suggestive emblem

for the kind of aesthetic sympathy the play probes and questions. The lords, and the sonnets they write, have so far been all surface and no depth; they are easily satisfied and easily confused by outward signs and masks. We shall discover in a moment, too, that Holofernes' doctrine of imitation remains at the same superficial level. The best art will work both ways. But Navarre's sonnet fails its own test; some of its imagery is rich and complex—perhaps too complex—but the tedious periphrases of "night of dew" and "transparent bosom of the deep" are dead weight.

Navarre will scorn the poems of Dumain and Longaville, but he is himself exposed by Berowne, who mocks the King's very language:

> *Ber.* Good heart! what grace hast thou, thus to reprove
> These worms for loving, that art most in love?
> Your eyes do make no coaches; in your tears
> There is no certain princess that appears:
> You'll not be perjur'd, 'tis a hateful thing:
> Tush! none but minstrels like of sonneting.
> (IV.iii.151–6)

Berowne has singled out for scorn the most "conceited" elements of the poem, especially the "eye" and "tears" imagery. Navarre seems to have taken the advice Proteus gives to Thurio in *The Two Gentlemen of Verona* on how to compose "wailful sonnets . . . full-fraught with serviceable vows":

> Say that upon the altar of her beauty
> You sacrifice your tears, your sighs, your heart.
> Write till your ink be dry, and with your tears
> Moist it again, and frame some feeling line
> That may discover such integrity.
> (*TGV*, III.ii.69–76)

The Princess' view of Navarre's "feeling" lines is jaundiced; she remarks that he has sent, along with diamonds,

> . . . as much love in rhyme
> As would be cramm'd up in a sheet of paper,
> Writ o' both sides the leaf, margent and all,
> That he was fain to seal on Cupid's name.
>
> (V.ii.6–9)

Like the others, Navarre cannot control his own unleashed energies. His poetry, like that of his friends, has a way of falling flat when he most wants it to soar. The only art he has so far mastered is that of sinking.

LONGAVILLE

Longaville follows the King in IV.iii, entering "like a per-jure, wearing papers" stuck in his hat (l. 46). Shaken by colossal sighs of melancholy, "Ay me! I am forsworn," Longaville worries,

> I fear these stubborn lines lack power to move.
> O sweet Maria, empress of my love!
> These numbers will I tear, and write in prose.
>
> (IV.iii.55–7)

Disregarding for the moment Berowne's salacious rejoinder to this sentiment, we should note that while these verses are primarily intended as vehicles of praise for the beloved, they are also, like all poetry, supposed to "move" the listener. Sidney argued that "moving" is "wel nigh the cause and the effect of teaching. For who will be taught, if hee bee not mooved with desire to be taught? and what so much good doth that teaching bring forth . . . as that it mooveth one to doe that which it dooth teach? for, as *Aristotle* sayth, it is not *Gnosis* but *Praxis* must be the fruit" (Smith, I,171). The point, then, is to stir the affections of the listener, to excite in him certain emotions which will lead him to emulate, say, a heroic action, or in this case, to respond in kind to the lover.[12]

Longaville has something rather more literal and trivial in

mind, and the allusion to the traditional doctrine seems ironic.
His lines remain "stubborn," moving no one:

> Did not the heavenly rhetoric of thine eye,
>   'Gainst whom the world cannot hold argument,
> Persuade my heart to this false perjury?
> Vows for thee broke deserve not punishment.
> A woman I forswore; but I will prove,
>   Thou being a goddess, I forswore not thee:
> My vow was earthly, thou a heavenly love;
>   Thy grace being gain'd cures all disgrace in me.
> Vows are but breath, and breath a vapour is:
>   Then thou, fair sun, which on my earth doth shine,
> Exhal'st this vapour-vow; in thee it is:
>   If broken then, it is no fault of mine:
> If by me broke, what fool is not so wise
>   To lose an oath to win a paradise?
>
>   (IV.iii.58–71)

This is the densest and wittiest of the poems so far, and the
most "Petrarchan." The mistress is "heavenly," a "goddess,"
the "fair sun." She has total power over the poet. Her "eye"
controls him. In a series of reversals, he claims she has forced
him, by her beauty, to perjure himself. The "heavenly rhetoric" of her eye anticipates Berowne's Promethean Fire
speech, and the final rhetorical question, "what fool is not
so wise / To lose an oath to win a paradise?" foreshadows a
similar comment from Berowne later:

> Let us once lose our oaths to find ourselves,
> Or else we lose ourselves to keep our oaths.
>   (IV.iii.358–9)

Many of the ideas and images in Longaville's sonnet, however, find more interesting expression, as he himself predicted, in the "prose," and also in Berowne's speech. The
poem depends on a number of familiar oppositions: heavenly-

earthly, sun-earth, truth-perjury, fool-wise, and that old stand-by, grace-disgrace. We sense not a perception of truth in these dualisms, but simple manipulation according to traditional formulae. The poem is an elaborate "argument," a self-justification ("what fool is not so wise") of prior and present folly. Berowne's immediate comment focuses on the poem's hyperbole:

> This is the liver vein, which makes flesh a deity;
> A green goose a goddess; pure, pure idolatry.
> God amend us, God amend! we are much out o' th' way.
>
> (IV.iii.72–4)

"Idolatry" and deification—false evaluations, false praise—are at the heart of all these poems; such perceptions inevitably produce shallow poetry. Like Navarre, Longaville has an instinct for euphemistic periphrasis; thus his oral spray of rhetorical froth is awkwardly termed "this vapour-vow," which is as insubstantial as his original vow. Transferring all responsibility for broken oaths to his mistress, Longaville pursues the conceit with admirable energy and lamentable logic. He finally takes refuge in a rhetorical question. The terminology of logic is evident throughout the poem, as Longaville says that he (indeed, "the world") has lost an "argument," unwillingly "persuaded" to "false perjury" (as if there were any other kind). Longaville will therefore attempt to win his mistress over with another argument: "I will prove" a paradox. The poem proceeds through statement and syllogism, lines six through nine introducing the premises, line ten springing the conclusion ("Then . . ."). The consequences of the argument are then prophesied in two successive "if" clauses of the "heads I win, tails you lose" variety. But the mechanics of logic produce nothing more than sophistry. Navarre had said of Berowne's logical wit, "How well he's read, to reason against reading!" (I.i.94), but the description applies to all of the lords, for they are enamored of the mere trappings of wisdom.

Dumain

Dumain enters last, making the fourth; in a passage quoted in full in the previous chapter, his sighing exclamations are punctuated by Berowne's mocking echoes:

Dum. O most divine Kate!
Ber. O most profane coxcomb!
Dum. By heaven, the wonder in a mortal eye!
Ber. By earth, she is not, corporal; there you lie.
                                                    (IV.iii.81–4)

Corporeal or not, the love of her is a "fever" which "reigns" like a queen in Dumain's blood; the metaphor of the "fever" of love has a lengthy tradition behind it and was taken literally by many writers to mean an actual disturbance in the blood. But Berowne's suggestion to "let her out in saucers," a "sweet misprision" for which he congratulates himself, destroys any possible romantic sentiment. The familiar tropes of Petrarchanism are again and again brought low by a comic literalness.

Dumain's "ode" was collected in both *The Passionate Pilgrim* and *England's Helicon*. In the latter, it was entitled "The passionate Sheepheards Song" and was transformed into even more of a pastoral: the "lover" of line 105 became a "shepherd"; lines 113–14, which tie the poem more closely to the play, were omitted; and there were other minor changes. The poem, in any event, comes from a different tradition than do the others:

> On a day, alack the day!
> Love, whose month is ever May,
> Spied a blossom passing fair
> Playing in the wanton air:
> Through the velvet leaves the wind,
> All unseen can passage find;
> That the lover, sick to death,
> Wish'd himself the heaven's breath.
> Air, quoth he, thy cheeks may blow;

Air, would I might triumph so!
But alack! my hand is sworn
Ne'er to pluck thee from thy thorn:
Vow, alack! for youth unmeet,
Youth so apt to pluck a sweet.
Do not call it sin in me,
That I am forsworn for thee;
Thou for whom Jove would swear
Juno but an Ethiop were;
And deny himself for Jove,
Turning mortal for thy love.

(IV.iii.99–118)

This is in a quieter pastoral vein, more akin to Herrick than to Donne. Longaville's proposal "to lose an oath to win a paradise" and Berowne's "Let us once lose our oaths to find ourselves" are echoed in Dumain's "Vow, alack! for youth unmeet." Berowne had argued that "we lose ourselves to keep our oaths," and Dumain justifies the forswearing of the first oaths on the grounds of decorum—that "youth" is "so apt" to pluck sweets. Dumain defends himself against the accusation of "sin" as well, a mock blasphemy which will be taken to an extreme at the end of Berowne's Promethean Fire speech: "It is religion to be thus forsworn; / For charity itself fulfils the law" (IV.iii.360–1). Though Dumain proposes to send, in addition to his ode, "something else more plain," it is the poem's simplicity which is attractive, though the last four lines indulge in a familiar kind of excess.

Dumain is surprised first by Longaville, then by Navarre, who mocks both of them and their poems:

King. Come, sir, you [Longaville] blush; as his
     [Dumain] your case is such;
  You chide at him, offending twice as much:
  You do not love Maria! Longaville
  Did never sonnet for her sake compile,
  Nor never lay his wreathed arms athwart
  His loving bosom to keep down his heart.

I have been closely shrouded in this bush,
And mark'd you both, and for you both did
    blush.
I heard your guilty rhymes, observed your
    fashion,
Saw sighs reek from you, noted well your
    passion:
Ay me! says one; O Jove! the other cries;
One, her hairs were gold, crystal the other's eyes:
You [Longaville] would for paradise break faith
    and troth;
And Jove, for your [Dumain] love would
    infringe an oath.

(IV.iii.129–42)

Navarre satirizes their affected melancholy, their sighs, their very language, though neither of their poems actually includes the old clichés of golden hair and crystal eyes. Speaking specifically of the poems Dumain has sent her, Katharine terms them,

Some thousand verses of a faithful lover;
A huge translation of hypocrisy,
Vilely compil'd, profound simplicity.

(V.ii.50–2)

The love-sonnets of the four noblemen may have been anthology-favorites of the day, but the context of the play repeatedly demonstrates their limitations. We hear the same complaints, even from those who write the poems, over and over again: the poems are too hyperbolical, too exaggerated. They make flesh a deity, they are idolatrous, and they are only imitations. They are precisely what self-deceived academics of the day would probably be writing, and depend on an uncritical infatuation with the machinery of Petrarchanism. The noblemen are not poets, but poetasters.

Moreover, there is a sameness about their poems that is deliberate, though Berowne's sonnet is thematically appropriate to him—its emphasis on study looks back to his comments in I.i on the proposed academy, and forward to his Promethean Fire speech. Navarre's poem, with its celestial imagery of sun and moon, is suited to a king in love with a princess. The poems of Longaville and Dumain, however, are not thematically or psychologically related to their characters at all, and might be switched with no offense to dramatic propriety. In fact, despite the differences in detail, all the sonnets are interchangeable. Neither the poems nor their authors are really distinct. Only Berowne, in his flashes of self-consciousness, can be distinguished from his fellows, even if his poetry is similar.

The lords are somehow constrained and narrowed by their own affectation of worldliness and polish. But Armado and Moth—whose poems we will now examine—express by their very extravagance a freer and ampler spirit, and, although his case is more complex, Holofernes too seems more liberated than the lords. More important, these comic characters allow Shakespeare a freer rein of his imagination, for through their exuberance and wrong-headed zeal he can release his own fantastical energies. Shakespeare can be outrageous and extravagant even as he shows such powers run amuck in his characters. There is a Dickensian quality in this, an appreciation of the freedom granted by caricature, an abandonment to the joys of the bizarre, the low comic. The most startling transformations in the play occur here, at the lower end of the scale, whereas the more subtle and ambiguous changes occur at the higher end. With the zanies, at least, there can be no confusion about whose poetry is being heard, for their voices are as singular as the lords' are conventional.

Moth

> *Arm.* Sing, boy: my spirit grows heavy in love.
> (I.ii.115)

One of Moth's functions, as Armado's page, is to sing for his master, to help relieve his melancholy. Armado bids him, "make passionate my sense of hearing" (III.i.1), and Moth obliges with "Concolinel," which the *Arden* editor tells us was probably the title of an Irish song. Moth also sings the following song to illustrate for Armado a point about lovers:

> If she be made of white and red,
> Her faults will ne'er be known,
> For blushing cheeks by faults are bred,
>   And fears by pale white shown:
> Then if she fear, or be to blame,
>   By this you shall not know,
> For still her cheeks possess the same
>   Which native she doth owe.

(I.ii.93–100)

The play on cosmetics and blushing will be discussed in the fifth chapter. I shall only note now that this song is unlike anything that Moth says elsewhere in the play; his prose style would not lead us to it. Yet it is appropriate for him, offering a light amalgam of the sophisticated and the "natural," just the sort of thing for a courtly audience. The simplicity of the verse-form and diction set off the point-of-view of the speaker, which is sophisticated: the perception of the Art-Nature opposition, the undercurrent of witty cynicism. It is the kind of song, in another play, that Touchstone might produce.

ARMADO

We have seen how Armado is meant to be an anachronism, an archaic figure from the romances of the previous decade. He has been brought to the court to entertain the academics. The "child of fancy" is to relate "In high-born words the worth of many a knight / From tawny Spain, lost in the world's debate" (I.i.171–2). As it turns out, we never hear any of these stories, but the promise is perhaps enough. Armado is to be a court bard, a teller of fabulous tales. Navarre concludes:

118

How you delight, my lords, I know not, I;
But I protest I love to hear him lie,
And I will use him for my minstrelsy.

(I.i.173–5)

Navarre plays on the word "lie"—the old charge that poets not only imitate, they also "feign" or "counterfeit," and hence "lie." Considering the degree of exaggeration and hyperbole expected from Armado, "lie" is probably the more accurate term anyhow. The noblemen are expecting tall tales of the "world's debate" while here in the court we are witnessing the smaller but no less intense war of each man against his own affections. The debate on poetry, in any event, soon takes precedence over the world's debate.

Before he can produce his celebrated lies, however, Armado falls in love with Jaquenetta and everything changes. He becomes the stereotype of the melancholic lover, as we have seen. Neal Goldstien suggests that in Armado's melancholy and literary pretensions "Shakespeare treats with open ridicule a notion that Sidney, through the persona of his agonized and doubtful lover, handled with tongue in cheek."[13] The little that we learn of Armado's literary taste indicates that it is predictably old-fashioned, as in this exchange:

> *Arm.* Is there not a ballad, boy, of the King and the Beggar?
> *Moth.* The world was very guilty of such a ballad some three ages since; but I think now 'tis not to be found; or, if it were, it would neither serve for the writing nor the tune.
> *Arm.* I will have that subject newly writ o'er, that I may example my digression by some mighty precedent.

(I.ii.103–10)

Neither the language nor the meter of the ballad is appropriate now, according to Moth, but Armado is undaunted—

he will rework the subject, just as Shakespeare himself reworked so many moldy old tales. But the result of Armado's
labor, his second letter, is depressing. We have already suffered through one rendition of "he came, saw, and overcame: he came, one; saw, two; overcame, three" (IV.i.70).
To quote any more verges on cruel and unusual punishment.

Earlier, we recall, Armado had promised to "turn sonnet":
"Devise, wit; write, pen; for I am for whole volumes in folio" (I.ii.174–5). The "whole volumes" turn out to be six
lines of Marlovian huff appended to the letter to Jaquenetta:

> Thus dost thou hear the Nemean lion roar
> 'Gainst thee, thou lamb, that standest as his prey;
> Submissive fall his princely feet before,
> And he from forage will incline to play.
> But if thou strive, poor soul, what art thou then?
> Food for his rage, repasture for his den.
>
> (IV.i.87–92)

The audience, no doubt, shares the Princess's astonishment
at this poem: "What plume of feathers is he that indited this
letter? / What vane? what weathercock? did you ever hear
better?" (IV.i.93–4). Everyone, fortunately, has heard better. Armado's poem is most notable for the "vane"-ness of
its author—in the analogy, Armado associates himself with
the Nemean lion, though it was conquered by Hercules—
and for the clumsiness of the inversion, "Submissive fall his
princely feet before," for the sake of the rhyme. "Repasture"
is meant to be elevated diction, an elegant variation on
"food," but it affords little nourishment. It is an old style,
one that Boyet and the audience have heard before. War-
burton concluded that it must be "a quotation from some
ridiculous poem of that time" (Var., p. 122), and he was
right. The author is Armado.

Later, Armado tells Holofernes, "the king would have me
present the princess, sweet chuck, with some delightful ostentation, or show, or pageant, or antic, or firework. Now,
understanding that the curate and your sweet self are good

at such eruptions and sudden breaking out of mirth, as it were, I have acquainted you withal, to the end to crave your assistance" (V.i.105–12). In an attempt to impress Holofernes with his sincerity, the imported Spanish fabulist ironically swears "By the world, I recount no fable" (l. 100). If it comes as a surprise to us that the "child of fancy" needs the assistance of the two "book-men," the time-worn pageant that Holofernes suggests comes as no surprise at all.

HOLOFERNES

> *"Imitari* is nothing."
>
> (IV.ii.124)

Holofernes' contribution to the "poetry" of the play is—how shall we put it?—a disappointment. The "extemporal epitaph on the death of the deer," quoted in the first chapter, is unspeakable. As he promised, Holofernes does indeed "affect the letter," and we are overwhelmed by the alliteration, which is Holofernes' way of demonstrating "facility" in the use of rhetorical schemes and figures. It is his recurring obsession, and the play's standing joke. Unable to see Moth's rhetorical joke in the fifth act, for example, he asks him, "What is the figure? what is the figure?" (V.i.61). And he compliments one of Costard's unexpected puns as "a good lustre of conceit in a turf of earth" (IV.ii.86–7). With his own predilection for synonymy and figures, and a brain crammed with scraps of schoolboy grammars and Latin poets, Holofernes presents a conception of poetry that is fairly simple: poetry is something to be learned from rhetoricians like Sherry or Peacham or Erasmus, and it is as easy and as mechanical as learning the multiplication tables. "Base authority from others' books" is good enough for this continual plodder.

Although Holofernes' openly theoretical pronouncements are occasionally vague, they are of some importance in the play. In IV.ii, Jaquenetta and Costard enter with Berowne's misdelivered sonnet and give it to Nathaniel to read. While he is doing so, Holofernes hums to himself and peeks over Nathaniel's shoulder:

> *Facile precor gelida quando pecus omne sub umbra*
> *Ruminat*, and so forth. Ah! good old Mantuan. I may
> speak of thee as the traveller doth of Venice:
> > *Venetia, Venetia,*
> > *Chi non ti vede, non ti pretia.*
> Old Mantuan! old Mantuan! who understandeth thee
> not, loves thee not. *Ut, re, sol, la, mi, fa.* Under pardon,
> sir, what are the contents? or, rather, as Horace says in
> his—what, my soul! verses?
>
> (IV.ii.92–101)

After Nathaniel reads the sonnet, Holofernes confidently delivers his judgment on it: "Here are only numbers ratified; but, for the elegancy, facility, and golden cadence of posey, *caret*. Ovidius Naso was the man: and why, indeed, *Naso*, but for smelling out the odoriferous flowers of fancy, the jerks of invention? *Imitari* is nothing; so doth the hound his master, the ape his keeper, the tired horse his rider" (IV.ii.118–26).

What does all this mean for the play's debate on poetry? Possibly very little, for Holofernes garbles the familiar schoolboy quotation, and makes an error in the musical gamut, as well as making other mistakes in his Latin elsewhere in the play. Still, he mentions Mantuan, Horace, and Ovid; along with Virgil, these were the central poets studied in the grammar school, the chief authorities for the study of figures, the *flores rhetorici* or, in Holofernes' rendering, the "odoriferous flowers of fancy." Holofernes says that Berowne's sonnet is mechanically correct in meter, but that the essence of poetry is missing. With this much we can agree. Holofernes identifies this essence with Ovid; Berowne fails where Ovid triumphed.[14] Holofernes is undoubtedly the greatest fool in the play, but in this allusion to Ovid he is also unwittingly the most revealing, for in the midst of all the allusions to literary and historical worthies, to prior and higher authorities, he points us to the poet who seems to have been Shakespeare's favorite.

It seems to me that Holofernes is right in his criticism of Berowne's sonnet, but that, because of his conception of Ovid, we must take his remarks in two different and opposed ways. First of all, for Holofernes—for the pedant—the Ovid of Erasmus' *Copia* was the supreme example of "copy" in poetry. This Ovid was copious in a specific sense. As L. P. Wilkinson notes, " 'Copy' of *words* was the faculty of varying the same *sententia* . . . it depended, of course, on richness of vocabulary."[15] In short, Holofernes' unfavorable comparison of Berowne with Ovid concerns not what we might now term the essence of the poem, involving some verbal transformation or metaphor, but its lack of varied epithets. Holofernes' comments must therefore be strictly construed. The schoolmaster is summoning up one version of Ovid in order to criticize Berowne for not writing the kind of poem that he, Holofernes, approves of. "Richness of vocabulary," and the willingness to employ it, become the primary poetic virtues. "Smelling out the odoriferous flowers of fancy" is made the highest act of the imagination.

Keeping this narrow viewpoint in mind, we can now approach Holofernes' next comment: *"Imitari* is nothing." On the face of it, this is an astonishing thing for any literary critic of the 1590s to be saying.[16] A quotation from Puttenham's *Arte* is typical of the whole orthodox tradition, from Ascham to Ben Jonson: "And neverthelesse without any repugnancie at all, a Poet may in some sort be said a follower or imitator, because he can express the true and lively of every thing is set before him, and which he taketh in hand to describe: and so in that respect is both a maker and a counterfaitor: and Poesie an art not only of making, but also of imitation."[17] Both Sidney and Puttenham make a distinction between the lower kind of imitation, which captures only the external and no more, and the higher kind which describes the universal or inner qualities through the external. But both agree that "imitation" in some form is indispensable.

The point is that, although there may in fact be some classical precedent for Holofernes' comment,[18] it would still have been shocking to an audience accustomed to hear just the opposite. Once again, however, the pedant's analogies betray his superficiality: "so doth the hound his master, the ape his keeper, the tired horse his rider." These are equivalent comparisons, but the ape-keeper metaphor has a distinguished heritage. Ernst Curtius has shown how "ape" became a synonym for "imitator"; the identification seems to have resulted from a confusion of etymologies—*simulus* and *simius*. As Curtius notes, "The real ape (*simius*) becomes the *simia* when he imitates man. . . . An unintelligent imitator could thus be called *simia*" (Curtius, pp. 538–40).[19] This sense of the term may have been rare in the Middle Ages, but it was common in the Renaissance, and in Shakespeare. The "Third Gentleman" lauds the fictitious master-sculptor Julio Romano in *The Winter's Tale* as an artist who, "had he himself eternity and could put breath into his work, would beguile Nature of her custom, so perfectly he is her ape" (V.ii.92–4). And in *Cymbeline*, sleep is the "ape of death" (II.ii.31). The reference could be either contemptuous or approving, but in both cases it implied a mindless literal imitation; the pedant who gave us the "extemporal epitaph" thus stands self-condemned by his own creations. The sonnets of the four lords may be derivative, but they rise far above the relentlessly mechanical alliteration of Holofernes' poem. Berowne himself, picking up the term, will soon angrily refer to Boyet as "the ape of form, monsieur the nice" (V.ii.325), which suggests again how Boyet is a parody of the lords' foppishness.[20]

There is yet another interesting contemporary use of the ape-metaphor. Robert Greene, in his famous attack on Shakespeare, called him an "upstart Crow, beautified with our feathers," in his own conceit thinking himself "the onely Shake-scene in a countrie." Greene continues the warning to his "fellowe Schollers": "O that I might intreate your rare wits to be imployed in more profitable courses; & let those Apes imitate your past excellence, and never more acquaint them with your admired inventions. . . . For it is pittie men of such rare wits, should be subject to the pleasures of such rude groomes" (Greene, XII, 144). Harold White long ago showed how the "strutting crow" of Horace represented "the superficial, mechanical imitator," little better than a sneak thief.[21] In Greene's attack, Shakespeare—who was both actor and playwright—is thus "crow" and "ape," the non-university man stealing success from the "Schollers" who deserve better. It is tempting to speculate that, by allowing Holofernes to ridicule Berowne, Shakespeare gains a measure of ironic revenge against the pedants who had attacked him.

None of this can be proven, of course, and there is a certain amount of truth in Holofernes' charge against Berowne. The pedant is charging that Berowne's sonnet is only a barren replica, which should have been more gaily festooned with "jerks" and "flowers" of his own—that is, like those of Ovid. Holofernes therefore contradicts himself, offering as models Mantuan, Horace, and especially Ovid at one moment, denying something similar to Berowne in the next, while commending his own favorite. I argued in the first chapter that Holofernes comes closest to living in a totally solipsistic world of words, and the inevitable pun "nothing"="note-ing" suggests again that for Holofernes there can be no coherent relationship to the world around him, for if imitation involves "noting," then the schoolmaster will remain forever blind.

I suggested earlier that there were at least two ways of looking at Holofernes' comments on Ovid and imitation. The first, then, is that from a literal, pedantic point of view Holofernes is correct; Berowne's sonnet is an imitation, and it is not particularly Ovidian. The second way of approaching his words is to see them as ironic: the very mention of Ovid, even in Holofernes' narrow sense, inevitably reminds

us of everything else Ovid meant to the Elizabethans, and to
Shakespeare in particular, and thus Holofernes is again un-
done by his own words. The pedant is unintentionally
revelatory.

As J.A.K. Thomson points out, Shakespeare himself was
repeatedly linked with Ovid: "Shakespeare was regarded by
his contemporaries as the most brilliant master in a school of
classical art. He was the new Ovid—one of the new Ovids—
of his time."[22] The standard proof of this is Francis Meres'
famous description, in 1598: "As the soule of Euphorbus was
thought to live in Pythagoras: so the sweete wittie soule of
Ovid lives in mellifluous and hony-tongued Shakespeare, wit-
nes his *Venus and Adonis*, his *Lucrece*, his sugred Sonnets
among his private friends, &c" (Smith, II, 317). This sentiment is echoed again and again in surviving documents. One
of the more interesting examples is in the First Part of *The
Returne from Parnassus* (c. 1599–1600), where Ingenioso
gives Gullio imitations of verses in the style of Chaucer,
then Spenser, and then one in "Mr. Shakspeares veyne," to
palm off as his own:

> Faire Venus, queene of beutie and of love,
> Thy red doth stayne the blushinge of the morne,
> Thy snowie neck shameth the milke white dove,
> Thy presence doth this naked worlde adorne,
> Gazing on thee all other nymphs I scorne.
> When ere thou dyest slowe shine that Satterday,
> Beutie and grace muste sleepe with thee for aye.[23]

The anonymous author of this parody assumed that his audience, admittedly an academic one, would recognize as most
typically Shakespearean such obviously Ovidian imagery. It
is just this flavor which is missing from the sonnets of the
noblemen, but more evident in Moth's song.

Love's Labour's Lost is in fact permeated with other reminders of Ovid: from the echo of *tempus edax rerum* in
"cormorant devouring Time" (I.i.4), through the imagery
of love's warfare and hunt,[24] to the whole theme of transfor-

mation. *This* Ovid, the Ovid of the *Metamorphoses*, stands behind the play. It is unnecessary to document here the general influence of Ovid on Shakespeare, or the numerous specific references and echoes in the early plays, especially in *The Taming of the Shrew*, *Titus Andronicus*, and *The Two Gentlemen of Verona.* But the famous reference in *As You Like It* casts light on *Love's Labour's Lost*:

> *Touchstone.* I am here with thee and thy goats, as the most capricious poet, honest Ovid, was among the Goths.
>
> *Jaques.* (aside) O knowledge ill-inhabited, worse than Jove in a thatched house!
>
> *Touchstone.* When a man's verses cannot be understood, nor a man's good wit seconded with the forward child, understanding, it strikes a man more dead than a great reckoning in a little room. Truly, I would the gods had made thee poetical.
>
> *Audrey.* I do not know what poetical is. Is it honest in deed and word? Is it a true thing?
>
> *Touchstone.* No, truly; for the truest poetry is the most faining, and lovers are given to poetry, and what they swear in poetry may be said, as lovers, they do feign.
>
> (III.iii.5–18)

Holofernes links the right words—Ovid and imitation—but with too narrow a meaning. The rest of us, however, should understand how poetry "lies," how the truest poetry is the most feigning, and therefore by these criteria how the poetry of the noblemen in *Love's Labour's Lost* fails.

Berowne's sonnet is only slightly more precious than the average lyric poem of the 1590s. By comparison, Navarre's poem is inferior, its conceits forced and awkward. But we do well to remind ourselves that Shakespeare wrote *everything* in *Love's Labour's Lost*, from the good to the awful. If the lords' sonnets are inferior to the final songs, as they clearly are, there may be a thematic explanation for this difference. The noblemen are, above all, everywhere glib, devoted to "fashion." They speak in witty paradox, they choose to present a sophisticated masque, they compose "correct" but languid Petrarchan sonnets. Everything they do and say is an uninspired imitation of some other art form, to which they add nothing; if the ape imitates his keeper, as Holofernes testifies, the lords follow whatever is current. Berowne had promised, "I will love, write, sigh, pray, sue, and groan" (III.i.201), and his list of verbs could have been lifted directly from any Renaissance handbook of love. Their poetry is "faining"—it reveals desire, though not quite in Touchstone's sense—but there is not enough "feigning" in it.[25] Holofernes' epitaph is simply a more extreme version of the problem of imitation they all face, his devotion to alliteration no different from the lords' devotion to, say, "eye" imagery. Neither involves an adaptation or transformation of what is given. But we will hear, in the final songs, a remarkable metamorphosis of the medieval literary debate.

What is most interesting about the lords' sonnets is that Shakespeare transforms them simply through context. Their limitations and virtues, our expectations about them, are all drastically altered when considered against the background of the sonnet-reading scene in particular, and the play as a whole. This figure/ground phenomenon has recently found dramatic expression in Borges' story, "Pierre Menard, Author of the *Quixote*," where two identical passages are juxtaposed, one from Cervantes, the other from the imaginary twentieth-century author who is rewriting the *Quixote*. "Cervantes' text and Menard's are verbally identical," the narrator tells us, "but the second is almost infinitely richer." A lengthy analysis of the differences between them follows.[26] The love-sonnets of the noblemen in *Love's Labour's Lost* underwent a similar sea-change when they were separated from the context which sets them off and were submerged in uniform collections of similar sonnets. The genius of their creation lies precisely in how Shakespeare has captured the clichéd tropes and wearisome sentiments of the stereotypical "lovers." It is a high irony that anthology editors overlooked the context and took the poems perfectly seriously. The most dramatic contrast imaginable, after all, is seen in the difference between Shakespeare's own sonnet-sequence and the lords' poems.[27] Though Shakespeare may once or twice have sounded like Navarre, the reverse could never be true.

The Masque of Muscovites and the Pageant of the Nine Worthies are aesthetic failures for the same reasons the poems are: they are not artificial enough, they do not "feign" enough. They pretend instead to the kind of literal "imitation" Holofernes understands, and as a result they fall apart once their feeble illusions are shattered. Two senses of "imitation" are involved in this theatricality. There is, first, the imitation of a previously existing art form; both the lords with their masque and the low characters with their pageant incorporate wholesale what they take to be a fashionable form. Part of the ensuing failure results from not transforming what is given to suit the needs and expectations of a new audience and a new context. The second sense of "imitation," reproducing nature, is parallel to the first. The pageant, especially, attempts the kind of verisimilitude that even photographs cannot capture, and that must have been even more difficult to attain in Renaissance art forms. "Feigning" has no place in such an attempt.

But the thrust of the play, Shakespeare's evident intention, is gradually to reveal the necessity for such feigning, the inevitability of transformation. The Princess quite rightly expects the greatest comedy to result from those actions in which "zeal" exceeds ability: "That sport best pleases that doth least know how" (V.ii.512). The converse of this is that the greatest satisfaction must come from those who most "know how," from those who "feign"—invent, pretend, transform, imagine—the best. Touchstone does not hesitate, nor would the audience, to identify this power with Ovid, and, possibly, with Marlowe; but ultimately with Shakespeare himself, the new Ovid. We therefore owe a great debt to Holofernes for "smelling out" Ovid. He speaks more wisely than he can know, for the advice to follow Ovidius Naso ironically proves to be correct.

Moreover, it is precisely the self-consciousness of Touchstone's carnal desires, as acknowledged through puns, which is missing from the conceited sonnets of the noblemen, who have not yet acknowledged the reality of those desires, comically personified in Costard, ludicrously in Armado. They pretend to ignore all such "affections." On a basic level, the loosely "Ovidian" impulse toward the flesh works against the assumed sophistication of the noblemen's sonnets, which remain unalterably naive. The difference between what we may term the Ovidian and the Petrarchan impulses is partly a matter of perception ("eyes" again), but mostly a question of self-knowledge. The lords' sophisticated style is an attempt to sublimate carnality, to ignore the "world's debate" that takes place in man, the "war against your own affections." They try to assume the appearance of "special grace" in order to imagine that they have "by might master'd" their "affects" (I.i.150). The attempt fails for lack of self-knowledge. Holofernes unwittingly points to a truer mode of perception, and of style, but it is something to be cultivated from within rather than donned from without.

Holofernes' final aesthetic choice is to select the Pageant of the Nine Worthies as the subject for entertaining the court. We assume that he wrote the lines for the various actors, with some help from Nathaniel. He certainly wrote the "apology" for Moth-Hercules' diminutive size, which runs as follows:

Hol. (dressed as Judas)
 Great Hercules is presented by this imp,
 Whose club kill'd Cerberus, that three-headed
  canus;
 And, when he was a babe, a child, a shrimp,
 Thus did he strangle serpents in his *manus*.
 Quoniam he seemeth in minority,
 Ergo I come with this apology.

          (V.ii.581–6)

It is a perfect example of Holofernes' own ideas about "copy"—a line-filling, rhyme-completing epithet for Cerberus (and if the Quarto "canus" is right, his spelling is wrong), and four varied "epithets" for the word "child," not to mention the clumsiness and affectation of the four Latin words. As we saw in chapter two, the rest of the verses in the pageant are hardly any better ("The armipotent Mars, of lances the almighty" etc.). Shakespeare can capture and parody the sound of stilted archaicism as easily as he can the glib tropes and slick antitheses of the sonneteers.

Virtually every chapter in this study ends with a look ahead to the final songs, and this one is no exception. At the end of the play we are left with a range of poetic modes: archaic, Petrarchan, Ovidian, topical. None of these satisfy as does the "dialogue" between Spring and Winter concluding the play which, Armado says, "should have followed in the end of our show" (V.ii.877–8). The songs do not seem to echo any immediately recognizable style from elsewhere in the play. Embodying still another poetic prototype, one which has been almost unanimously praised by critics of the play, the final songs are in a sense *the* exemplum towards which the play has been working. They supply the "special grace" which, aesthetically if not religiously, masters and shapes man's passions. In the final chapter I shall examine in detail how the songs work. Enough for now to note that the "songs of Apollo" are the best poetry in a play filled with "poetry."

CHAPTER FOUR

Transformations

The characters in *Love's Labour's Lost*, as we have seen, differ in their choice of prose styles, their attitudes toward language and theatrical representation, and their preferences in poetry. Virtually all these differences arise from variations in the characters' imaginations, for even though the poets, lovers, and lunatics of this play are of imagination all compact, there are still important distinctions to be made among them. In *A Midsummer Night's Dream*, Theseus elaborates upon the ways in which imagination operates in each of the three types, and somewhat disparagingly reveals how the distortions in each stem from warped perceptions:

> One sees more devils than vast hell can hold:
> That is the madman. The lover, all as frantic,
> Sees Helen's beauty in a brow of Egypt.
> The poet's eye, in a fine frenzy rolling,
> Doth glance from heaven to earth, from earth to heaven;
> And as imagination bodies forth
> The forms of things unknown, the poet's pen
> Turns them to shapes, and gives to airy nothing
> A local habitation and a name.
> Such tricks hath strong imagination
> That, if it would but apprehend some joy,
> It comprehends some bringer of that joy;
> Or in the night, imagining some fear,
> How easy is a bush supposed a bear!
>
> (V.i.9–22)

Although there are differences in what the avatars of the imagination "see," still the essential activity of the imagination is perceptual, and the differences grow out of various ways of seeing. The emphasis is the same in *Love's Labour's Lost*. The objects seen may vary—from "devils" and "beauty" to "the forms of things unknown"—but the activity of vision remains constant. It is on this theme that Shakespeare rings changes, allowing distinctions in perception to yield the transformations—unique, surprising, beautiful, bizarre—which characterize the figures in the play. The "sweete wittie soule of Ovid" does indeed live in Shakespeare, as Meres noted, for he has filled the play with his own metamorphoses.

As Theseus' tone suggests, "imagination" or "phantasy" was not always viewed with approval. An ambiguous, potentially dangerous faculty, it was, as Murray W. Bundy puts it, "the same power which, allied to the appetites, passions, temperaments, and humours, was prone to false reports concerning the external world, responsible for bad behavior, and as likely to fabricate monsters and delusions as perfect heroes and ideal Commonwealths."[1] For John Davies, the "Phantasie," which was often identified functionally with the imagination, but sometimes distinguished from it physiologically, was "wits looking glasse."[2] Not only did distortions in this "glasse" alarm moralists, Baconians, and Puritans, among others, but it was also frequently observed that man's reason might fail to control the imagination. Especially "in time of sleep," Robert Burton warned, the imagination "is free, and many times conceives strange, stupend, absurd shapes, as in sick men we commonly observe" (Burton, pp. 139–40).

The terms "phantasy" and "phantastical" were often used interchangeably to refer to both the controlled and the uncontrolled imaginations at work.[3] Sidney made a distinction, however, between good and bad poetic imaginations: "For I will not denie but that mans wit may make Poesie (which should be *Eikastike*, which some learned have defined, figuring foorth good things) to be *Phantastike*: which doth, contrariwise, infect the fancie with unworthy objects" (Smith, I, 186). Again, the idea of "infection." Yet Sidney also asked, "shall the abuse of a thing make the right use odious?"—a question well worth asking with respect to *Love's Labour's Lost*.

Sidney's distinction is one only of degree, not of kind, for the good and the bad are separated only by the regulation of the reason. Puttenham admits the same link between lunatics and poets when he tries to describe the potential powers of the phantasy. If the "phantasticall part of man" is not disordered, then it is "a representer of the best, most comely and bewtifull images or apparances of thinges to the soule" (*Arte*, p. 19). But if it is disordered, it breeds "*Chimeres & monsters.*" Like Sidney, Puttenham terms those with disordered phantasies *phantastici*, and those of the ordered phantasy are *euphantasiote*: "of this sort . . . are all good Poets, notable Captaines stratagematique, all cunning artificers and enginers, all Legislators Polititiens & Counsellours of estate, in whose exercises the inventive part is most employed and is to the sound & true judgement of man most needful" (pp. 19–20).

These definitions are helpful in analyzing the major characters in *Love's Labour's Lost*, for each represents a different, often startling refraction of "wits looking glasse," from the fun-house distortions and grotesqueries of Armado to the "most comely and bewtifull images" of Berowne at his best. Shakespeare, as usual, shows both sides of the question—both the *phantastici* and the *euphantasiote*. I shall begin with a brief look at the lower end of the scale, at two of the *phantastici* of the play or, in their own terms, the "phantasimes."

Armado is most obviously possessed by a diseased phantasy. Holofernes elaborately characterizes the knight's dubious gifts: "*Novi hominem tanquam te*: his humour is lofty, his discourse peremptory, his tongue filed, his eye ambitious, his gait majestical, and his general behaviour vain, ridiculous, and thrasonical. He is too picked, too spruce, too affected, too odd, as it were, too peregrinate, as I may call it." Even worse, the pedant continues, "he draweth out the thread of his verbosity finer than the staple of his argument. I abhor such fanatical phantasimes, such insociable and point-devise companions; such rackers of orthography" (V.i.10–20). What began as praise of Armado has quickly become an attack on his affectation and verbosity, and he is properly labeled a "phantasime." It takes one to know one, however, and no sooner does Holofernes deliver his attack than he slides into still another defense of his own orthographical theories.

Earlier, once Armado's letter to Jaquenetta was read aloud, Boyet offered a similar description to the ladies:

> This Armado is a Spaniard, that keeps here in court;
> A phantasime, a Monarcho, and one that makes sport
> To the prince and his book-mates.
>
> (IV.i.97–9)

The references to the "Monarcho," along with "phantasime," are important because they indicate just how archaic a character Armado would have seemed to Shakespeare's audience. We learn from the *Arden* and *Variorum* notes that the Monarcho was an actual court hanger-on in the mid-1570s and dead by 1580. He was, by all accounts, utterly vain and more than a little mad. Francis Meres (*Wits Commonwealth*) confirms the vanity of "*Monarcho* that lived about the Court" as one of a type: "As a Chamaelon is fedd with none other nourishment, then with the ayre, and therefore shee is always gaping: so popular applause dooth nourish some, neither doe they gape after any other thing but vaine praise and glorie" (Nashe, IV,155–6). The Monarcho claimed to be "soveraigne of the world," and was, inevitably, of "melancholike humor" (Nashe, IV,338). Thomas Churchyard even wrote an epitaph entitled "The Phantasticall *Monarkes* Epitaphe" (1580):

> Come poore old man that boare the *Monarks* name,
> Thyne Epitaphe shall here set forthe thy fame.
> Thy climyng mynde aspierd beyonde the starrs,
> Thy loftie stile no yearthly titell bore:
> . . .

135

And though thy pride and pompe was somewhat vaine,
The *Monarcke* had a deepe discoursyng braine;
. . .

His forme of life who lists to look upon,
Did shewe some witte, though follie fedde his will.

(*Var.*, p.124)

"Vaine praise," "glorie," "phantasticall," "loftie stile," "melancholike humor," "follie fedde his will"—these terms apply to virtually all of the men in the play. But they best describe Armado, who marches to his own fantastic tune. His private inner vision, of a world still peopled by knights errant and damsels, corresponds to little beyond his own turbulent imagination. Jaquenetta becomes his Enchanted Dulcinea del Toboso; this compliant "wench" undergoes a transformation in Armado's phantasy as remarkable as Alonza Lorenzo—she of the garlic breath—does in Don Quixote's.

Holofernes' mind—I use the term loosely—represents an unusually oblique refraction of phantasy's mirror. Almost everything that he says about Armado can be taken to apply to himself as well, and Armado directs the same terms against Holofernes that were used at his expense earlier: "I protest, the schoolmaster is exceeding fantastical; too, too vain; too, too vain" (V.ii.524–5). Holofernes has condemned Armado for having too little matter for his verbosity, but he considers himself bursting with imagination, ingenuity, and wit. The "jerks of invention" are his obsessive specialty. But we have seen that his use of "invention," the "varying" of the words of a formula, has a narrow rhetorical definition, as in Sonnet 105:

> Fair, kind, and true is all my argument,
> Fair, kind, and true, varying to other words;
> And in this change is my invention spent.

Murray W. Bundy has shown in detail the metamorphosis of the term "invention," from its place in the Trivium through a gradual evolution into a synonym for "imagination." He notes that the pejorative connotations of the phantasy were a concern to poets and critics of the day: "The Renaissance thus reached a kind of impasse in its thought about the poetic imagination or phantasy. Ronsard, Puttenham, and Sidney had tried to find one way out by their identification of 'imagination' and 'phantasy' with rhetorical 'invention'."[4] This association seems to be parodied in Holofernes' narrow notions. Although Shakespeare may have used the term in its older sense, as in the sonnet, he was certainly not confined to it.

Untroubled by the inhibitions of conventional modesty, Holofernes is good enough to give us a complete description of his own powerful mind (this after his alliterative epitaph on the pricket): "This is a gift that I have, simple, simple; a foolish extravagant spirit, full of forms, figures, shapes, objects, ideas, apprehensions, motions, revolutions: these are begot in the ventricle of memory, nourished in the womb of *pia mater*, and delivered upon the mellowing of occasion. But the gift is good in those in whom it is acute, and I am thankful for it" (IV.ii.66–72). With its complex physiology, its sexual metaphor, and its impressive string of synonyms, this extraordinary description is a virtuoso demonstration of the very power which Holofernes is describing. The metaphor of gestation and birth is fairly common in Shakespeare, and is found elsewhere in *Love's Labour's Lost*.[5] But Holofernes makes much of it here. Wit is "sharp," "piercing," or "cutting" in the play; hence, masculine. The forms and figures which swirl about in Holofernes' brain are begotten *in* the female ventricle, presumably *by* his wit.

Though Holofernes has not really given us a physiology of the imagination, he has at least offered a description of another faculty, the memory. Bundy has summarized the traditional textbook psychology of the brain: "The brain was divided into three cells or ventricles: in the foremost were common sense and imagination; in the middle, fantasy and judgment; and at the rear was memory."[6] Thus Davies and Burton clearly separate the function and location of the phantasy from that of memory. The forms that phantasy can no longer see, Davies says,

> To Memory's large volume she commends.
> The ledger-book lies in the brain behind,
> Like Janus' eye, which in his poll was set;
> The layman's tables, storehouse of the mind,
> Which doth remember much, and much forget.[7]

Holofernes' mind is exactly such a "storehouse," crammed full of arcane words, dusty ledgers, and pedantic trivia. His power, "begot in the ventricle of memory," therefore depends not on the imagination or the phantasy but on a large remembered vocabulary which may be summoned up for "variation," yet for nothing that we could term a genuine transformation of language.

Armado and Holofernes thus represent the most obvious cases of the infected phantasy—terminal cases. Their minds are full of those "*Chimeres* & monsters" Puttenham feared. Most of the other characters are also afflicted by some special quirk of vision which alters whatever is seen, and yields the transformations that resemble in kind if not in quality those of the artist. Any discussion of poetry and the imagination, and especially one that has already touched on Ovid, must consider the idea of metamorphosis in a broad sense, involving as it does a theory of metaphor. As we will see, transformation becomes another source of thematic unity in *Love's Labour's Lost*, like the idea of "worthiness."

There are three distinct but related senses of transformation to be examined, and I have borrowed my categories from Theseus' speech. Lunatics, lovers, and poets people *Love's Labour's Lost*. The categories are somewhat arbitrary, and a character may belong to all three. But they serve useful distinctions. Transformation may be broadly visual— an external object altered in the act of perception by the "lunatics" and changed into another shape; this is perhaps the broadest application of the term. Or it may be a psychological transformation—the "lover" is perceptibly changed by the power of his "affection." The transformation may, finally, be a verbal one—the "poet" takes words, offers them to his "invention," mechanical and otherwise, and alters "words" into "songs," as the final line of the play notes. Phantasy, the "imagination" as Theseus says, is the primary force in each category. And it is Love, in most cases, which first activates this power.

THE LUNATICS: VISUAL TRANSFORMATION

"This is abhominable, which he would call abominable, it insinuateth me of insanie: *ne intelligis domine?* to make frantic, lunatic."

(V.i.25–7)

Holofernes' lunacy is caused both by some obscure internal infection and by his belief that all reality challenges his linguistic theories; his mania is self-induced. Moreover, we have just seen how Armado's mind alters Jaquenetta from a lowly "wench" to one "more fairer than fair, beautiful than beauteous, truer than truth itself" (IV.i.64–5). The recurring impulse of the love-stricken lords is also to idealize the lover as well as the loved one, making Alonzas into Dulcineas and Don Quixotes into romance heroes.

In *Love's Labour's Lost* this power of idealization is frequently expressed by the verb "to make." "Poet" is derived from *poiein*—"to make"—as Puttenham reminds us in his first sentence, "A Poet is as much to say as a maker" (p. 3). What the lords succumb to is a parodic Incarnation:

Ber. This is the liver vein, which makes flesh a deity;
   A green goose a goddess; pure, pure idolatry.

(IV.iii.72–3)

To idealize a mistress in the Petrarchan mode is indeed idle, and to make a god of man is to invert God's making. Dumain, while ragging Armado-Hector in the pageant, jokingly voices the traditional view: "He's a god or a painter; for he makes faces" (V.ii.634). The wit of this line glances in several directions at once. Armado's grimaces of irritation are equated, by way of a pun, with the highest acts of creation. The physical and the ideal collapse together in this joke, whereas they have elsewhere been left wholly separate. Superhuman "making" is often invoked in *Love's Labour's Lost* as a standard by which to measure human "makings." Boyet turns it all to flattery when he tells the Princess that Nature was "prodigal . . . in making graces dear / When she did starve the general world beside, / And prodigally gave them all to you" (II.i.10–12). The Princess herself is only half-jesting when she first hears Armado: "A' speaks not like a man of God's making" (V.ii.522). Perhaps only a poet could make such folly.

The lords are seen from the beginning to be endowed with the power of imaginative transformation, and the action of the play is partly a record of their attempts to control the gift of "making." Dumain, for example, is described as having great power to do harm because of his innocence: "he hath wit to make an ill shape good, / And shape to win grace though he had no wit" (II.i.59–60). "Ill" may simply mean "imperfect" or "faulty" here, but the predominant sense is "evil," in opposition to "good." This potential to make the appearance of what is evil or vile pleasing is common to all lovers, as Helena makes explicit in *A Midsummer Night's Dream*:

> Things base and vile, holding no quantity,
> Love can transpose to form and dignity.
> Love looks not with the eyes, but with the mind,
> And therefore is winged Cupid painted blind.
>
> (I.i.232–5)

When Berowne is confused by the women's jesting, he will complain to Rosaline, "Your wit makes wise things foolish" (V.ii.374). The reverse is also true: the lords' misdirected wit makes them foolish. The "wit to make" is a powerful and often unpredictable energy, for in the very act of changing others, one may change oneself. This is the overt significance of the penance Rosaline imposes on Berowne, who must use his wit to make the sick and impotent laugh. The lesson he must learn is one of aesthetic responsibility:

> A jest's prosperity lies in the ear
> Of him that hears it, never in the tongue
> Of him that makes it.
>
> (V.ii.851–3)

The "lunatics" of the play tend to recreate reality in their own images; the "idolatry" they commit is finally a form of self-worship. The men—high and low alike—are primarily narcissists, projecting their own desires and images onto those about them. "Love looks not with the eyes," as Helena noted, "but with the mind"; but the men's wit tends to be, like Pope's in "An Essay on Criticism," "*Something*, whose Truth convinc'd at Sight we find, / That gives us back the Image of our Mind." The lords in particular, who like children "tumble on the ground, / With such a zealous laughter" (V.ii.114), expect to find no more than the image of their minds reflected back at them in the ready compliance of the ladies. The lords have been living in a "curious-knotted garden" of their own making, a protected space of instant wish-gratification. It is this garden of the mind, however, which has enabled them to cultivate the unusual flora and fauna we hear throughout the play, the "odoriferous flowers of fancy" which sprout up unsupervised. They have rarely been required to play the role of good gardener, pruning and shearing the excess; and even when one of them tries, "He weeds the corn," as Longaville notes, "and still lets grow the weeding" (I.i.96). It is with the greatest surprise and consternation that the lords find in the ladies not the image of their own minds but the image of strong, independent, superior minds which have a life and will of their own. It is the beginning of the movement which will lead the lords out of their solipsism into a position where they can put the social and verbal gifts cultivated in solipsism to the best uses. The "lunatics" will continue to "transpose" many things "base and vile," but the power which dominates them shifts from self-generated illusions to the external manipulations of a superior force. Unbeknownst to them, the noble "lunatics," as befits the term, have become bound to "Dictynna . . . to Phoebe, to Luna, to the moon."

"Thus change I like the moon" (V.ii.212) Rosaline tells the King as she confounds his expectations of wooing. She has chosen a familiar but still inexhaustible simile to make her point—emblem of change and mutability, "the governess of floods" (*MND*, II.i.104) and seasonal change on earth, the first mover of lovers and madmen. The moon not only undergoes continual metamorphosis herself, but effects change on earth, on the "dull sublunary lovers" Donne describes. Holofernes and Nathaniel produce four synonymic names under which she is known, yet they could have gone on to Hecate, Diana, and others. Rosaline's verb is therefore both transitive and intransitive, for in changing herself she also changes others, and vice versa. The lords who had sought the defeat of time and a transcendence of change did not bargain for this kind of reversal. Navarre tries to make a quick recovery from this latest setback:

> *King.* Will you not dance? How come you thus
>   estranged?
> *Ros.* You took the moon at full, but now she's changed.
> *King.* Yet still she is the moon, and I the man.
>   (V.ii.213–5)

But Navarre's clever riposte is seen, on closer inspection, to have backfired, for if he is the man in the moon then he is, according to the popular legends, a sabbath-breaker, a blasphemer; in Dante and other writers, the man in the moon is specifically Cain.[8] Perhaps there is some point, then, in Dull's substitution of the name of Cain for that of Adam in the riddle posed by him in IV.ii. Navarre, at any rate, is certainly not "the man" for the disguised Rosaline (he takes her for the Princess); and to say "Yet still she is the moon" is to utter both truth and paradox, hinged on a pun in "still"—it is yet the same woman in disguise, but the moon is not the moon if it is "still."

Rosaline's rebuke must shock Navarre in particular, for he has shown a real fondness for moon-imagery. His sonnet describes the Princess's face as shining through his tears: "Not shines the silver moon one half so bright / Through the transparent bosom of the deep" (IV.iii.29–30). And he replies to Berowne's praise of Rosaline in the same terms: "My love, her mistress, is a gracious moon; / She [Rosaline] an attending star, scarce seen a light" (IV.iii.227–8). In the Masque of Muscovites, the ladies' faces are "clouded" with masks, and it is to Rosaline that Navarre addresses his request for revelation:

> Vouchsafe, bright moon, and these thy stars, to shine,
> Those clouds remov'd, upon our watery eyne.

Rosaline's reply reduces the celestial imagery to its proper level:

> O vain petitioner! beg a greater matter;
> Thou now requests but moonshine in the water.
> (V.ii.205–8)

"Moonshine in the water" is a proverbial expression for "a waste of time" (V.ii.208n.), but it is also a metaphor for the lords' folly. "Moonshine" means foolishness; the water is a reflecting surface; thus folly sees its own reflection. The ladies hold up a mirror, as it were, to reflect the men's own inconstancy. And so we are led back to our starting-point, to the question of perception and the power to "transpose." We have already intruded upon Theseus' second category in discussing the subtle energies of the moon. In *A Midsummer Night's Dream* "young Cupid's fiery shaft" is "quenched in the chaste beams of the wat'ry moon" and no harm is done to the "imperial vot'ress" who passes on "fancy-free" (*MND*, II.i.161–4). But no one in *Love's Labour's Lost* escapes Cupid's aim, and, like the moon, the "lovers" undergo radical change. Berowne ironically laments that he is "betray'd," because he must keep company "With moon-like men, men of inconstancy" (IV.iii.178).

THE LOVERS: PSYCHOLOGICAL TRANSFORMATION

> "By heaven, I do love, and it hath taught me to rhyme,
> and to be melancholy."
>
> (IV.iii.12–3)

Berowne's confession in the sonnet-reading scene comes as no surprise to the audience. Love has strange effects on everyone; psychological transformations are common, and Berowne is not the last to become "melancholy" as a result (we have already heard his ability "to rhyme"). The other lords also find themselves shifted into the roles of melancholy lovers, into walking clichés. But the low characters experience more startling changes—or rather, they embody such changes in their guises as legendary heroes. The transformation of such legendary heroes broadly parodies the changes wrought in the noblemen.

The theme of great heroes transformed by the power of love is announced in the second scene with Armado's question: "Comfort me, boy. What great men have been in love?" (I.ii.61–2). Moth mentions only Hercules and Samson here, but the play is filled with other allusions: "mad" Ajax, Jove "turning mortal for thy love" (IV.iii.118), Achilles and Solomon. We should take special note of the comic potential in this theme. The hero, as Ernst Curtius points out, was usually known specifically for his self-control, and Cupid is traditionally the only force that can conquer him (Curtius, p. 167). Self-discipline and control, moreover, are the very things the noblemen in *Love's Labour's Lost* had asserted in their edicts of abstinence and denial. But most men succumb to love. Sidney takes up the famous case of Hercules: "so in *Hercules*, painted with his great beard and furious counte-

nance, in woman's attire, spinning at *Omphales* commaunde-
ment, it breedeth both delight and laughter. For the repre-
senting of so strange a power in love procureth delight;
and the scornefulnes of the action stirreth laughter"
(Smith, I,200). Burton, as we might expect, dwells more on
the "scornefulnes" and especially on the loss of self-control
which marks the hero's undoing: "The major part of Lovers
are carried headlong like so many brute beasts . . . this
furious lust precipitates, counterpoiseth, weighs down on the
[reason] . . . [Lovers] degenerate into dogs, hogs, asses,
brutes; as Jupiter into a Bull, Apuleius an Ass, Lycaon a
Wolf, Tereus a Lapwing, Callisto a Bear, Elpenor and Gryl-
lus into Swine by Circe" (Burton, p. 737). Ovid's *Metamorphoses* is undoubtedly the source of most of these
stories.

The more terrifying implications of transformation are
largely absent from *Love's Labour's Lost*, which emphasizes
instead the comic. To begin with, a physical transformation
—or rather deformation—is comically evident in the Pageant of the Nine Worthies; Moth, after all, must play Hercules "in minority," and the other actors hardly measure up
to their namesakes. Berowne alludes to the theme of the hero
reduced when he mocks his three comrades, after they have
revealed themselves to be in love:

> O! what a scene of foolery have I seen,
> Of sighs, of groans, of sorrow, and of teen;
> O! me with what strict patience have I sat,
> To see a king transformed to a gnat;
> To see great Hercules whipping a gig,
> And profound Solomon to tune a jig,
> And Nestor play at push-pin with the boys,
> And critic Timon laugh at idle toys!
>
> (IV.iii.161–8)

"Dumain transform'd" (IV.iii.80) and now "a king transformed"—this is the stuff of comedy.

A pompous parody of the four noblemen, Armado actively seeks "some mighty precedent" by which to justify his own comic transformation from soldier of war to soldier of love. In his first soliloquy, by means of false syllogism, he succeeds with little effort: "Love is a familiar; Love is a devil: there is no evil angel but Love. Yet was Samson so tempted, and he had an excellent strength; yet was Solomon so seduced, and he had a very good wit. Cupid's buttshaft is too hard for Hercules' club, and therefore too much odds for a Spaniard's rapier" (I.ii.162–7). Self-justification apparently knows no bounds. That final collection of phallic weapons notwithstanding, Armado makes a good case, and our response is complex. We laugh at those who say that love will not touch them, but also at those whom it has already touched, and who are thus transfigured. In both cases, the power of the force itself is greater than anyone can estimate. If Cupid can conquer Hercules, then Berowne and Armado offer small challenge. The fun of the play comes in seeing what form the inevitable defeat will take. Armado visualizes the "green goose" Jaquenetta as a "goddess," and this transformation, as well as the transformation of Armado in love, parallels the lords' misconception of the ladies, and the changes that are wrought in them.

Love effects subtler psychological transformations in addition to such broadly comic ones. Boyet immediately notices an interesting internal change in Navarre. After the first meeting of the lords and ladies, Boyet tells the Princess that Navarre is "infected"/"affected" with love. His evidence is "the heart's still rhetoric," as disclosed through Navarre's eyes:

> *Boyet.* Why all his behaviours did make their retire
> To the court of his eye, peeping thorough
> desire:
> His heart, like an agate, with your print
> impress'd,
> Proud with his form, in his eye pride express'd:
> His tongue, all impatient to speak and not see,

Did stumble with haste in his eyesight to be;
All senses to that sense did make their repair,
To feel only looking on fairest of fair:
Methought all his senses were lock'd in his eye,
As jewels in crystal for some prince to buy;
Who, tend'ring their own worth from where
    they were glass'd,
Did point you to buy them, along as you pass'd:
His face's own margent did quote such amazes,
That all eyes saw his eyes enchanted with gazes.
I'll give you Aquitaine, and all that is his,
An you give him for my sake but one loving
    kiss.

(II.i.234–49)

This is a virtuoso speech, and the ladies are quite right to suspect that "Boyet is dispos'd" to playfulness, and that he is himself an "old love-monger." The eight couplets, mostly with eleven-syllable lines, contain a number of ingenious conceits, beginning with the metaphor of a castle. Navarre's "behaviours" crowd together inside the fortress, peeping out for a view. All his senses are said to be composed into his eyes, "as jewels in crystal," and presumably just as helpless to escape and express themselves. His face and eyes are then likened, in the familiar trope, to a book. Throughout the passage there is a consistent and familiar emphasis on "eyes" and vision. Boyet describes the effects of some striking internal change (presumably for the good), a summoning and concentrating of social and sexual energy. In the final scene, Berowne uses a similar image in a speech to Rosaline:

Studies my lady? mistress, look on me.
Behold the window of my heart, mine eye,
What humble suit attends thy answer there.

(V.ii.827–9)

In both cases, the appeal is through the eyes, to the "heart's still rhetoric," not the tongue's tinkling eloquence. Whether these are the desired transformations remains to be seen. It is ironic that the men reveal themselves so openly through their eyes, for their Petrarchan fascination with women's eyes— with vision and therefore the superficial generally—has para- doxically blinded them.

Perhaps the most celebrated moment in *Love's Labour's Lost* occurs in the sonnet-reading scene when, after all the noblemen have been discovered and exposed, Berowne makes his Promethean Fire speech. The speech glorifies the psycho- logical transformations that result from the inspiration of love and women; my discussion of it will intrude upon the third category of change, for the speech contains brilliant verbal transformations as well. But the first thing to be noted is that it is intended to be sophistical, witty, and paradoxical. Like Armado's search for "precedent," it is a justification, and still another ironic bow to "authority":

> *King.* . . . good Berowne, now prove
> Our loving lawful, and our faith not torn.
> *Dum.* Ay, marry, there; some flattery for this evil.
> *Long.* O! some authority how to proceed;
> Some tricks, some quillets, how to cheat
> the devil.
> *Dum.* Some salve for perjury.
> (IV.iii.281–6)

Given this introduction, it is difficult to construe, as some readers have done, the following speech as Shakespeare's own voice. But it is Berowne at his best. For reference, it is quoted in its entirety, omitting the shorter section (lines 293–314) which appears to have been revised and expanded in the rest (*Arden*, p.xx):

> O! 'tis more than need.
> Have at you then, affection's men-at-arms:
> Consider what you first did swear unto,
> To fast, to study, and to see no woman;
> Flat treason 'gainst the kingly state of youth.

Say, can you fast? Your stomachs are too young,
And abstinence engenders maladies.
. . . .

O! we have made a vow to study, lords,
And in that vow we have forsworn our books:
For when would you, my liege, or you, or you,
In leaden contemplation have found out
Such fiery numbers as the prompting eyes
Of beauty's tutors have enrich'd you with?
Other slow arts entirely keep the brain,
And therefore, finding barren practisers,
Scarce show a harvest of their heavy toil;
But love, first learned in a lady's eyes,
Lives not alone immured in the brain,
But, with the motion of all elements,
Courses as swift as thought in every power,
And gives to every power a double power,
Above their functions and their offices.
It adds a precious seeing to the eye;
A lover's eyes will gaze an eagle blind;
A lover's ear will hear the lowest sound,
When the suspicious head of theft is stopp'd:
Love's feeling is more soft and sensible
Than are the tender horns of cockled snails:
Love's tongue proves dainty Bacchus gross in taste.
For valour, is not Love a Hercules,
Still climbing trees in the Hesperides?
Subtle as Sphinx; as sweet and musical
As bright Apollo's lute, strung with his hair;
And when Love speaks, the voice of all the gods
Make heaven drowsy with the harmony.
Never durst poet touch a pen to write
Until his ink were temper'd with Love's sighs;
O! then his lines would ravish savage ears,
And plant in tyrants mild humility.

(IV.iii.286–346)

149

If Berowne's logic is shaky, and sometimes dependent on quirky associations, his choice of language is nonetheless subtle and often exquisite: "as sweet and musical / As bright Apollo's lute, strung with his hair." This is the kind of line that the noblemen have been vainly reaching for in their own verse. The women's inspiring influence is heard as it is described. Here, finally, is a genuinely poetic transformation through language. Berowne's description of Love's powers —his use of an increasingly inventive list of attributes, culminating in Cupid's personification—becomes by the end a self-evident demonstration of Apollo's power as well. One metamorphosis inspires another. The poet himself seems to have a "double power," as he ranges through all the senses, hearing the lowest sounds, his feeling more soft and sensible, his eyes and ears exquisitely attuned, subtle as a sphinx himself, sweet and musical, and, in the person of Berowne, still climbing trees after mythical fruits—conventional emblems of poetic power. Berowne's list, working through the forms of Cupid's powers, becomes increasingly imaginative. The catalogue and others like it are meant to parallel the lists of synonyms produced by Holofernes and Nathaniel, and the extravagantly varied invocations of Armado. Once we recall the sterility of Holofernes' variations and mechanical manipulations, we can recognize Berowne's genuine fertility.

There is ample evidence in the speech that Berowne, even in his flight of inspiration, has not forgotten his special audience. If, for example, the "fiery numbers" of line 319 refer, as seems likely, to the love-sonnets the men have just read aloud, then we may legitimately suspect some irony in Berowne's tone. So, too, with the probable double-entendres in "the tender horns of cockled snails." And Berowne's description of Love as "a Hercules, / Still climbing trees in the Hesperides" reminds us of Berowne's own comic ascent into the tree only moments before. The speech, as promised, is full of "tricks" and "quillets." What Berowne says is in itself unexceptional, for he continues to play on Petrarchan conceits dealing with eyes, light, and fire, and he will soon summon the traditional authority of Prometheus, fire-giver and emblem of knowledge, for extra support. But the way in which Berowne changes the clichés and reinvigorates what was lifeless engages our attention and delights us. The reworked imagery of the speech contrasts sharply with the tired invocations of the lords' Petrarchan sonnets.

The Promethean Fire speech once again makes explicit the link between love and poetry. The conventional idea of love as an inspirational force is augmented by the notion that it preternaturally heightens sensibility at the same time. Calderwood notes that Berowne's speech "does not regard love as a social phenomenon between man and woman but as a vivifying inner event, an intensification of sensory powers."[9] To the extent that it is not "social," Calderwood sees this experience as needing some correction. But it would be difficult to reject the charm of the speech—especially its suggestion that the creation of beautiful poetry sometimes arises directly from such a private intensification. "Bright Apollo's lute" rings throughout the speech itself. And when, in lines 341–6, Berowne paraphrases the myth of Orpheus, the father of poets who can "ravish savage ears," we are impressed by the seriousness of this power. The effect of it is not to "Make heaven drowsy with the harmony," or to lull the audience either, but rather to "make," in Titania's words, "music . . . such as charmeth sleep" (*MND*, IV.i.82)—to attract and bewitch us into the greatest attention. Earlier, Rosaline had said of Berowne's power of speech,

> . . . his fair tongue (conceit's expositor)
> Delivers . . . such apt and gracious words
> That aged ears play truant at his tales,
> And younger hearings are quite ravished;
> So sweet and voluble is his discourse.

> (II.i.72–6)

The recurrence of the word "ravish" suggests that these passages are to be compared, for both testify to the lyric, "poetic" potential in Berowne, who is successful in his great speech though he may go astray elsewhere. With the play's lack of the conventional marriages at the end, the only "ravishing" done (aside from that of Jaquenetta) is sublimated through language.

If Berowne's speech touches on serious issues, particularly on the play's debate about the claims of poetry and art, it does not do so for long. As Berowne continues, his speech becomes ever more rhetorical and self-consciously clever, until the final outrageous paradox:

> From women's eyes this doctrine I derive:
> They sparkle still the right Promethean fire;
> They are the books, the arts, the academes,
> That show, contain, and nourish all the world;
> Else none at all in aught proves excellent.
> Then fools you were these women to forswear,
> Or, keeping what is sworn, you will prove fools.
> For wisdom's sake, a word that all men love,
> Or for love's sake, a word that loves all men,
> Or for men's sake, the authors of these women,
> Or women's sake, by whom we men are men,
> Let us once lose our oaths to find ourselves,
> Or else we lose ourselves to keep our oaths.
> It is religion to be thus forsworn;
> For charity itself fulfils the law;
> And who can sever love from charity?
>
> (IV.iii.347–62)

Again, an interesting mixture of tones reverberates in the speech. "Let us once lose our oaths to find ourselves"—this rings true on the deepest level, for the movement of the entire play has been towards such a self-discovery. Yet it is also a self-justification, and to some extent another self-deception; its sincerity is undermined by the over-elaborate patterning and repetition of the "or" construction. The last few lines, with the obvious echo of Romans 12.8, are just short of being blasphemous, and yet we enjoy the wit that brings us to this point without being cozened by it. Barber aptly describes the tone of these last lines: Shakespeare "has turned the word 'fool' around, in the classic manner of Erasmus in his *Praise of Folly*; it becomes folly not to be a fool . . . the speech concludes with overtones of Christian folly in proclaiming the logic of their losing themselves to find themselves and in appealing from the law to charity. But Berowne merely leaps up to ring these big bells lightly; there is no coming to rest on sanctities; everything is in motion" (Barber, p. 92).

What we have, then, is virtuosity. Wooing the ladies of France becomes, through sleight-of-hand, identified with Christian charity; Navarre's edicts become harsh Mosaic law; and it seems the most "natural" thing in the world when Berowne argues that the old law exists only to be superseded. Our reactions to this must be complex. On the one hand, our comic expectations have all along been that this foolish law will eventually be broken, that it should be broken. But the manner of its breaking—the sophistic cleverness of Berowne's speech—indicates that, although the oath may indeed be lost, the young men have yet to find themselves. Berowne's speech continually moves toward various truths of human nature, but is deflected from them by its own parabolic irony.

Like Hercules and the other great heroes, the lords are in the grip of a force stronger than themselves. Moreover, they sometimes seem to be unaware of it; oaths are dropped and directions reversed without comment. But the audience and the ladies notice the changes that they do not. Helena complains about similar events in *A Midsummer Night's Dream*:

> For ere Demetrius looked on Hermia's eyne,
> He hailed down oaths that he was only mine;
> And when this hail some heat from Hermia felt,
> So he dissolved, and show'rs of oaths did melt.
>
> (*MND*, I.i.242–5)

Resolve dissolves and melts just as easily in *Love's Labour's Lost*. And so does language—for we are presented with a paradigm of the linguistic process in the shift of meaning from "hailed" to "hail," a paranomasia which was anticipated in *Love's Labour's Lost*:

> *King*. All hail, sweet madam, and fair time of day!
> *Prin*. Fair in all hail is foul, as I conceive.

Navarre's plaintive reply—"Construe my speeches better, if you may" (V.ii.339–41)—represents every reader's critical byword. I shall now attempt to construe the verbal metamorphoses more closely.

THE POETS: VERBAL TRANSFORMATION

> *Dum*. Will you vouchsafe with me to change a word?
> *Mar*. Name it.
> *Dum*.   Fair lady,—
> *Mar*.   Say you so? Fair lord,—
> Take that for your fair lady.
>
> (V.ii.238–41)
>
> *Prin*. We arrest your word.
>
> (II.i.160)

Dumain's query is accepted and turned back at him faster than he can react. To "change a word" is social intercourse, but if words change their meanings and contexts, communication temporarily breaks down. The word "change" itself changes here, for a figurative sense is supplanted by a literal one. The Princess' declaration is characteristic of all the ladies, beyond this single incident—they will take words for their literal meaning, "arrest" them, in dealing with the lords. Once again they confront them with a reflection of their own folly. In *Love's Labour's Lost* everything that Bacon feared can be found thriving—words continually "beget" other words, other meanings.

We have already seen this promiscuous fertility at work in the word "fame" in the first chapter. The extremes of transformation are also revealed in the word "turn." Like so many important terms in *Love's Labour's Lost*—"fame," "affection," "worth," "make"—"turn" is a charged word whose meaning depends on its context and the energies surrounding it. The play exploits the capacity of language to be unstable and free. Far from being meaningless, certain words are, because of changes in context, magnets which draw to themselves a wide range of possible meanings. This multiplicity is a linguistic equivalent to the structural design of contrasting but interwoven plot-lines.

"Turn" is capable of the same wide applications. The simple physical sense of the word, describing movement in space, is extended into a number of complex, figurative applications. Costard, for example, attempts a linguistic evasion of responsibility in the first act, substituting "demsel," "virgin," and then "maid" for the term "wench"—but in vain:

> King. This maid will not serve your turn, sir.
> Cost. This maid will serve my turn, sir.
>
> (I.i.282–3)

The idiomatic meaning of "to serve one's turn" is "to answer one's purpose or requirement; to suffice for or satisfy a need" (*OED*). But Navarre also means "turn" as "a subtle device of any kind; a trick, wile, artifice, stratagem" (*OED*)—he is referring to Costard's turn of phrase, his attempt to obscure meanings by piling up synonyms. Costard neatly demonstrates this ability to twist words once more by giving "turn" a sexual meaning—as an euphemism for intercourse. The whole exchange exploits a "trick" or "artifice."[10]

The most common figurative meaning of "turn," however, is "to shape, form, or fashion artistically or gracefully" (*OED*). Armado, for example, promises "I shall turn sonnet" (I.ii.174). He means "shape" or "fashion," but there is more than a hint that, in his enthusiasm, he will become what he beholds. Rosaline says of Berowne that every object caught by his eye his wit "turns to a mirth-moving jest" (II.i.71), with the same potential for abuse we saw in the "wit to make." Berowne, for his part, claims of Rosaline that her dark complexion "turns the fashion of the days"

(IV.iii.259). The Princess' judgment that "None are so surely caught, when they are catch'd, / As wit turn'd fool" (V.ii.69–70) describes the quintessential metamorphosis of comedy. It prepares us for Berowne's ignorant complaint that Rosaline's "wit makes wise things foolish" (l. 374). When the lords' Masque of Muscovites is exposed, Dumain tries to escape responsibility as Falstaff might: "Let us confess, and turn it to a jest" (V.ii.390). But the joke is on the lords, as always. When wit turns unwitting fool, no mere jest will suffice to resolve the comic tension or save face.

In Berowne's final plea to the ladies, the whole vocabulary of metamorphosis is summoned up in an attempt to displace responsibility and effect an easy transition toward the happy ending the men (and audience) had expected. It is a speech of tortured and fallacious logic. If we have betrayed our oaths and seemed foolish, Berowne argues,

> Those heavenly eyes, that look into these faults,
> Suggested us to *make*. Therefore, ladies,
> Our love being yours, the error that love *makes*
> Is likewise yours: we to ourselves prove false,
> By being once false for ever to be true
> To those that *make* us both,—fair ladies, you:
> And even that falsehood, in itself a sin,
> Thus purifies itself and *turns* to grace.
>
> (V.ii.759–66; my emphasis)

Even Berowne can't follow all this: he must resort to the awkward suspension of "fair ladies, you" to identify the mysterious agents of all these transformations. By a remarkable "turn" of language, the ladies become the cause of everything—the "makers" gone awry. It is hardly Berowne's finest moment. His last two lines invoke once again the religious terminology used so wittily at the end of the Promethean Fire speech, where it was "religion" to be "forsworn," and "charity" to fulfill the "law." Berowne anticipates prematurely the purification that will take place during the "year and a day" of imposed penance. He assumes an easy

156

spiritual transformation because he is still unaware of the full extent of the comic metamorphosis in which he is implicated. If there is any doubt about his shortsightedness, it is dispelled by his statement that "falsehood" already "turns" to that ubiquitous and too-easily summoned "grace" which throughout the play alternates between religious and courtly meanings, neither of which the lords have attained. In addition, the word has a slippery connection with its homophonic cousin, "grease." And yet in another sense Berowne is unwittingly correct, for the shape and movement of the entire play show how certain kinds of falsehood are being turned to "grace" in the sense of beauty and order. For Shakespeare, at least, has the "wit to make" things right again. That fact reminds us that the vocabulary of metamorphosis must not be lightly invoked, that it entails serious artistic responsibilities. Under the pressure of "love"—or at least the love of love—the lords both rise and fall to the occasion, unaware that they themselves are changing.

"Form" is another word with strange alter egos. As a verb, it usually has the sense of "to shape" or "create." In one of Berowne's speeches, it occurs twice: "Form'd by the eye, and therefore, like the eye, / Full of strange shapes, of habits, and of forms" (V.ii.752–3). And Holofernes has described his "foolish extravagant spirit" as "full of forms, figures, shapes" (IV.ii.67). As verb or noun, it is associated with the active power of the imagination. But, like the word "fame," it is also trivialized, as in Berowne's complaint about Boyet: "This is the ape of form, monsieur the nice" (V.ii.325). Holofernes is horrified at Dull's appearance: "O! thou monster Ignorance, how deform'd dost thou look" (IV.ii.23). And "form" becomes nonsensical in Costard's "In manner and form following" (I.i.202), where it sinks to the sense of "bench" (l. 204).[11] The insubstantial shapes of the imagination petrify in matter.

Something similar happens to the word "fashion." In its active sense, it could also mean "to create" or "shape," as in Spenser's intention to "fashion a gentleman or noble person in virtuous and gentle discipline," or in Berowne's "fashioning our humours" (V.ii.747). More often, however, the verb has solidified into a noun. Armado is "a man in all the world's new fashion planted" (I.i.163), and "a man of fire-new words, fashion's own knight" (I.i.177). Berowne boasts that Rosaline's dark "favour . . . turns the fashion of the days" (IV.iii.259). Still another parallel is found in the use of the word "figure." Holofernes' spirit is "full of forms, figures, shapes." "Figures," the *Arden* editor tells us, here means "imagination." But the word usually is deadly literal in this play, referring to the specific figures of rhetoric, as in Holofernes' "What is the figure?"

The male characters in *Love's Labour's Lost* seem therefore to trivialize the imagination. It is contracted to matter and cliché in the persons and poetry of Holofernes, Armado, and to a lesser extent in the four noblemen. The *commedia* figures are themselves "deformations" of the legendary Nine Worthies, comically reduced in scale—Hercules could only be presented "in minority" whether Moth plays his part or not. The same kind of trivialization is evident in the language of the play, for the traditional forms of the imagination have become mere formalities, dead conventions. The whole vocabulary of metamorphosis itself seems peculiarly liable to change. The figures of the mind have congealed into figures of rhetorical invention to be memorized. In the fate of such words as "turn," "form," and "fashion" we can see a paradigm of other changes in the play. Each of them is a synonym for the active shaping force of the imagination, but each is brought low by comic misuse. The play's interest in archaic forms of style, diction, and poetry brings into relief the contrast between static forms and active formation. In their adopted roles as melancholy-lovers, the noblemen themselves are merely the apes of form, acting an old part no longer very interesting, and consequently seeming "deformed" in contrast to their superior women. The breakdown of imagination generally is reflected in the parallel cases of the lords' language and their social behavior.

Cupid: The Wimpled, Whining, Purblind, Wayward Boy

"Love" is the power behind all of this change and confusion, leading ultimately to clarification. But "love," as a word and as a personification, undergoes dramatic transformations of its own in the course of the play. During Berowne's Promethean Fire speech, possibly at line 334, "love" is no longer simply the abstract force which "courses as swift as thought" through the mind and body—an "affection"—but it also becomes "Love," or Cupid. The personification takes on greater and greater life, as Costard's "one Frances" does, until once again a word becomes a moral agent, with a local habitation and name. When Berowne's speech is over, love's full metamorphosis is revealed by Navarre: "Saint Cupid, then! and, soldiers, to the field!" (IV.iii.363). Before this abrupt canonization, Cupid has already been the most impressive "Worthy" in the play, from the militant conqueror of Samson, Solomon, and Hercules, to the paradoxical but powerful opponent of Berowne's soliloquy in III.i:

> O! and I forsooth in love!
> I, that have been love's whip;
> A very beadle to a humorous sigh;
> A critic, nay, a night-watch constable,
> A domineering pedant o'er the boy,
> Than whom no mortal so magnificent!
> This wimpled, whining, purblind, wayward boy,
> This signor junior, giant-dwarf, dan Cupid;
> Regent of love rhymes, lord of folded arms,
> The anointed sovereign of sighs and groans,
> Liege of all loiterers and malcontents,
> Dread prince of plackets, king of codpieces,
> Sole imperator and great general
> Of trotting paritors: O my little heart!
> And I to be a corporal of his field,
> And wear his colours like a tumbler's hoop!
>   (III.i.170–85)

The wit of this passage is brilliant: the ascending metaphors of royalty, the references to love's war, the comic use
of alliteration, the juxtaposition of the regal and carnal—
all point to the growing, contradictory power of love.
Throughout the play, whether described as an abstract force
or a personification, love comes in fact to resemble, by its
paradoxes and effects, the power of poetry. And here again,
as in the inventive lists in the Promethean Fire speech, Berowne achieves powerful verbal transformations. In lines
170–4, he creates a list of his own roles with respect to Love
—beadle, critic, constable, pedant—which correspond, inter-
estingly, with at least three of the *commedia* figures in the
play: Nathaniel (the "hedge-priest" or beadle), Dull (the
constable), and Holofernes (the pedant),[12] indicating, once
again, the special mirroring function of the subplot.

Berowne's personification of Cupid, like the statue of Her-
mione in *The Winter's Tale*, comes gradually to life under
the pressure of his continually inventive imagination. Cupid
is known first as a state of mind: one is "in love." Cupid is
born, as it were, in the next line (l. 171), and we see him as
the helpless child, love in the lower case. Berowne has flogged
and dominated the child in the past, but he knows that "no
mortal" is as proud or as formidable as Cupid. Like all children, however, Cupid will grow up and overthrow his
"father." Berowne is the parent who has lost control in this
parodic family myth. At the end of this scene, he describes
his new plight as "a plague / That Cupid will impose for my
neglect / Of his almighty dreadful little might" (ll. 198–200).
In a comic version of Freud's family romance, the neglected
child seeks revenge against the now helpless adults.

From line 175 on, the "wayward boy" becomes increasingly powerful and, in line 177, his identity and reality are
confirmed when he is first given a name—"dan Cupid," the
boy who is also master and lord. This is already the third
paradox in that line, for Cupid's age—signor (senior)/ju-
nior—and his size—giant/dwarf—have already been described. These paradoxes play on the discrepancy between

the boy's symbolic attributes and his real power, his presumed youth and age-old influence over men, and his small size and immense strength. In this last paradox he is analogous to Hercules "in minority" (V.i.129), the babe in the cradle who strangles serpents and performs heroic feats (Berowne forges the identification in the Promethean Fire speech— "For valour, is not Love a Hercules?"). Berowne's description makes Cupid something of a freak, to be sure, something powerful but deformed and possibly unnatural. Yet the darker implications of this power are not dwelt on. Instead, Berowne chooses in the next eight lines to create an increasingly grand sequence of titles which remind us by contrast of Holofernes' synonymic poverty, but which are connected with an increasingly ludicrous sequence of possessives. The tables are more than turned, for the greater Cupid's power becomes, the more absurd his subjects seem. The second list —of "love rhymes," "sighs and groans," "loiterers and malcontents"—defines the stereotypes of the courtly lover. The link with the lords is explicit, as the "folded arms" of l. 178 recalls Moth's satiric portrait of the lover earlier in this scene —"with your arms crossed on your thin-belly doublet like a rabbit on a spit" (ll. 16–7)—and looks forward to Navarre's mockery that Longaville "never lay his wreathed arms athwart / His loving bosom to keep down his heart" (IV.iii.133–4).[13] If the description of Cupid begins with the lords as melancholy-minded lovers, it also veers downward to take in the other extreme—"plackets" and "codpieces," portions of the dress and, by transference, the anatomy more familiar, in this play, to Costard, Armado, and Jaquenetta. The sexual metaphor here is more than ever deflationary. The extremes of love, foolish etherealism and blunt carnality, are shown to draw their power from the same source. Cupid's metamorphoses, like those Berowne describes in IV.iii.324–46, are analogous to the changes the characters themselves experience. Love is still a "Hercules," a giant-dwarf; the "king of codpieces" stands erect through Berowne's language, undergoes Protean changes of shape, and becomes himself an emblem for creating change. Metamorphosis as a power of love is analogous to, and here indistinguishable from, the transformations of art created by the imagination through language.

Cupid has become a "saint" and ally by the end of Berowne's Promethean speech, the exemplification of the religion of love, of the "liver vein." The canonization is literally, according to Berowne's earlier terms, "pure, pure idolatry." This attitude, along with the strong sexual overtones of Berowne's exhortation—

> Advance your standards, and upon them, lords!
> Pell-mell, down with them! but be first advis'd,
> In conflict that you get the sun of them—
>
> (IV.iii.364–6)

severely limits the extent to which the speech might be taken as Shakespeare's own words, as some readers of the play have done. Above all, Berowne's speech impresses us with how much can be done with language, simultaneously reminding us that even more remains to be done. Berowne has only to lose his self-conscious sophistry and pick up Apollo's lute.

At the end of the pivotal sonnet-reading scene, Cupid undergoes still another transformation as the lords plan "some strange pastime" for the ladies: "For revels, dances, masks, and merry hours, / Forerun fair Love, strewing her way with flowers" (IV.iii.376–7). Appropriately enough, the metamorphosis is sexual. Love becomes a Flora-like goddess of social gathering, a kind of vegetation-deity ushered in like royalty. In the final scene, before the Masque of Muscovites, Cupid as Love appears in his most mysterious form yet. Boyet is warning the ladies that the masked lords are approaching them:

> Love doth approach disguis'd,
> Armed in arguments; you'll be surpris'd:
> Muster your wits; stand in your own defence;
> Or hide your heads like cowards, and fly hence.
>
> (V.ii.83–6)

Love is here the armed warrior, whose main weapon is expected to be verbal sophistry. But the sexual edge of "stand" hints at the underlying carnality of the mock-assault. The Princess exclaims: "Saint Denis to Saint Cupid!" (l. 87), summoning the patron saint of France to counter the patron saint of the libido.

Cupid—in every form—is present everywhere in the play, designating for us both concupiscence and conspicuous folly. Armado vows to "outswear Cupid" (I.ii.61), but admits that "Cupid's buttshaft" (l. 165) will overpower his own rapier. Katharine calls Boyet "Cupid's grandfather" (II.i.255), rather a misnomer in light of Boyet's apparent impotence. Berowne sees the "wayward boy" as a kind of stage-manager directing the folly: "Proceed, sweet Cupid: thou hast thumped him [Navarre] with thy bird-bolt under the left pap" (IV.iii.22–4). A moment later, Berowne reminds us of Cupid's power as the "king of codpieces": "O! rhymes are guards on wanton Cupid's hose: / Disfigure not his shop" (ll. 58–9). "Shop" means "phallus," and it is obvious that the cause-and-effect relationship described here is actually reversed in the play. The lords are the ones who have been "disfigured" sexually and emotionally.

Cupid is referred to by name often enough in the play, but not with the frequency that the word "love" is used.[14] Although most of the occurrences of the latter are unremarkable, the usage is crucial when "love" becomes the active agent of a sentence, for the personification elevates it to a synonym for Cupid. The bewildered Armado, for example, hopelessly declares, "Love is a familiar; Love is a devil; there is no evil angel but Love" (I.ii.162–3). He explains his human "weakness" as the result of demonic possession.[15] Such a power is immense and seems arbitrary. Berowne goes even further: "By the Lord, this love is as mad as Ajax: it kills sheep, it kills me, I a sheep" (IV.iii.6–7). Here the irrational fury of madness associates Love by distant allusion with *Hercules furens*. Berowne goes on to describe Cupid as comic pedant: "it [love] hath taught me to rhyme, and to be melancholy" (ll. 12–3). This is the ruling passion, as it were, of almost every character. When Dumain steps forth in IV.iii, Berowne comments: "Once more I'll mark how love can vary wit" (l. 98). His remark could be taken as an epigraph for the play generally, a description of the ways in which transformation alters the human shape. That the word "vary" should be used here is revealing for, in its strict rhetorical sense, the word has a complex history in the play. It suggests still another link between the transformation of personality and attempted verbal transformations, as in Holofernes' "sweetly varied" (IV.ii.8) synonyms.

The metamorphosis of Berowne and his comrades at the end of the play is as incomplete and unsatisfying as their poetry. But the men have at least begun to change, however gradual their transformation. In a speech filled with the terms of metamorphosis, Berowne tries in the final scene to mount a defense of his folly:

> Your beauty, ladies,
> Hath much deform'd us, fashioning our humours
> Even to the opposed end of our intents;
> And what in us hath seem'd ridiculous,—
> As love is full of unbefitting strains;
> All wanton as a child, skipping and vain;
> Form'd by the eye, and therefore, like the eye,
> Full of strange shapes, of habits, and of forms,
> Varying in subjects, as the eye doth roll
> To every varied object in his glance:
> Which party-coated presence of loose love
> Put on by us, if, in your heavenly eyes,
> Have misbecom'd our oaths and gravities,
> Those heavenly eyes, that look into these faults,
> Suggested us to make.
>
> (V.ii.746–60)

Berowne tries to make the ladies responsible for the vagaries of his own imagination simply because they came into his line of sight and prompted these phantasms. He tries again to evade aesthetic responsibilities by personifying and summoning "love" to his defense. Neither the militant conqueror nor the irate madman, love becomes—through Berowne's wish not to offend the women—the charming "wanton," the wayward boy again, "skipping and vain." It is this power, generated in part by the women's "heavenly eyes," which prompted the lords "to make" (l. 760) all that they did, "varying" (l. 754) the objects of their vision, "fashioning" (l. 747) their humours the wrong way. It becomes apparent, to the audience at least, that Cupid's mutations are also the lords'—that the personifications are, in part, self-betraying projections. The repertoire of Cupid's roles and masks can be viewed as a descriptive catalogue of the lords' obsessions, for they too are "skipping and vain" in their modes of imagination.

The Princess, quite rightly, rejects Berowne's specious argument. His lack of social and artistic responsibility, his sophistical cleverness at an inappropriate time, above all his faulty understanding of his own imagination demonstrate that he and his friends are not yet "worthy" of the ladies, that they are still too fantastical, too much like Armado. After sending Berowne to a hospital for his year-long penance, Rosaline says:

> if sickly ears,
> Deaf'd with the clamours of their own dear groans,
> Will hear your idle scorns, continue then,
> And I will have you and that fault withal;
> But if they will not, throw away that spirit,
> And I shall find you empty of that fault,
> Right joyful of your reformation.
>
> (ll. 853–9)

It is no coincidence that Rosaline answers Berowne's admission of being "deform'd" (l. 747) with a look toward his eventual "reformation" (l. 859). *Love's Labour's Lost* as a whole is vitally concerned with "formation" in all its aspects: with the metamorphosis of personality, with the education of the noblemen, with the transformation of Nature into Art. What is needed, as Rosaline makes clear, is a genuine re-formation on all fronts. Much of *Love's Labour's Lost* can therefore be seen as a prelude to the eventual true metamorphoses of the noblemen and their language. The process has begun, but it will require "a year and a day" yet. In that year, the men must learn certain artistic and moral responsibilities; chief among them, how language is not a subterfuge but a medium through which truth is revealed.

Love's Labour's Lost is in part a record of the lords' attempt to control imagination. But most of the play records their falling short. They are moving in the right direction at the end, but the transformation is incomplete. The audience, however, has already reached this outer boundary of knowledge and experience, always a step ahead of the lords. As if to guarantee the final re-formation, and to reward the audience for its efforts, the final songs afford us immediate proof that language can be used well, even magnificently. To anticipate further changes in the lords would require at least a year. But "that's too long for a play," as Berowne admits, and besides, it would require another play altogether, none other than *Love's Labour's Won*. The rest is silence.

CHAPTER FIVE

Living Art

The structural movement of *Love's Labour's Lost* takes an expansive form. The play seems to proceed from the inner ring of concentric circles to the outer, from the less to the more inclusive, from "artifice" and "illusion" to "reality." The play begins in Navarre's mind, as he details in his opening speech a plan for defeating time with a "little academe." The constricted world of the academe is forcibly widened, however, by the arrival of the women, and the setting moves to the park, away from the court itself. The introduction of the various low comic characters contributes to a continuing expansion as the play progresses, and more and more reminders of time and death impinge on the secluded park. The Princess' embassy implies another world beyond the court, another dimension where wars are fought, debts must be settled, old men sicken and die. With the entrance of Marcade in the final scene, announcing the death of the Princess' father, death itself enters the play. Whatever remained of the plan for the ascetic academe has long since vanished. The various levels of awareness and self-knowledge so schematically outlined in the sonnet-reading scene are found mirrored in the larger structure of the entire play. We move from the innermost ring, in the opening speech, to something like the outermost with Marcade's entrance and the imposition of the year-long penances.

Recent critics of *Love's Labour's Lost* are virtually unanimous in their appraisals of the meaning and implications of this outward movement. It represents, in its broadest terms, what is usually called the victory of "reality" over "illusion," of "nature" over "art." This verdict is all the easier to reach because of the extraordinary complexity of the play's language; it is simpler to call it "affected" or "artificial" than to understand what it achieves. As Ralph Berry sums it up, the movement of the play is "towards an acceptance of reality. 'Reality' is a term that (however unsatisfactory philosophically) critics agree upon as a convenient designation for the target of the play's probing. The word . . . designates all those phenomena of life that are symbolized by the entry of Mercade. That entry is the key fact of the play . . . the final Act makes sense only as a reversal of the first Act: the themes of light-darkness, folly-wisdom, fantasy-reality are initiated and resolved in the exposition and conclusion." These themes are "resolved" on only one side, that of Mercade, according to Berry, and others. He concludes that this "movement towards reality" should be seen as "a set of reversals, refutations of the untenable positions taken up in Act I—just as, perhaps, the logic of the final Winter-song refutes Summer" (Berry, p. 69)[1] I hope to show that such interpretations severely oversimplify the play's complex balance of opposites.

If there is agreement on the general movement of the play, not everyone is agreed on its precise turning-point. For one thing, the theme of death runs throughout the play, from the opening words of Navarre to Armado's lament for the dead Hector. But death is finally embodied in Mercade, another verbal allusion made flesh. The build-up is gradual, from witty references to plague "tokens" or a "death's-face in a ring" (V.ii.605) to the movement in the fifth act stage-time from early afternoon to the gathering darkness of twilight, in which Holofernes-Judas stumbles. Most readers of the play, however, see Mercade's entrance, quite properly, as the chilling and dramatic high-point in the play. It never fails to shock in performance.[2]

But the brilliance of Mercade's *coup de théâtre* may blind us to the fact that his entrance is not yet the end of the play, that there are some 200 lines left, and that the play actually ends, not with a chilling note of death or with a harsh penance but with a much more complex tone, in a highly artificial debate or "dialogue." Schematic structures of all sorts are continually being dissolved and re-created during the play—outer circles suddenly become inner, exclusive points of view are shattered into multiplicity. I suggest that a similar enlargement of meaning occurs at the end of *Love's Labour's Lost*, after Marcade's entrance, and that recent criticism of the play has largely failed to take this expansion into account.

The use of multiple rings of perception is a basic principle of construction in the play. It structures the whole and, as we saw in chapter two, it is the governing form of individual scenes. We think of the rings as extending past the audience to the dramatist, occupying the outermost circle, who is the "demi-god," the *primum mobile* which turns the universe of the play, with the elements near the center (Dull, Costard) slower and heavier than those near the edges (Moth, the ladies). Shakespeare's method everywhere is to set opposites in conflict, worlds in collision, to bring contrary viewpoints into contention with one another. The first chapter showed several stylistic examples of this method, with high and low diction alternating, one prose style clashing with another, and a frequent use of figures of rhetoric such as antithesis and chiasmus. Jonas Barish finds that Shakespeare's habitual syntactical arrangement, in prose, is disjunctive in a similar way: "What we find in Shakespeare and in writers like him is a tendency to insist on the points of disjunction, to hold up the two pieces of the sentence side by side, in full view, to symmetrize them and brandish them in their matched antagonism" (Barish, pp. 27–8). In the second chapter we saw a similar juxtaposition of dramatic styles, the "sophisticated" masque set against the "naive" pageant, for example, although they have the same aesthetic effect on their audiences. In the third chapter, an even greater variety of poetic styles was displayed, with sheer opposites—topical versus archaic—and everything between. In each of these chapters on "style," Shakespeare's dramatic practice was seen to be basically the same. It is an insistence on giving us the many rather than the one, on showing us multiple-colored refractions of Nature rather than a single narrowly focused image. He shifts, to continue the optical metaphor, from telescopic to microscopic views, from a wide scan to a contracted highlight, and then back again. In the fourth chapter we saw how the images tended to dissolve and melt into one another, how the shapes in question shifted their outline in passing from one mirroring station to the next. All this arises from the same recurrent technique. I intend, in this chapter, to isolate one of these patterns—the juxtaposition of two logically opposite themes or ideas—and to show how "theme" and "structure" are different aspects of the same phenomenon.

THE WORLD'S DEBATE

The final "dialogue" or debate between Hiems and Ver serves as a suggestive emblem of the basic structural principle of *Love's Labour's Lost*. Two opposite powers of myth literally appear on stage to contend in mock-struggle, each making claims for itself which exclude the other. It is a rudimentary form of the dramatic impulse. This "dialogue" is conducted throughout the play on a number of levels. *Love's Labour's Lost* is a debate on the nature of poetry and the imagination in the sense that two or more conflicting attitudes and examples are again and again placed in opposition so that contrary claims can be more starkly revealed and evaluated. G. K. Hunter has argued, for example, that the play is "based . . . on a debate-theme of learning against experience (the principal experience being love)," and notes as well a parallel debate about love-wit.[3] He goes on to connect this debate structure specifically with Lyly's habitual dramatic practice. I believe that the debate about the use of imagination and language is the chief one in the play, though there are to be sure many more debates conducted at the same time. A list of all the contending dualisms in the play would be long; the following are those most frequently heard:

Spring vs. Winter
Learning vs. Experience
Rhetoric vs. Simplicity
Affectation vs. Self-Knowledge
Wearing a Mask vs. Revealing Oneself
Playing a Role vs. Being Oneself
Style vs. Matter
Words vs. Things
Form vs. Content
Mind vs. Body
Paradox vs. Common Sense

In the very beginning of the play, for example, Navarre's edicts are premised on an untenable mind-body dualism which is quickly shattered. Longaville makes a joke of it at first:

The mind shall banquet, though the body pine:
Fat paunches have lean pates, and dainty bits
Make rich the ribs, but bankrupt quite the wits.

(I.i.25–7)

These lines in themselves are evidence enough of a starved mind and bankrupt wits, but the men who agree to "war against your own affections" (l. 9) are already too self-divided and addled to notice. One of the first and most important things Navarre, and the audience, will learn is that experience is not so easily categorized, and that simplistic assumptions about human nature make flimsy foundations for an academy or any other enterprise.

If recent criticism of Shakespeare's comedies has taught us anything, surely it is that these plays are more complex than we at first suspect, that Shakespeare's structures and his ideas are occasionally simple but never simple-minded. All the more surprising, then, to find almost unanimous agreement among recent readers of *Love's Labour's Lost* that the play clearly affirms the "victory" of the right side of this list over the left, of russet and honest kersey over taffeta and silk, of Winter-Reality over Spring-Illusion, of, most generally, Nature over Art. At its worst, this traditional reading of the play finds Shakespeare in Berowne, renouncing gimmickry and artificiality once and for all. Some readers continue, moreover, to say that Shakespeare "prefers" or sides with Winter's song over Spring's on the grounds that it is more realistic. Yet a reading of the tradition of the debate form does not support such conclusions, apart from the evidence of the play itself.

The debate or *conflictus* is an archaic, primitive device of great appeal, dating back at least to the ninth century. Its origin lies in a perception of the rhythm of nature itself, and its use of dualistic opposites, we might argue, reflects similar divided impulses in man. It is an older and even more venerable dramatic model than the Pageant of the Nine Worthies, but unlike the pageant it is not at all comic or ludicrous in *Love's Labour's Lost*. Literary debates, including pastoral rhyming contests, generally avoided reaching either-or decisions. The contrary forces of such debates—the owl and the nightingale, winter and summer—are too complex to admit one-sided resolutions. Madeleine Doran argues that such topics "admit only of practical decision in the course of living, not of theoretical and absolute conclusion." She goes on to say that "It is the airing of the issues that has been important, not the conclusion."[4] In "The Debate and Stryfe Betwene Somer and Wynter" (1530?), for example, the two seasonal forces exchange arguments about their respective desirabilities, ranging over such topics as love, human fellowship, the harvest, and so on. Summer's arguments are strong, but Winter reminds him that "The hyest day in the yere is the Nativyte." Summer, in the next and last stanza, calls a halt to the debate by arguing for a point of agreement between them:

> Wynter, by one assent / our great stryfe let us ceas,
> And togeder agre we / and make a fynall peas;
> God that create this worlde / & made bothe the & me,

172

Let us pray to hym to send us a good ende / Amen
for charité.[5]

This debate ends with "one assent," not a one-sided victory,
on the grounds that God made both seasons, and therefore
both must be good. A similar "assent," I will argue, ends the
final debate in *Love's Labour's Lost*.

Winter's song comes after Spring's in *Love's Labour's
Lost*, but there is no evidence in the text that one song is
superior to the other (I will consider them in detail in the
next chapter). But Catherine McLay, among others, has recently argued to the contrary, in part by appealing to the
play's structure: "Like the Song, the play too moves from
spring to winter, from art to nature, from illusion to reality.
And the movement in the Song from the folly of the cuckoo
to the wisdom of the owl has its counterpart in the handling
of the several strands of the play's action, of its plots and
subplots."[6] This does justice neither to the play nor to the
songs, both of which are far more complex than McLay
allows. In those *débats*, festivals, and fertility rituals in which
one side is declared a victor over the other, moreover, it is
Spring or Summer, not Winter, whose victory is celebrated.[7]
But no such either-or decision is made in *Love's Labour's
Lost*. It is the interplay between the dualistic forces which
is of interest; the stress in the play is now to one side, now to
another, but one side never achieves complete dominance
over the other—the entrance of Marcade comes close to such
a victory, only to fall short.

A similar case may be made for the other dualisms listed
above. To stress only the right side of the list—matter,
things, experience—is naive, not to say materialistic. It is a
curious ontology (and meteorology) which allows "reality"
and "nature" to be identified exclusively with Winter. To
emphasize only the left side of the list, however—learning,
style, words—is equally perverse. Shakespeare advocated
neither of these sides alone, though it is not difficult to find
theoretical proponents in the Renaissance of one side or the

other, from Chapman, say, to Montaigne.[8] But in *Love's Labour's Lost*, easy dualisms are suspect; they are flourished and
emphasized, only to be rigorously examined. Differences between the opposites always turn out to be less than we
thought. As Jonas Barish has remarked, in an article on
Lyly's antithetical prose style, "the more absolute of its kind
a thing may appear to be, the more certain it is that somewhere within it lies its own antithesis, its anti-self."[9] Nowhere
is the interrelatedness of apparent opposites more evident
than in the most important and inclusive opposition of the
play, Art versus Nature.

ART AND NATURE

Armado tells Navarre that he discovered Costard and Jaquenetta "north-north-east and by east from the west corner of
thy curious-knotted garden" (I.i.239–40). We immediately
look forward to Milton's Eden, where there are

> Flours worthy of Paradise, which not nice Art
> In Beds and curious Knots, but Nature boon
> Powrd forth profuse. . . .
>
> *(P.L.,* IV,241–3)

We never actually see Navarre's garden, nor could we even
find it from Armado's directions, but it is easy to imagine the
"curious" and ornately sculpted labyrinths and mazes which
"nice Art" has created. Moreover, there is a strong family
resemblance between Navarre's garden and his rhetoric; the
hortus conclusus is inevitably also the *hortus mentis*.[10]
When Milton wishes to initiate a distinction between Art
and Nature, the garden is a handy emblem, as it was for
Shakespeare. In both Eden and Navarre, there is an apple (a
"costard") and a fall. Jaquenetta is described as "a child of
our grandmother Eve, a female" (I.i.253) and, continuing
the allusions, Berowne says of Boyet, "Had he been Adam,
he had tempted Eve" (V.ii.322). In an imperfect world,
largely of their own making, the lords attempt to reinstitute

a golden age, first by study, then through love. "What fool is not so wise," Longaville asks, "To lose an oath to win a paradise?" (IV.iii.70–1). So Adam thought, losing what he didn't know he had for breaking an oath. The garden motif continues through the play, comically reincarnated in a verbal form in Costard's "gardon," a monetary paradise. There is a classical analogue in the garden of the Hesperides, alluded to in Berowne's Promethean Fire speech (IV.iii.338). Hercules' labor is to enter the garden and pick the apples from the tree, the converse of the Biblical injunction.[11] Costard's fall in Navarre's garden, at any rate, reenacts Adam's and anticipates the comic stumbles of the lords about to come. The metaphor of the garden is invoked as a means of revealing the actions of the mind, Nature in the service of Art.

The Art-Nature relationship is central to any debate about the function of the imagination and the role of the artist. Everything depends on which side of the dualism one comes down on—the imagination may be severely circumscribed if "Nature" is held morally superior to "nice Art." The ideal relationship is usually a balance or dialectic—Art supplies what Nature lacks, it encourages and complements what is given.[12] In Spenser's Temple of Venus the standard formula is given:

> For all that nature by her mother wit
> Could frame in earth, and forme of substance base,
> Was there, and all that nature did omit,
> Art playing second natures part, supplyed it.
>
> (*F.Q.*, IV.X.xxi)

Puttenham similarly describes Art first as "an ayde and coadiutor to nature," then as "an alterer . . . and in some sort a surmounter" of nature, then as "a bare immitatour of natures works." He goes on to distinguish the "maker or Poet" from the painter, who can "counterfaite the naturall by the like effects and not the same"; from the "gardiner aiding nature to worke both the same and the like"; and from the carpenter who works "effectes utterly unlike" nature. The poet is rather "*even as nature her selfe* working by her owne peculiar vertue and proper instinct and not by example or meditation or exercise as all other artificers do" (my emphasis). The poet, Puttenham concludes, "is then most admired when he is most naturall and least artificiall. And in the feates of his language and utterance, because they hold as well of nature to be suggested and uttered as by arte to be polished and reformed. Therefore shall our Poet receave prayse for both, but more by knowing of his arte then by *unseasonable* using it, and be more commended for his naturall eloquence then for his artificiall, and more for his artificiall well desembled, then for the same overmuch affected and grossely or undiscretly bewrayed" (*Arte*, p.307; my emphasis). This is a rich and important passage, but we must concentrate for the moment on the fact that Puttenham resolves and at the same time affirms the Art-Nature dualism, declaring that the correct use of Art by the poet is "even as nature her selfe," while a misuse is "unseasonable." We can already hear Polixenes's assertion, in *The Winter's Tale*, that "the art itself is nature." If it seems surprising to say that this kind of sophistication is also evident in such an early play as *Love's Labour's Lost*, that is the result of decades of patronizing criticism. The sophistication and complexity of this play can best be demonstrated by a closer examination of two special cases of the Art-Nature problem, the concepts of the garment of style, and of *ut pictura poesis*.

THE GARMENT OF STYLE

> Expression is the *Dress* of *Thought*, and still
> Appears more *decent* as more *suitable*;
> A vile Conceit in pompous Words exprest,
> Is like a Clown in regal Purple drest;
> For diff'rent *Styles* with diff'rent *Subjects* sort,
> As several Garbs with Country, Town, and Court.
> ("Essay on Criticism," 318–23)

176

In case we have forgotten, Pope's lines remind us of one
of the enduring clichés of aesthetic theory—the garment of
style.[13] The metaphor saturated the Renaissance, so frequently used as to be virtually unconscious. In its usual formulation, style, and specifically the use of rhetorical figures,
is described as external ornament and decoration or, in Puttenham's words, "the flowers as it were and colours that a
Poet setteth upon his language by arte, as the embroderer
doth his stone and perle, or passements of gold upon the
stuffe of a Princely garment" (p. 138). When ornament is
used improperly—with affectation—the metaphorical results
are predictable. Dame Rhetoric, usually described in medieval allegories as a stately woman dressed in "jewels" and
"colours," the figures of speech, is transformed (here, in
Sidney) into a fallen woman of the night: "So is that honny-
flowing Matron Eloquence apparelled, or rather disguised,
in a Curtizan-like painted affectation: one time with so farre
fette words, they may seeme Monsters" (Smith, I,201–2).

The metaphor of clothes operates everywhere in *Love's
Labour's Lost*. After the ladies have described the noblemen,
the Princess marvels,

> God bless my ladies! are they all in love,
> That every one her own hath garnished
> With such bedecking ornaments of praise?
>
> (II.i.77–9)

Such "ornaments" glitter in most of the speeches. Holofernes' judgment of Armado also relies on the trope: "He
draweth out the thread of his verbosity finer than the staple
of his argument" (V.i.17–8). After Marcade's entrance and
Navarre's fumbling condolences, Berowne tries to explain
things to the ladies in "honest plain words," but the Princess' reply is sharp: they have "rated" the lords' letters and
favors "as bombast and as lining to the time" (V.ii.770–1).
A style full of "bombast" is one literally stuffed with wool
padding. Berowne brings the metaphor to earth when he
tells us that "rhymes are guards on wanton Cupid's hose"

(IV.iii.58)—merely the ornamental trimmings of fashion, serving a dubious function.

The most famous use of the clothes metaphor in the play occurs in Berowne's supposed renunciation of fancy speech. After confessing and revealing himself to the "sharp wit" and "keen conceit" of the ladies, Berowne concludes:

> O! never will I trust to speeches penn'd,
> Nor to the motion of a school-boy's tongue,
> Nor never come in visor to my friend,
> Nor woo in rhyme, like a blind harper's song,
> Taffeta phrases, silken terms precise,
> Three-pil'd hyperboles, spruce affection,
> Figures pedantical; these summer flies
> Have blown me full of maggot ostentation:
> I do forswear them; and I here protest,
> By this white glove (how white the hand, God knows),
> Henceforth my wooing mind shall be express'd
> In russet yeas and honest kersey noes:
> And, to begin: Wench,—so God help me, law!—
> My love to thee is sound, sans crack or flaw.

Rosaline trips him up immediately—"Sans 'sans,' I pray you" —and Berowne confesses,

> Yet I have a trick
> Of the old rage: bear with me, I am sick;
> I'll leave it by degrees.
>
> (V.ii.402–18)

More sheer nonsense has been written about this speech than of any other part of the play. Philip Parsons, for one, terms it "a turning to reality that helps prepare for the harsh intrusion of death into the summer enchantment," [14] Shakespeare's own renunciation of false rhetoric. But Berowne, like Shakespeare, retains more than just "a trick" of the old madness. Berowne is still of the "wooing mind," still witty and paradoxical, still a poseur. For one thing, the last fourteen lines of his speech (ll. 402–15) form a regular "Shakespearean" sonnet, hardly a "natural" form for a renunciation to take. The speech is liberally sprinkled with the very ornaments and "figures pedantical" which Berowne is in the act of forswearing. "Maggot ostentation" still feeds off itself, an overblown metaphor far more powerful and grisly than necessary. And Berowne is a master of the clothes metaphor, forswearing "taffeta," "silken," "three-pil'd," and "spruce" terms—all of the elegant trappings of poetry.[15] But what else is "three-pil'd hyperboles" if not a three-pil'd hyperbole? The "old rage" rages on, as we hear in Berowne's French "*sans.*" Even while renouncing, Berowne still comes "in visor to my friend," wooing "in rhyme," his self-knowledge only pretended. He rejects the more overt "figures pedantical," such as Holofernes might use, but he has only exchanged them for another variety.

If "Art" is represented by fine silk and taffeta, elaborate dress of body and language, its logical opposite "Nature" should be represented by nakedness, by poor, bare, forked man. But the metaphor is not literal in practice, and at this point the analogy collapses. There neither is nor can be any such thing as unadorned verse. The metaphor founders on the most ancient of shoals—the old distinction between form and content, between style and matter. To call a speech or a poem "natural" in the Renaissance, or now, is to say no more than that it exhibits a different *kind* of artifice, rather than eschewing artifice altogether. It has been made, after all. The hand one swears upon is always concealed by a "white glove" of some kind, as in Berowne's case, and we never quite know "how white the hand" may be underneath.

Berowne forswears taffeta and silk, not for nakedness then, but for "russet" and "honest kersey." He will substitute a supposedly sincere low style for a bombastic high style. We hear the change immediately when he uses the homely native word, "wench," instead of some latinate synonym. He is learning Holofernes' lessons in reverse. Berowne tries to become more like Costard (who had countered Armado's "child of our grandmother Eve, a female" with "wench" at

I.i.252), and less like Armado. But he has not done away with style, only changed it, and not very successfully. Yet many theoreticians of the Renaissance and some current readers of the play speak as if Nature, devoid of attributes, were something one could know directly.

It is an appealing but quite arbitrary convention that finds a low style more "natural" than a high one. There is an equally conscious, and hence artificial, choice behind the use of either style, especially when it is a courtly or sophisticated speaker who makes the choice. The low style is often used in *Love's Labour's Lost* to balance or to puncture the principal affectation of the play, an overblown high style. But the low style can be an affectation in itself. Berowne is still of a "wooing mind," and his stylistic excesses are a symptom, not a cause, of that state of mind. He affects for a moment a low style to express the same thoughts. We have seen sophisticated affectations of primitiveness elsewhere in the play. In defending his mistress, Berowne resorts to the usual hyperbole:

> Who sees the heavenly Rosaline
> That, like a rude and savage man of Inde,
> At the first opening of the gorgeous east,
> Bows not his vassal head, and strooken blind,
> Kisses the base ground with obedient breast?
>
> (IV.iii.218–222)

In his Promethean Fire speech, Berowne says that a poet should not write until he has been touched by love: "O! then his lines would ravish savage ears, / And plant in tyrants mild humility" (IV.iii.345–6). And in the final act, he begs Rosaline, "Vouchsafe to show the sunshine of your face, / That we, like savages, may worship it" (V.ii.201–2). These references to the "savage" are still further instances of "pure idolatry,"[16] and they remind us again of the lords' comically blasphemous attempts to elevate the human to the divine. Berowne would rather be Caliban than Ariel, begging Stephano and Trinculo to "be my god" (*Tmp.*, II.ii.145). It is an affectation of the same order as the resort to russet and kersey. Assuming the role of the noble savage—shorn of the superfluous trappings of civilization, struck blind by the "sunshine" of the "first opening of the gorgeous east," bowing down before them in humble worship—Berowne would have us believe that he has abandoned pretension and insincerity, but only the gullible will swallow the conceits he serves up now. Berowne's toying with this facet of the Art-Nature question is sophisticated in the extreme. His manipulations of the concept, as distinguished from Shakespeare's, suggest that he is still playing, still posing. The question then arises whether it is possible not to play or to pose, as the dualism suggests, or whether it is rather a matter of choosing the best role among many.

The metaphor of clothes finds a visual corollary in the varied and elaborate costumes the play demands.[17] The fancier the clothes, the fancier the speech. The obviousness of matching stage costume and verbal style indicates the ubiquity and familiarity of the clothes metaphor. It is only "natural," we say, that the style of aristocrats is higher than that of rustics. But it isn't; it is only more conventional. A more subtle instance of suiting dress to words is found in the use of masks in the play. When the Masque of Muscovites enters, Moth greets the ladies, "All hail, the richest beauties on the earth!" to which Boyet sardonically replies, "Beauties no richer than rich taffeta" (V.ii.159). The masks worn in the play are made of "taffeta" (or silk), the material which Berowne forswears for "honest kersey." Recalling the discussion of the mask in chapter two, we can see the richness of the analogy at once. Masks (or roles) cover and disguise the face (the true, "natural" self) just as rhetoric and ornament, in the standard reading of the metaphor, cover the "matter" of speech or poetry. Stephen Gosson seizes on this image of the mask as a symbol of deceit and trickery in poets (as it is in fact intended to be in the Masque of Muscovites), and concludes, "pul off the visard that poets maske in, you shall disclose their reproch, bewray their vanitie, loth their wantonnesse, lament their folly, and perceive their sharpe sayinges to be placed as pearles in dunghils, fresh pictures on rotten walles, chaste matrons apparel on common curtesans."[18] What Gosson implicitly desires—what the metaphor, literally read, demands—is a dis-covery, an un-masking, the ornament stripped off—something like Bacon's ideal, a completely perspicuous language, no ornament, no "style," just abstract counters and symbols. This is impossible. The Art-Nature "dualism" is not, like the shirt of Nessus, a burning question; it is rather, like the shirt of Armado, nonexistent. It is certainly not worth fighting over. The "naked truth" (V.ii.699) is that Armado has no shirt, but he does have "a dishclout of Jaquenetta's, and that a' wears next his heart for a favour" (V.ii.702–4). There is always some "clothing," some garment of style, no matter how seedy.

UT PICTURA POESIS

> Poets like Painters, thus, unskill'd to trace
> The *naked Nature* and the *living Grace.*
> With *Gold* and *Jewels* cover ev'ry Part,
> And hide with *Ornaments* their *Want of Art.*
> ("Essay on Criticism," 293–6)

Pope describes the abuse of a second great critical commonplace, but the terms of abuse are analogous to those of the first one.[19] A literal reading of the metaphor (as in Pope's ll. 294–6) again seems to imply the usual form-content dichotomy, where "style" is like color, smeared onto a "subject" as onto a canvas. The poet thus deceives; he covers up the ugly or plain beneath a pleasing façade, "fresh pictures on rotten walles," as Gosson said. It is a naive and crudely limiting vision of the function of art.

"Painting," by extension, almost automatically included the use of cosmetics. Renaissance writers loved to argue the moral merits of a woman's painting herself,[20] and Shakespeare's sonnets are filled with scornful references:

For since each hand hath put on nature's power,
Fairing the foul with art's false borrowed face,
Sweet beauty hath no name, no holy bower,
But is profaned, if not lives in disgrace.

(Sonnet 127)

On the side of Art, and in league with Ovid, Ben Jonson's
Truewit is exemplary: "I love a good dressing, before any
beautie o' the world. O, a woman is, then, like a delicate
garden; nor, is there one kind of it: she may varie, every
houre; take often counsell of her glasse, and choose the
best" (Jonson, V,167–8). Herrick strikes a balance in an
epigram aptly titled "Painting Sometimes Permitted": "If
Nature do deny / Colours, let Art supply." This parallels
Puttenham's summary of the functions of Art with respect
to Nature and the orthodox notion that the two are
complementary.

A great deal is made in *Love's Labour's Lost* of "painting"
in the sense of cosmetics. Armado claims that to be a gentleman and a gamester "are both the varnish of a complete
man" (I.ii.41). He goes on to boast that his love is "most
immaculate white and red," to which Moth responds, "Most
maculate thoughts, master, are masked under such colours" (I.ii.87–8). The "colours" masking Armado's impure
thoughts are presumably the "red" in the cheeks.[21] A false,
"painted" blushing is metaphorically equivalent to wearing
a mask, concealing the "maculate" reality beneath. The
truth of Moth's comment is proved later by Jaquenetta's
pregnancy. "Colours" may also be "poetic ornaments" here,
though the hint is slight. The "colours" red and white are
themselves colours (ornaments), however, and Moth's comment is also a punning (hence concealing) reference to the
power of rhetorical ornament to conceal.

A moment later, Moth sings his song, which is worth
quoting again:

If she be made of white and red,
Her faults will ne'er be known,

183

For blushing cheeks by faults are bred,
    And fears by pale white shown:
Then if she fear, or be to blame,
    By this you shall not know,
For still her cheeks possess the same
    Which native she doth owe.

                    (I.iii.93–100)

Moth suggests that the appearance of things is no longer a reliable guide to moral qualities. The natural blush of a maiden is now artificially created by the painting of cosmetics, and her cheeks are always ("still") the same colors, beneath which maculate thoughts may lurk, although no one is able to tell. What was "native," by Nature, has been supplanted by the man-made, or Art. The scene continues ironically when Jaquenetta enters and Armado confesses, "I do betray myself with blushing" (I.ii.124).

The Princess, as we have already seen, is firm on the subject of undeserved praise, condemning the "painted flourish" of Boyet's flashy stylistic devices (II.i.13–4). This is the conventional distrust of "painting," predictably uttered in a speech no less elaborately (only differently) patterned than the one she is criticizing. With the Forester later, the Princess is in a jovial mood, and trips him up:

> *Prin.* What, what? first praise me, and again say no?
>   O short-liv'd pride! Not fair? alack for woe!
> *For.*   Yes, madam, fair.
> *Prin.*   Nay, never paint me now:
>   Where fair is not, praise cannot mend the brow.
>
>   (IV.i.14–7)

Rejecting undeserved praise, and a certain kind of hyperbolic compliment, as false painting, she reaffirms her position as a moral guide.

A more complex and self-conscious use of the painting-metaphor occurs in the sonnet-reading scene. Longaville exposes Dumain's hypocrisy, saying to him:

Long. You may look pale, but I should blush, I know,
    To be o'er heard and taken napping so.
King. (advancing) Come, sir, you blush; as his
      your case is such . . .
    . . . for you both did blush.

                           (IV.iii.127–9,136)

With the pun on "case" as both "situation" and "face," we
are given a hierarchy even of blushing. The idea is quickly
developed in the next lines. Defending his dark mistress, who
is the antithesis of the golden-haired Petrarchan ideal, Berowne boasts,

> Of all complexions the cull'd sovereignty
> Do meet, as at a fair, in her fair cheek;
> Where several worthies make one dignity.

Inspired, he begs assistance:

> Lend me the flourish of all gentle tongues,—
> Fie, painted rhetoric! O! she needs it not:
> To things of sale a seller's praise belongs;
> She passes praise; then praise too short doth blot.
>   (IV.iii.231–8)

His mistress needs no painting, therefore he won't use any
in his rhetoric. Yet we know that her "native" complexion is
like painting, and Berowne still uses a complicated rhetoric
himself. In the subtle reversal which follows, her beauty is
termed such that it "doth varnish age, as if new-born"
(l. 241), and is presumably not varnished itself, though we
know it is.

Navarre is unimpressed. Rosaline has a dark complexion,
he says in a famous passage seized on by the interpreters of
topical allegory,[22] and he pretends shock at Berowne's
sophisms:

> O paradox! Black is the badge of hell,
> The hue of dungeons and the school of night;
> And beauty's crest becomes the heavens well.

But Berowne has only begun, and he now replies to Navarre
with the greatest of his paradoxes:

> Devils soonest tempt, resembling spirits of light.
> O! if in black my lady's brows be deck'd,
> It mourns that painting and usurping hair
> Should ravish doters with a false aspect;
> And therefore is she born to make black fair.
> Her favour turns the fashion of the days,
> For *native blood is counted painting now*:
> And therefore red, that would avoid dispraise,
> Paints itself black, to imitate her brow.
>
> (IV.iii.251–62; my emphasis)

This passage is a triumph of complexity, in a play filled with
such moments. Associating hell, in an echo of 2 Corinthians
11.14, with light rather than dark, as Navarre had done,
Berowne laments that some "doters," otherwise unidentified,
will be deceived by cosmetics and wigs. On the other hand,
Rosaline's darkness, which seems confined mostly to her hair
and eyes, will inspire a whole new set of imitators. In a complete reversal of the Art-Nature dualism, "native blood"—a
flushed or naturally red complexion—is now considered
painted, or artificial, and, ironically, those who have such
complexions must now "paint" themselves black in order to
avoid the charge of "painting." Consequently, Rosaline's
complexion now seems "natural." Berowne has completed
the reversal implicit in Moth's song—one can no longer mark
a distinction between Art and Nature. Whether a "god or a
painter" (V.ii.634) has made a face is impossible to say.
Although Berowne maintains that his mistress is dark by
"nature" and others are dark by "painting," Moth's song
suggests that the effect is still the same on the viewer. The
implications of this passage reach out to take in the larger
Art-Nature question, for it is suggested that there is always
some sort of painting, that even the "natural" may be considered artificial, or, finally, that the distinction is simply
arbitrary.

186

This interchange continues in a lower vein, when the other noblemen mockingly comment on Rosaline's darkness:

Dum. To look like her are chimney-sweepers black.
Long. And since her time are colliers counted bright.
King. And Ethiops of their sweet complexion crack.
Dum. Dark needs no candles now, for dark is light.
Ber. Your mistresses dare never come in rain,
For fear their colours should be wash'd away.

(IV.iii.263–8)

As the conversation spirals down into boyish naughtiness ("O vile!"), we recognize a familiar pattern in the structure of this set-piece: the whole section is built on paradoxes and dualisms. From Berowne's "to make black fair," to his "O wood divine," to his reversal of the Art-Nature problem, virtually every line depends on a semantic or intellectual paradox, a confusion of normal opposites. We recall, too, that a rarefied discussion ("O wood divine") punctured by a contrast in diction and sentiment ("what upward lies / The street should see as she walk'd overhead") is a recurring pattern in the play as a whole.

An equally complex reversal of the usual relationship between Art and Nature occurs when, in response to Katharine's description of Rosaline as "Fair as a text B in a copybook" (i.e., of a dark complexion, because that letter required more ink to form than others), the following exchange occurs:

Ros. Ware pencils, ho! let me not die your debtor,
My red dominical, my golden letter:
O! that your face were not so full of O's.
Prin. A pox of that jest!

(V.ii.42–6)

Rosaline picks up the terms of one art—writing—and, through a double meaning in "pencils," transfers them to the art of painting. She refers first to Katharine's "amber" complexion (cf. IV.iii.85) with "red," but then goes on to de-

187

scribe the "O's" of Katharine's "pox" scars, suggesting that they have been painted on. The effect would again be as Moth sings: "still her cheeks possess the same / Which native she doth owe." Katharine's "native blood," in Rosaline's densely witty riposte, "is counted painting" again.

The painting metaphor finds literal expression in *Love's Labour's Lost* not only in the cosmetics which the actors would wear, but also, again, in their masks. Such masks were dark, probably black,[23] and there are several references to them as "clouds" concealing light. We recall Rosaline's irony against Berowne here: "that superfluous case / That hid the worse and show'd the better face" (V.ii.387–8). It is no longer possible at this point, to tell what is hidden, what revealed.

The clothing and painting metaphors cannot be read literally, then. They are at best imprecise, and in this play they are continually being qualified, even reversed in meaning. Sigurd Burckhardt notes that the essential difference between poets and all other artists, and hence the flaw in the interchanged metaphors, is that the other artists have basically neutral mediums in which to work, but the poet "must deal in an already current and largely defaced coinage. In fact it is not even a coinage, but rather a paper currency." The poet, he continues, is not only "denied the creative privilege of coining his own medium; his medium lacks all corporeality, is a system of signs which have only a secondary, referential substance."[24] Shakespearean vestiges of the coinage theory are still evident in Navarre's description of Armado as a "man of fire-new words," with a "mint of phrases in his brain" (I.i.177,164) and, most graphically, in the remunerative guerdons which Costard tosses in the air. Coins, clothing, painting—unlike other artists, the poet has only "style" and "technique." They are not simply effected with metaphorical needle or figurative brush. They inhere. They are the work itself. In *Love's Labour's Lost*, Shakespeare seems continually to work toward a resolution of the extremes implied in the metaphor. Yet two centuries later,

188

Wordsworth would still be struggling with the imprecise trope: "If words be not (recurring to a metaphor before used) an incarnation of the thought, but only a clothing for it, then surely will they prove an ill gift."[25]

Pope's passage on the garment of style says nothing about the possibility of an "un-dressed" thought. He understands the comparison in a broader, less literal sense. There are "several" (separate) styles suitable for different subjects: low for "Country," middle for "Town," and high for "Court." Judgment is crucial in determining which level is appropriate. The overflowing of an exuberant wit (in both Pope's and Berowne's sense of that word) must be checked by an adherence to the rules of decorum. It was an automatic theoretical requirement of Renaissance authors, as indicated for example in Richard Edwards' Prologue to *Damon and Pithias*: "In comedies the greatest skill is . . . to touch / All things to the quick, and eke to frame each person so / That by his common talk you may his nature rightly know."[26] Edwards continues that:

> Correspondent to their kind their speeches ought to be.
> Which speeches, well-pronounc'd, with action lively
> framed—
> If this offend the lookers on, let Horace then be blamed,
> Which hath our author taught at school, from which
> he doth not swerve,
> In all such kinds of exercise *decorum* to observe.

Recent scholars have shown how deeply this concept—applied broadly to choice of subject, audience, style, manner of treatment, genre, and the matching of character and action —penetrated all Renaissance literature, how naturally and effortlessly authors and critics nodded obedience to the theory, and yet how many arguments arose over individual examples. Rosemond Tuve reminds us, however, that "it was the demand that decorum be observed which was inflexible, not the definition of decorum."[27]

Decorum

A glance at *Love's Labour's Lost* will suggest how decorum, in its broadest and narrowest senses, is at the heart of the play. A large part of the linguistic fun examined in the first chapter depends on assumptions of decorum and the hierarchy of style; these must first be recognized for their violation to be significant. My second chapter showed how the concept of dramatic decorum was investigated through the three theatrical scenes, the humor in these scenes depending largely on literalistic misconceptions of what is required. The Pageant characters worry about the physical correspondence or discrepancy between actor and Worthy: "none so fit as to present the Nine Worthies" (V.i.118), Holofernes brags. In the process they forget all about the more important imaginative correspondence. They try to fill in gaps that are better and more successfully bridged in the mind of the audience.

This interest in decorum is evident in the minutiae of the text in addition to the broader concerns just mentioned. Armado selects an "epitheton" (synonym) which is, in his own words, perfectly "congruent" in its application to its subject (I.ii.13), and Moth responds that the title he has himself just used is "appertinent" (l. 16). Later, using the knight's same term, Holofernes loudly congratulates Armado on another of his linguistic choices: "The posterior of the day, most generous sir, is liable, congruent, and measurable for the afternoon: the word is well culled, chose; sweet and apt, I do assure you, sir; I do assure" (V.i.86–9). Holofernes, as usual, pompously demonstrates the very thing he is praising in another—seven "choice" epithets for a single idea. The minor characters seem obsessed with the need for observing decorum. Armado knows that his sexual behavior is wrong, on grounds of hierarchy, but in a blizzard of specious logic he tries to make it decorous with "base": "I will hereupon confess I am in love; and as it is base for a soldier to love, so am I in love with a base wench" (I.ii.54–6). He spends most of his time seeking a "mighty precedent" for his digression. Later, Moth puns on his own role as messenger for Armado: "A message well sympathized: a horse to be ambassador for an ass" (III.i.49–50). And Nathaniel unwittingly says, "it would ill become me to be vain, indiscreet, or a fool" (IV.ii.30), when he is already all these things. A moment later, Holofernes describes his "foolish extravagant spirit" in which his synonyms are best "delivered upon the mellowing of occasion," at the most suitable moment (IV.ii.70–1). In this comic underworld, everything must be apt, congruent, becoming, appertinent, well culled, well sympathized. The low characters are fussily concerned about the rules and models of polite behavior and poetry, but ironically they turn out to be the grossest violators of imaginative decorum. The lords are not far behind, continually breaching decorum of manner.

Maria, for example, had described Longaville as "A man of sovereign parts . . . / Well fitted in arts, glorious in arms" —a latter-day Worthy, in effect. He combines, in this description, both the contemplative and the active virtues.[28] Uniting these powers in a single person was, for the Renaissance, perhaps the ultimate goal of the moral life. The fusion described here is considerably premature, however, and none of the other lords is able, in the course of the play, to effect a proper balance between these antinomies. Maria's continuation of her portrait of Longaville immediately qualifies the initial praise:

> Nothing becomes him ill that he would well.
> The only soil of his fair virtue's gloss,
> If virtue's gloss will stain with any soil,
> Is a sharp wit match'd with too blunt a will;
> Whose edge hath power to cut, whose will still wills
> It should none spare that come within his power.
>
> (II.i.44–51)

Dumain similarly has too blunt a will and no sense of propriety, as Katharine reports. He is well accomplished, but has

191

Most power to do most harm, least knowing ill,
For he hath wit to make an ill shape good,
And shape to win grace though he had no wit.
I saw him at the Duke Alençon's once;
And much too little of that good I saw
Is my report to his great worthiness.

(II.i.58–63)

Of great potential, these men are both naive and innocent
("least knowing ill"), and crude ("too blunt a will"). They
need an education, but in a far different sense than they
originally proposed. Rosaline goes on to describe "another
of these students," Berowne:

His eye begets occasion for his wit;
For every object that the one doth catch
The other turns to a mirth-moving jest.

(II.i.69–71)

"A merrier man," she says, "Within the limit of becoming
mirth, / I never spent an hour's talk withal" (II.i.66–8). But
Berowne is constitutionally unable to stay within the limits
of what is "becoming," of what is proper and decorous;
Rosaline is willing to spend an "hour" with him, but balks,
like the other ladies, at the "world-without-end bargain"
(V.ii.779) proposed at the end. As we have seen, a great
deal of charm and excitement is associated with the licentious
wit and blunt wills of the noblemen—which in Berowne's
case become something poetic. But the women identify the
concurrent problems early on. The Princess at first fears she
too may be breaching decorum ("To teach a teacher ill
beseemeth me"—II.i.108) but it proves to be the only way
in which the men will learn anything.

Simultaneously more and less sensitive to propriety than
his comrades, Berowne is particularly associated, in this respect, with imagery of Nature. He notes the mind-body
dualism implicit in the idea of the ascetic academy, and de-
rides the rules as "barren tasks" (I.i.47). The "necessity" of

the flesh, Costard's "sinplicitie," will force them to break
their oaths (I.i.148). Sure enough, when all the noblemen are
exposed, Berowne makes this appeal:

> Sweet lords, sweet lovers, O! let us embrace.
> As true we are as flesh and blood can be:
> The sea will ebb and flow, heaven show his face;
> Young blood doth not obey an old decree:
> We cannot cross the cause why we were born;
> Therefore, of all hands must we be forsworn.
>
> (IV.iii.211–6)

The appeal is to the catch-all Nature, to the sea and the flesh,
but also to decorum: it is more fitting, more appropriate for
them to woo, in accordance with their innate desires (affections). Navarre had earlier accused Berowne of thwarting
Nature by his gibes and witticisms: "Berowne is like an envious sneaping frost / That bites the first-born infants of the
spring." Berowne's reply is unequivocal, and he describes a
natural rhythm, the force that energizes human desires,
which must be obeyed:

> Well, say I am; why should proud summer boast
> Before the birds have any cause to sing?
> Why should I joy in any abortive birth?
> At Christmas I no more desire a rose
> Than wish a snow in May's new-fangled shows;
> But like of each thing that in season grows.
> So you, to study now it is too late,
> Climb o'er the house to unlock the little gate.
>
> (I.i.100–09)

In spite of his profound insight into the cyclical rhythm of
nature, the deep-felt desire "of each thing that in season
grows," Berowne continues to violate decorum. In his attempt to prove that "black is fair," he wishes no less than to
reverse all conventional propriety. "O paradox!" Navarre
bellows, in mock-astonishment at such audacity.

At the very end of the play, after Marcade's message, the

men reveal that their flaws have not yet been overcome. Navarre stumbles along in a clumsy, last-ditch appeal based upon his mistaken sense of decorum. The awkwardness of his rhetoric betrays the fallacious logic he proposes:

> The extreme parts of time extremely forms
> All causes to the purpose of his speed,
> And often, at his very loose, decides
> That which long process could not arbitrate:
> And though the mourning brow of progeny
> Forbid the smiling courtesy of love
> The holy suit which fain it would convince;
> Yet since love's argument was first on foot,
> Let not the cloud of sorrow justle it
> From what it purpos'd.
>
> (V.ii.730–9)

Admitting one breach of decorum, Navarre goes on to urge still another, and the Princess does not understand his intention. Berowne, turning to a plain style again in his own appeal, says that "honest plain words best pierce the ear of grief" (V.ii.743). But we have seen again and again that words are never wholly honest or plain, that words, as Bacon said, "beget" other words, that connotations cannot be repressed. Still, Berowne tries, and begins to lay much of the blame for his own actions on the beauty of the ladies. He notes that "love is full of *unbefitting* strains," that the ladies' love-infected fancies have warped their behavior into folly:

> Which party-coated presence of loose love
> *Put on* by us, if, in your heavenly eyes,
> Have *misbecom'd* our oaths and gravities,
> Those heavenly eyes, that look into these faults,
> Suggested us to make.
>
> (V.ii.756–60; my emphasis)

"Unbefitting," "misbecom'd": the noblemen have "put on" the wrong garments of style—literally, in the Masque—affected a foolish style, made errors in tact and propriety. The

194

fool's "party-coated" motley they have been wearing now seems out of place to them. That they recognize this is a necessary prelude to their reformation, but it is not the reformation itself.

The famous punishments at the end of the play are aimed at teaching the supposed students the nature of decorum, in addition to observing a suitable time of mourning. The Princess sends Navarre to "some forlorn and naked hermitage," where he should mature. In a cluster of vegetation images, reminding us of the "envious sneaping frost" exchange between Navarre and Berowne, the Princess once again links together the rhythms of Nature and the idea of propriety:

> If this austere insociable life
> Change not your offer made in heat of blood;
> If frosts and fasts, hard lodging and thin weeds,
> Nip not the gaudy blossoms of your love,
> But that it bear this trial and last love;
> Then at the expiration of the year,
> Come challenge me. . . .
>
> (V.ii.789–95)

There will be "hard lodging" instead of a fashionable court, "thin weeds" instead of the sumptuously elegant costume he is now wearing. Navarre is being required not only to talk, but also to live, in low style for a change, to learn the full range of possibilities of style. Berowne had exuberantly boasted earlier in the play of Rosaline's power to transform: "A wither'd hermit, five-score winters worn, / Might shake off fifty, looking in her eye" (IV.iii.239–40). But Navarre is somber when he realizes that his fate is to mature rather than to become younger: "Hence hermit, then—my heart is in thy breast" (V.ii.806). The man who had attempted to defeat "cormorant devouring Time" has suddenly found himself in time's grasp—not yet "wither'd" perhaps, but certainly aged and saddened. That Navarre sees himself as a "hermit" suggests that he still considers his quest for the Princess a quasi-religious one.

Berowne fares even worse than Navarre. Earlier in the play, Rosaline had threatened to make Berowne "fawn, and beg, and seek, / And wait the season, and observe the times" and become her "fool, and I his fate" (V.ii.62–3,68). No Petrarchan mistress could have desired more. Now at the end, in an attempt to make him observe the proper "season" and "observe the times," Rosaline announces the dreadful year-long penance which is his "fate":

> Oft have I heard of you, my lord Berowne,
> Before I saw you, and the world's large tongue
> Proclaims you for a man replete with mocks;
> Full of comparisons and wounding flouts,
> Which you on all estates will execute
> That lie within the mercy of your wit:
> To weed this wormwood from your fruitful brain,
> And there withal to win me, if you please,
> Without the which I am not to be won,
> You shall this twelve month term from day to day,
> Visit the speechless sick, and still converse
> With groaning wretches; and your task shall be,
> With all the fierce endeavour of your wit
> To enforce the pained impotent to smile.
>
> (V.ii.831–44)

In the shorter, presumably earlier version of this speech (ll. 807–12), Rosaline had said that Berowne needed to be "purged," implying that he was infected-affected, and that his own sickness could be cured only by confronting the physically sick. In the version above, the unruly garden of the "fruitful brain" must be "weeded." Berowne is horrified at the prospect:

> *Ber.* To move wild laughter in the throat of death?
> It cannot be; it is impossible:
> Mirth cannot move a soul in agony.
> *Ros.* Why, that's the way to choke a gibing spirit,
> Whose influence is begot of that loose grace
> Which shallow laughing hearers give to fools.

She will confront his glib fertility with the fact of the "impotent," his volubility with the "speechless." His "gibing spirit" was "begot," in another reference to the sexuality of wit, of "loose grace," not a "special grace." Berowne's "womb of *pia mater*," to borrow Holofernes' terms, has produced one "abortive birth" (I.i.104) too many, the very thing he himself was unable to "joy" in. The comic punishment of the Academy enforced one kind of silence—"Item: that no woman shall come within a mile of my court . . . on pain of losing her tongue" (I.i.119–22)—but confronting the "speechless sick" is a horrible irony Berowne could do without.

Rosaline goes on to explain decorum of behavior to Berowne. It involves a due consideration of one's audience, for those who must listen to "penn'd speeches":

> A jest's prosperity lies in the ear
> Of him that hears it, never in the tongue
> Of him that makes it: then, if sickly ears,
> Deaf'd with the clamours of their own dear groans,
> Will hear your idle scorns, continue then,
> And I will have you and that fault withal;
> But if they will not, throw away that spirit,
> And I shall find you empty of that fault,
> Right joyful of your reformation.
>
> (V.ii.845–59)

This is strong medicine, indeed. But like the other ladies, Rosaline is not trying to stamp out Berowne's wit; she is not a killjoy attempting to suppress his exuberant and vivid imagination. She is only trying to educate him in the right use of his gifts. Her targets are specific: he is a mocker, "wounding" others, a "gibing spirit," full of "idle scorns," wielding an indiscriminate scattergun of wit that sprays everyone who approaches. "All estates" are vulnerable, nothing is sacred. But Berowne's "fruitful brain," though it must be "purged," is the source of his great energy, the power in him which continually delights and surprises us, and which

Rosaline elsewhere speaks of admiringly (II.i.64–76). It is the abuse which must be corrected, in the same way that his rhetoric must be reformed.

The women themselves are the perfect emblem of that reforming force, completely fluent masters of rhetoric and decorum, superior to the noblemen at their own tricks, fit educators for the academics. Moth's ironic love advice to Armado—"Negligent student! learn her by heart" (III.i.34) —applies perfectly to the lords as well. A parody of their academic pretensions is found in Holofernes' "charge-house on the top of the mountain" (V.i.78), where there seem to be all sorts of extracurricular lessons—Nathaniel comments to the pedant that the daughters of his parishioners "profit very greatly under you," and Holofernes agrees that "if their daughters be capable, I will put it to them" (IV.ii.75,78–9). The Princess and her ladies are not averse to "greasy" sexual talk, and there is certainly a sexual aspect to their correction of the men. But they are considerably subtler than Holofernes in putting it to them.

As a balancing or correcting force against excessive artifice in the debate, the women would seem to be on the side of Nature rather than Art. But the ladies do not represent Nature alone any more than they do Art; rather, they suggest in themselves the most cunning and attractive blend of artifice and nature in the play, with the exception of the final songs. The women do not attempt to write poetry, but rather in themselves exemplify a special "grace" and beauty which is aesthetically significant. Their refusal to engage in the requisite sympathy for the men's shenanigans seems fundamentally in harmony with the play's concern for decorum; the ladies block and re-direct folly and excess, rather than creative force itself. It is of course the men who continually violate propriety and decorum, who must be guided to the right path. If there is something less of the lords' anarchic linguistic energy in the ladies' speeches, there is no diminution in wit and brilliance. They always have the last word, and the best.

The women are associated with fertility in general, and with vegetation imagery in particular. Boyet, we recall, flattered the Princess in arguing that "Nature" had made "graces" scarce "When she did starve the general world beside, / And prodigally gave them all to you" (II.i.11-2). Although she rejects the facileness of the compliment, the Princess does not deny the truth of the statement, and a moment later she notes a vegetative paradox in Longaville, "Such short-liv'd wits do wither as they grow" (II.i.54). At the end of the play, when she tells Navarre the penance he must endure, she uses the same kind of image (with the pun on "weeds" resonating against "blossoms"): "If frosts and fasts, hard lodging and thin weeds, / Nip not the gaudy blossoms of your love . . ." (V.ii.791-2). The voice of "Nature" in the play, perhaps, but no less that of civility and sophistication.

Navarre had proposed that his court become an academe, "Still and contemplative in living art" (I.i.14), but the plan proved sterile, "still" but not "living."[29] The "barren practisers," the young noblemen, "Scarce show a harvest of their heavy toil" (IV.iii.322-3). But the men come to realize, as the audience has, long before them, that the women are an exemplum of "living art," an art which is fruitful, judicious, not separated from Nature but indissolubly wedded to it. The "harvest" must be postponed a year, but there is no doubt that fruition will eventually come.[30] "Living art" is not an impossible paradox, then, but the very goal toward which the play drives. There is indeed a dazzling reversal in the play's movement. It is not, however, from "Art" to "Nature," but from a false, sterile art, in Navarre's original formulation, to a genuine "living art," one which is not less artificial (in the best sense) but more so. The women are irresistible. They are to become even more so when Rosaline becomes Rosalind, then Viola.

Most of us are instinctively on the side of Nature rather than of Art. There have never been many anti-primitivists around, and today they are an endangered species. In an argument, or in theory, we tend to side with Perdita rather than Polixenes. So too in the Renaissance. But the very perception of a division, or the possibility of one, between Art and Nature, places us in the camp of "Art." Self-consciousness and sophistication are not attributes of even the noblest savage; malaprops cannot consciously make a good pun. Thus, as many readers have noted, the theoretical positions taken by Perdita and Polixenes in *The Winter's Tale* are reversed in their practical behavior in the next moment. We prefer Nature to Art, but to say so is in effect to admit that we exist more in Art than in Nature. In *Love's Labour's Lost*, Shakespeare insists on this paradox. The opposition of Art and Nature, as well as the other contraries associated with them, is formed only to be dissolved. The metaphors of clothes and painting are a case in point. A literal reading of these analogies, a reading which takes the analogy in place of the idea it amplifies, creates a form-content opposition, an absolute distinction between style and subject. But it is the kind of reading that only a Holofernes makes.

We learn from the play's dialectic that all dualisms are suspect, that there is not an opposition but a continuum between the terms, that the relation between Art and Nature is necessarily not static but dynamic. We think of Blake: "Without Contraries is No Progression." The difference is that, unlike Blake, Shakespeare follows a constant impulse toward reconciliation. The noblemen in *Love's Labour's Lost*, and the audience, come to learn what a "living art" really is. They learn that to deny either of the two terms in the concept is to falsify and destroy both. The noblemen, at the beginning, have denied what is "living"; the critics, with few exceptions, have concluded that the play denies the "art." The women and the songs embody and exemplify both.

The concept which mediates between Art and Nature is decorum. It has been broadly used to refer to living in general, to some natural rhythm, and to a specific poetic requirement. Approaching the play from the standpoint of its views on society, one reader sums up: "Virtually all the men in the play violate, each in his peculiar way, the values of 'civility', which meant at once civilization, social polish, government, courtesy, decorum, manners, and simple human kindness. . . . The play lays particular stress on the virtue of decorum, which becomes here a sense of the conduct appropriate to a given situation."[31] Decorum means all this and even more. Specifically, the play forwards the debate about poetry by affirming a principle of poetic decorum. This can be narrowly construed as simply the process of matching social level with stylistic level, and the play has great fun with this. It can also include the broader suitability of poetic subject for a particular audience (Berowne's penance) or, reversed, the suitability of a poetic subject for a particular artist (the low characters present an imitation of the Nine Worthies). But in *Love's Labour's Lost* Shakespeare goes beyond these somewhat limited senses of decorum to probe the nature of a more mysterious, more significant kind of poetic decorum. This exceptional quality of imaginative propriety is finally elusive and indefinable; it is only suggested by example, and by analogy with other kinds of decorum. Holofernes has never heard of it. Puttenham is forced to describe Decorum as "comeliness" or "convenient proportion"; this proportion, he says, "hath nature her selfe first most carefully observed in all her owne workes, then also by kinde graft it in the appetites of every creature working by intelligence to covet and desire: and in their actions to imitate & performe: and of man chiefly before any other creature as well in his speaches as in every other part of his behaviour" (*Arte*, p. 262). Nature herself observes decorum. "Decorum" is the proportion observed in Nature. "Nature" is the well-proportioned and decorous. Man has an inner "appetite" which tries to imitate this proportion. "Art" is the well-proportioned, the decorous. And so on, in circles.

In Puttenham, as in *Love's Labour's Lost*, to say "Nature" is another way of saying "decorum," and vice versa. The real contrary to Art is not Nature but "un-decorum."

At the end of the play, the verbal debate ceases and the actual principle of decorum, of "imaginative"—not literal—decorum, is exemplified. The women represent the "living art" brought about through decorum in its social and intellectual, as well as verbal, form; the final songs represent "living art" as it applies to poetry in particular. That "grace" which the men so glibly refer to again and again lives only in the art of the women and the songs.

At the beginning of this chapter the larger structure of *Love's Labour's Lost* was described as the form of an expansive spiral, a gradual widening from the small, closed academe, that "curious-knotted garden" of the mind which the men are trying, without success, to nurture to growth through a denial of the principle of fertility. This movement climaxes with the entrance of Marcade, grimly announcing the death of the King of France. But the play then continues beyond that dramatic entrance and the penances to end in self-consciousness, with insistent reminders of artifice and the playwright's skills and limitations:

> *Ber.* Our wooing doth not end like an old play;
> Jack hath not Jill: these ladies' courtesy
> Might well have made our sport a comedy.
> *King.* Come, sir, it wants a twelvemonth and a day,
> And then 'twill end.
> *Ber.*   That's too long for a play.
> (V.ii.864–8)

Trapped in some kind of new artifice, Berowne looks to the "old play" as a dramatic and social model, a form in which, as Puck sings,

> Jack shall have Jill;
> Naught shall go ill;
> The man shall have his mare again, and all shall be well.
> (*MND*, III.ii.461–3)

Turning sport to comedy isn't as easy as Berowne thinks, but Shakespeare has managed the trick well enough here. Berowne had complained earlier that the ladies had mocked their Masque of Muscovites as one would "dash . . . a Christmas comedy" (V.ii.462); now he wishes he were in an old play or comedy after all. The lords wish, in fact, that they were in a play like *The Winter's Tale*, where the Shepherd tells his son, "thou mettest with things dying, I with things new-born" (III.iii.106–7). Navarre argues for a similar cyclical completion, noting that "love's argument" (a theatrical term) was "first on foot," and should be carried through,

> since, to wail friends lost
> Is not by much so wholesome-profitable
> As to rejoice at friends but newly found.
> (V.ii.737–41)

Navarre ironically argues for a dismissal of those who are "lost," who have succumbed to the "disgrace of death" he described in the first scene. So much for "fame." The Shepherd's comment occurs at the very center of *The Winter's Tale*, and there is still plenty of time for the romance pattern of reconciliation to work itself out. But we are at the end of *Love's Labour's Lost*, "at the latest minute of the hour," and it is too late, and the wrong play, for a conventional ending. "Form confounded" gives rise to a new but unsettling form.

The pattern of concentric circles has been disrupted a final time, then, just as it has been periodically throughout the play. The complexity of the interchange between Navarre and Berowne is fully acknowledged in David P. Young's analysis: "Biron's observation is nearly our own and reminds us that we are still in the presence of artifice, an artifice which has the strength to call attention to itself, and that this same artifice has been brought remarkably close to the real, the natural. The gap disappears, and one comic marriage—the marriage of art and reality—takes place at the expense of some others."[32] Still another "marriage" takes place when

Armado, who had "seen the day of wrong through the little hole of discretion," and had pledged to right himself "like a soldier" (V.ii.714–5), announces his union (already consummated) with Jaquenetta. The "deep oaths" and vows which the lords made in the first scene, and immediately broke, ironically find a more permanent counterpart in Armado's declaration: "I am a votary; I have vowed to Jaquenetta to hold the plough for her sweet love three year." The ethereal vows of the lords are brought down to earth once again. Navarre's "three years' term" (I.i.16) has been commuted; it is still "three year" for Armado, but it is a willing and thus a human duration. Armado's vow to "hold the plough" anticipates the "ploughman's clocks" soon to be mentioned in Spring's song; the chivalric knight is placed immediately in a pastoral landscape, and his conversion heralds that of the lords in the coming year.

The last songs, the most perfect "marriage" of opposites in the play, take us a final step away from the harsh "reality" of Marcade and the penances, toward a realm where dualisms vanish and death is transformed by art. This realm is the ideal form, a true golden world, of which the ascetic academy was only a grotesque parody. It is a place where Art, if only for a moment, on a stage with "living" actors, merges with Nature—where the oxymoronic "living art" finds its incarnation.

CHAPTER SIX

Hiems and Ver

Spring. When daisies pied and violets blue
  And lady-smocks all silver-white
And cuckoo-buds of yellow hue
  Do paint the meadows with delight,
The cuckoo then, on every tree,
Mocks married men; for thus sings he,
     Cuckoo;
Cuckoo, cuckoo: O word of fear,
Unpleasing to a married ear!

When shepherds pipe on oaten straws,
  And merry larks are ploughman's clocks,
When turtles tread, and rooks, and daws,
  And maidens bleach their summer smocks,
The cuckoo then, on every tree,
Mocks married men; for thus sings he,
     Cuckoo;
Cuckoo, cuckoo: O word of fear,
Unpleasing to a married ear!

Winter. When icicles hang by the wall,
  And Dick the shepherd blows his nail,
And Tom bears logs into the hall,
  And milk comes frozen home in pail,
When blood is nipp'd, and ways be foul,
Then nightly sings the staring owl,
     Tu-whit;
Tu-who, a merry note,
While greasy Joan doth keel the pot.

When all aloud the wind doth blow,
  And coughing drowns the parson's saw,
And birds sit brooding in the snow,
  And Marian's nose looks red and raw,
When roasted crabs hiss in the bowl,
Then nightly sings the staring owl,
                Tu-whit;
Tu-who, a merry note,
While greasy Joan doth keel the pot.
                    (V.ii.884–919)[1]

The final songs contain everything in the play. Though they are presented almost as an afterthought, *Love's Labour's Lost* is incomplete, and unimaginable, without them. They receive almost unanimous praise, even (or especially) from critics who dislike the rest of the play. The songs represent a magic moment in *Love's Labour's Lost*, a moment which seems of a different quality and order from what has come before it.

And yet the songs explicate what has preceded them and are themselves best explicated by it. The first chapter showed that in the range of stylistic parodies encountered in the play there seemed no obvious rhetorical center, no voice to be relied upon. But that voice is heard, triumphantly, in the final songs. Thomas M. Greene says that we must think of them "as rhetorical touchstones by which to estimate the foregoing funny abuses of language."[2] This is on the right track, but it does not take us nearly far enough. The songs are touchstones in a much deeper sense: they are not simply a standard by which to measure abuse, but an exemplum and model for the right use of language.

The songs are not simple or "natural," in the usual sense, but are perhaps the most carefully crafted things in the entire play. They represent not the rejection of Art for Nature, but the rejection of bad art for good art, for sophisticated stylistic devices are used with assurance in the songs:

rhyming, inverted word order, frequent alliteration, punning ("To-it" and "to-wit"), low to middle diction, and an insistent if uncomplicated syntax ("when"="then," with a free use of "and" connectors that carry us along effortlessly). The meter is a carefully regulated ground-tone of iambic tetrameter, and the planned irregularities—the spondee of "mocks married men" and the anapestic surprise of "When icicles hang by the wall"—are strikingly effective. Holofernes would be astonished.

The point, as in the first chapter, is that, to say anything, we have to use a common body of rhetorical constructs and devices, although some schemes, such as periphrasis, are suspect from the start. *Love's Labour's Lost* in effect has debated the use of such devices, and if the parody and exaggeration in the play show us how not to use them, the last songs show what can be done with them. The rhetorical devices are essentially the same in both cases; what makes the difference is the imagination employing them.

That the songs seem a moment out of or beyond the play constitutes their triumph. They *are* still in the play, in the realm of the imagination, without seeming to be. The play proper, we think, ended some moments ago and this is simply being tacked on. But it isn't. Where the three earlier theatrical sections were self-consciously emphasized, the songs are introduced on a more casual note. It is crucial that they follow immediately upon Berowne's comment, "That's too long for a play," for as the play begins to turn back to artifice, away from the harshness of Marcade's outer world, the songs are offered as the perfect fusion of Art and Nature, inner and outer. And, as Shakespeare announces that his materials are too long for the traditional dramatic model, he concludes his play with one of the most traditional of all dramatic models, the medieval *conflictus*.

The third and fourth chapters, describing the range of poetry and imaginations in the play, showed, as did the first chapter, that though there are fine moments in Berowne's great speech and the ladies' talk, still there is no unmistakable poetic voice, no touchstone which suddenly rings true and inevitable. The body of the play debates and displays a variety of poetic voices only to find them wanting. But "Apollo's lute" is suddenly heard in the final songs. They are thus the exemplum of poetry toward which the play's debate had been moving. They are, in a play self-consciously filled with abuses, the best example of "praise," a word which, when Armado uses it a final time at V.ii.876, has taken on a special and complex resonance.

I think it essential that we feel great surprise when we first hear the songs. Consider Armado's introduction: "But, most esteemed greatness, will you hear the dialogue that the two learned men have compiled in praise of the owl and the cuckoo? it should have followed in the end of our show" (V.ii.874–8). Given time to consider this offer, we might recall that the best Holofernes and Nathaniel have been able to produce so far is the extempore epitaph on the pretty pleasing pricket and the awkward embarrassments of the Pageant of the Nine Worthies. We have every right to expect a disaster in these songs. But instead, to our delight, we witness a small miracle, one that could not have been predicted. Shakespeare has previously given us the topical, the old fashioned, the witty and conceited—all kinds of styles that failed to satisfy. The songs are attributed to the two learned men, but the audience knows whose voice is being heard.

The fifth chapter of this study adopted the songs as an emblem of structure, the *conflictus* in which both sides of a dualism present their arguments, without either being finally victorious. The very presentation of the issues leads to their resolution. It seems fair to say that the songs as a single entity represent the reconciliation of all the opposites in *Love's Labour's Lost*: the perfect marriage of Art and Nature, the play's central example of the transforming power of the imagination.

CORMORANT DEVOURING TIME

The songs climax the play's concern with time. *Love's La-bour's Lost* begins with a scheme to defeat time, to reverse or at least halt the process of mutability. We laugh at the naiveté of Navarre's plan, but we are never allowed to forget "cormorant devouring Time" during the course of the play. The sickness of the King of France, the dead heroes of the past, the touching story of Katharine's dead sister, the plague "tokens," the "death's face in a ring" described by Berowne: the pressures of time and mortality are relentless, and they achieve a grim victory in Marcade's message— for the moment, that is.

The play begins with an exhortation—"Let fame"—which becomes "may" at line 5 and "shall" in line 6. It is a gram-matical confidence which soon proves unwarranted. "Let fame" is a fiat which aims for the superhuman and falls far short. The Word has become empty words because Navarre has no sense of his own finite limitations. The fiat fails, then, not because it is "rhetorical" but because Navarre and his lords do not know what is possible and what is not, what ought to be and what ought not to be. In Genesis, everything is possible; in the kingdom of Navarre, something less. Self-deception makes fruitful creation of any sort impossible.

The noblemen intended an evasion of time, which is im-possible. Their penance must therefore involve enduring a ritual length of time, a year and a day. They must stay away, the Princess says, until "the twelve celestial signs / Have brought about the annual reckoning" (V.ii.787–8). And, we expect, the men will have to endure, forever after, annual reckonings by these sharp-eyed ladies. As an ironic analogue to the lords' futile efforts to avoid time, we are given the Nine Worthies to consider. The Worthies have achieved true fame to the extent that they have defeated time; they live on in pageantry and on the stage centuries later. But Armado reminds us that their victory is not a literal one:

"The sweet war-man [Hector] is dead and rotten; sweet chucks, beat not the bones of the buried; when he breathed, he was a man" (V.ii.651-3). Their victory is, rather, an imaginative one. The Worthies live only in art, in words—still the best means of defeating time. When Nathaniel-Alexander begins his speech—"When in the world I liv'd"—he heralds both a physical death and an imaginative rebirth, as he paradoxically announces his own past life. As it appears in *Love's Labour's Lost*, of course, the Pageant of the Nine Worthies is a joke; the Worthies are scarcely visible beneath the rustic naiveté and foolishness. The parallel with the noblemen, who attempt to achieve the same sort of fame as the Worthies, is striking. They think they are sophisticated, but they do little better than the rustics. A sophisticated, skilled art is the only solution in both cases, one that avoids simplistic dualisms of all sorts, denials of the flesh or the mind, and accepts what is given—one that moves from acceptance in the literal to trust in the imagination. The songs, alone, do this.

Love's Labour's Lost insists on a distinction between timeliness and timelessness. The lords continually confuse the two, and so gain neither. The play fancies its own topicality, it revels in the *au courant*. The chic tastes of the courtly audience are thoroughly gratified—but the play insists on proceeding to question this mere timeliness. There are reminders throughout that the men have misjudged the nature of time; their pride goeth before a pratfall, at the least. Dumain's ode, for example, confidently affirms that love's "month is ever May" (IV.iii.100). It is the basic assumption of pastoral, and has a certain validity, but the songs will show that May is always balanced by its opposite, and vice versa; pastoral is a sojourn, always implying a return to a different world. Dumain seems to have forgotten as well Berowne's question, "why should proud summer boast / Before the birds have any cause to sing?" (I.i.102-3). Dumain's May surely hasn't any cause to boast yet, and it is based on ignorance. Berowne told his fellows in the first scene that to

study now "it is too late" (l. 108); too late for them, even
before they have begun. But Berowne forgets his own wisdom, as usual, and it isn't long (IV.iii.271) before he is
shouting in defense of his mistress, "I'll prove her fair, or
talk till doomsday here," a time which occurs sooner than
he thinks, since Marcade's entrance is in the next act. At the
end of the sonnet-reading scene, Navarre sweeps off stage
still confident about time: "Away, away! no time shall be
omitted / That will be time, and may by us be fitted"
(IV.iii.378–9).

The ladies know better. Punning about the sealing wax on
the back of a letter which bears "Cupid's name," Rosaline
mocks the traditional fiction of Love's eternal youth: "That
was the way to make his godhead wax; / For he hath been
five thousand year a boy" (V.ii.10–11). We can already hear
Rosalind, the metamorphosis of Rosaline in *As You Like It*,
as she corrects Orlando: "Say 'a day,' without the 'ever.' No,
no, Orlando; men are April when they woo, December when
they wed. Maids are May when they are maids, but the sky
changes when they are wives" (IV.i.133–6). In *Love's Labour's Lost* the hollowness of romantic claims such as Love's
eternal youth is emphasized immediately after Rosaline's
mock, when Katharine tells how Cupid "kill'd" her sister:

Kath. He made her melancholy, sad, and heavy;
        And so she died: had she been light, like you
          [Rosaline],
        Of such a merry, nimble, stirring spirit,
        She might ha' been a grandam ere she died;
        And so may you, for a light heart lives long.
                                          (V.ii.14–8)

The tone then changes quickly, with the inevitable jesting
about "light" as "wanton," but the point has been made.
Love's month is sometimes also December. It is fitting that
the women, and especially Rosaline, bring this experience
of time to the attention of the lords. Berowne comically

acknowledged this function earlier, when he admitted in
soliloquy that he was another of Cupid's victims:

> What! I love! I sue! I seek a wife!
> A woman that is like a German clock,
> Still a-repairing, ever out of frame,
> And never going aright, being a watch,
> But being watch'd that it may still go right!
>
> (III.i.186–90)

It is so typical of Berowne here, that he makes a point
against himself when he thinks he's making one against the
women; using a clever chiasmus again, he succeeds only in
crossing himself up. The women *are* like clocks—they are
the custodians of time, the guardians of that "common sense"
(I.i.57,64) the men lack—but unlike the elaborately constructed clocks Berowne refers to, their method is simplicity
itself. The women are always "aright," always in "frame,"
always watching the men so that they "still go right." The
barbs and arrows of sharp wit have a way of rebounding
against the "shooter"—a word which, we learned in IV.i, is
the punning pronunciation of "suitor," a particularly apt
verbal coupling. No wonder that Longaville, hearing of his
year-long penance, whines, "I'll stay with patience; but the
time is long" (V.ii.825). Indeed it is. Even at the end of the
play, the lords haven't learned much more about time than
has their parody, Armado, who asked for the verbal assistance of "some extemporal god of rhyme" (I.ii.173). All of
them have yet to learn that not even the god of rhyme is
ex tempore; only his words are.

Navarre's final request shows how much the men still
have to learn about "the extreme parts of time" and why a
penance of "a twelvemonth and a day" is necessary:

> *King.* Now, at the latest minute of the hour,
>   Grant us your loves.

The princess' reply is unequivocal:

Prin. A time, methinks, too short
To make a world-without-end bargain in.
(V.ii.777–9)

This is the heart of the issue: minutes and hours on the one hand, and, on the other, a conception of time as "world-without-end." This day versus "doomsday," to put it at its most dramatic. The parallel with the play's debate on the nature of poetry is manifest—it is a struggle between the topical and the timeless.

The final songs confound all our initial expectations. After all, what could be more old-fashioned, more archaic, than the debate between Spring and Winter? Yet what affects us more deeply? Like Armado, Shakespeare takes a subject familiar "some three ages since," and gives it to us "newly writ o'er" (I.ii.103–10). But unlike Armado's ballad, or the Pageant, Shakespeare's songs are brilliant. The oldest subject in the world is suddenly fresh, transformed anew, timely once more. The most fashionable device in the play, the Masque of Muscovites, was a miserable failure because there was not enough "feigning," not enough art in it. The songs succeed because there is just enough. It is exactly this kind of rich and tantalizing complexity which is so distinctly characteristic of the late plays, not to mention the rest of Shakespeare's best work.

"Cormorant devouring Time" represents all that is most unbearable for man: his own ultimate decay and death. "For your fair sakes have we neglected time," Berowne tells the ladies (V.ii.745). But time has not neglected them. Nor has Shakespeare neglected time, as we realize at the end of the play. The final scene is masterfully arranged so that stage-time and real-time coincide and merge; the growing shadows of late afternoon, which cause Holofernes to stumble, are both figurative and actual. The play and the performance of the play in the theater end neither in light nor in darkness, but in a twilight world where the two are delicately balanced, reminding us of the compromises of the songs. Marcade, who mars Arcadia,[3] enters the play from the outer world of darkness, and his message is shocking and brutal.

Yet we are left not with Marcade's revelation but with an emphasis on artifice. Marcade is, after all, an actor, usually dressed in a black costume; he enters an incredibly stylized play at its most melodramatic moment, offering us a "tale." All in all, he is rather a poor choice to symbolize the total victory of Nature over Art. For Art is the victor, in one sense at least: Berowne's comments about the play in which he exists begin immediately to transform the threat posed by time and death into something more bearable, and prepare us for the songs.

The seasonal songs, above all, re-establish a sense of time as cyclical, not linear and therefore hopelessly irretrievable. Consider too the basic syntax of the songs. The "when-then" construction assures us, in its logical format, that it is describing something "natural" and inevitable. It suggests that there is a clearly defined time and place for certain activities, as in the normal cycle of the seasons. "Time" is transformed in the songs: here, "merry larks" serve as "clocks" for the ploughman. "Time" is therefore not outside Nature, as Navarre supposed, but part of it. The emphasis on the cycle of the seasons reminds us that time has its own proportion and decorum:

> Why should I joy in any abortive birth?
> At Christmas I no more desire a rose
> Than wish a snow in May's new-fangled shows;
> But like of each thing that in season grows.
>
> (I.i.104–7)

At the end of the play we see Christmas and May literally on the stage, in debate, each putting forth his own mixed claim. The songs offer us a cliché, but it is a profound one. Winter is inevitable, but so is Spring. So too with Art and Nature and the other antitheses.

PAINTING WITH DELIGHT

The songs seem merely to be describing the rhythm of nature and various rustic activities, but they reflect a skillful
artifice. Many of the larger themes in the play are represented in the songs in some form, as one critic has recently
shown.[4] But even single words and phrases from the rest of
the play are remembered and taken up in the songs. The
"staring owl" in Winter first appeared in Boyet's "Good
night, my good owl" (IV.i.138), and the cuckoo in Spring
was first known by its namesake, when Moth referred to a
"cuckold's horn" (V.i.65). The sexual verb "tread" is found
both in Spring and earlier in a "greasy" passage at IV.iii.276.
We exchange three kinds of apple in the rest of the play—
costard, pomewater, and crab—for the "roasted crabs" of
Winter. It is worth noting, too, how often the word "mock"
or some variant has occurred in the play; some fifteen instances before the last songs, according to my count. In
Spring's song, however, it goes beyond the usual sense of
scorning or making fun of something to mean "imitating" or
"copying." If the cuckoo "mocks married men," it both
ridicules those who have been cuckolded and, by the loose
grammar, itself imitates those who have done the cuckold-
ing. It is a familiar ambiguity. This kind of imitation—one
which implies self-consciousness and sophistication—contrasts starkly both with Holofernes' mechanistic notion of it
and with Berowne's description of the "fashion of the days,"
which supposedly "imitates" the dark coloring of his mistress. Here the imitation is fresher, more subtle. Moreover, it
requires but the slightest shift in pronunciation to change
the "lady-smocks" into the "ladies' mocks"—for it is precisely the ladies in Love's Labour's Lost who have "mocked"
the lords in every sense of that term. "Mock for mock is
only my intent" (V.ii.140), affirms the Princess.

There are still further connections to the ladies. Berowne
had confessed that he must "love, write, sigh, pray, sue, and

groan: / Some men must love my lady, and some Joan"
(III.i.201–2). But later he tries to deceive his friends by
arguing "When shall you see me write a thing in rhyme? /
Or groan for Joan?" (IV.iii.179–80). Rosaline's penance for
Berowne is to "converse / With groaning wretches"
(V.ii.841–2), to learn the nature of real as well as pretended
pain. The songs give us still another picture of Joan: "While
greasy Joan doth keel the pot." She is a link to all the women
in the play, but especially to the ladies and to Rosaline, who
is Berowne's Joan. And it is the ladies, after all, who "talk
greasily" (IV.i.136) with Costard and Boyet.

"Greasy Joan" also throws us back to the lubricity of
Jaquenetta and to the intended and unwitting "greasy" talk
of the low characters. Jaquenetta is never on stage at the
same time the ladies are, but an actual meeting is unnecessary
to reveal the link between them. The ladies have everywhere
been frank about their sensuality, their recognition of the
"sinplicitie" of the flesh; Rosaline is, according to Berowne
at least, "one that will do the deed" (III.i.195). But the ladies'
sense of "season" and "place" forestalls marriage and birth;
Jaquenetta rushes to the second before the first. Considering
Berowne's avowed sexual interests, it is quite appropriate that
his letter to Rosaline, miscarried by Costard, finds its way
to Jaquenetta in IV.ii. And Jaquenetta's influence over Armado, finally, parallels that of the ladies over the lords—the
"hermit" Navarre becomes in Armado "a votary"; Berowne
is described elsewhere as "one of the votaries with the king"
(IV.ii.136). The "vows" and "three year" period Armado
accepts look back to the opening scenes of the play where
the academe is proposed. Armado vows, under Jaquenetta's
influence, "to hold the plough for her sweet love" (V.ii.873);
a moment later, the songs anticipate this pastoral life with
the "ploughman's clocks" (l. 894).

Other connections between the songs and the play are
plentiful. The cuckoo appears "on every tree," just as Berowne became Cupid/Hercules, "still climbing trees in the
Hesperides" in the sonnet-reading scene. In Winter, more-

over, the "blood is nipp'd"—not "frozen" in the pail like the milk—but only restrained until the season is right. The lords, however, had tried first to deny their "blood" or passions; when Berowne tells Rosaline of his "sick" heart, she advises him to "let it blood" (II.i.186). Berowne remembers this advice, for when Dumain describes his mistress as "a fever [who] / Reigns in my blood," Berowne gives this off-stage advice: "A fever in your blood! why, then incision / Would let her out in saucers" (IV.iii.93–6).

Berowne can laugh about it for the moment, but he soon lurches to the other extreme with his defiant assertion that "young blood doth not obey an old decree" (IV.iii.214). He goes on to condemn their academic efforts in medical terms: "Why, universal plodding poisons up / The nimble spirits in the arteries" (ll. 302–3). The ladies serve as loyal physicians to the lords. The Princess may feel sad when she seeks "to spill / The poor deer's blood" (IV.i.34–5) in the deer-shooting scene, but none of the women hesitates to spill her dear's blood later. The Princess begins her order of penance to Navarre in these terms: "If this austere insociable life / Change not your offer made in heat of blood" (V.ii.789–90). Thus another transformation is anticipated, but this one will not, we are confident, occur. The lords' blood "is nipp'd," but only for a time and a season. It will thaw soon enough. There is, as Winter shows, a middle way.

The songs offer us a vision of true pastoral to contrast with the false pastoralism Berowne and his friends had espoused earlier. The song of Spring describes, with the most sophisticated art, a rustic "naturalism," a bucolicism mostly literary in its origin but still convincing. It represents activities which take place outside, moving from the colorful vegetation in the first stanza up to human and animal activities in the second. It is the same landscape seen later in Milton's "L'Allegro":

> While the Plowman near at hand,
> Whistles o'er the Furrow'd Land,

And the Milkmaid singeth blithe,
And the Mower whets his scythe,
And every Shepherd tells his tale
Under the Hawthorn in the dale.

Here, too, is a shepherd-poet, as "natural" as anything else, a part of the landscape, his creative activity an analogue to the general process of fertility. Spring's song shows us that "shepherds pipe on oaten straws"; their art, like that of the "larks" who tell time for us, is part of a larger natural rhythm. The second stanza of Spring lists man and animal together without distinction, for they exist in a perfect, idealized harmony.

Winter's song, on the other hand, is an "Il Penseroso" vision; it is literally darker ("nightly") and it takes place indoors, in "the hall," rather than outdoors. It represents another side of pastoral, a retreat from the harshness of a fallen world, where the "penalty of Adam" is felt most concretely in "The seasons' difference . . . the icy fang / And churlish chiding of the winter's wind," as the Duke describes it in *As You Like It* (II.i.5–8). The other part of Adam's penalty was to labor in the fields, and Winter's song reveals the necessity for such action in bearing logs, milking cows, keeling the pot. This pastoral retreat contrasts with the naive, escapist retreat the noblemen had proposed with their academe; the ladies will counter that by making them all "hermits" for a year. The Princess will confine herself "in a mourning house" (V.ii.798) during that time. Against this kind of retreat, Winter's song offers us a seasonal and therefore temporary sojourn "into the hall," a pulling back indoors while outside "all aloud the wind doth blow," "icicles hang by the wall," and the "ways be foul." The key word, again, is "when." There is a time for this kind of withdrawal, when nature is less friendly. The withdrawal, like all pastoral, seems to be both physical and psychological, for the "blood" which is "nipp'd" finds outlet in the feeling of community and warmth, of human action muted but still vital. The owl's song is "merry," not sad; he may be "star-ing" at the unsuspected activity beneath him. In this kind of retreat, there is little tolerance for abstraction; the *sen-tentiae* of the curate Nathaniel, Costard, and Holofernes have little place in a world where "coughing drowns the parson's saw." That coughing may be the result of a cold but it may also represent an impatience with institutional-ized knowledge when authentic wisdom seems embodied in the very process of living. There is considerable warmth in the hall in the hot "roasted crabs," the suggested fire, the pot Joan keels to keep it from boiling over. Nothing will boil over in Winter, we feel, but the potential is there, waiting only for the "due season."

Several of the words and phrases in the songs bear conno-tations of art or imaginative activity. In Spring, the flowers "paint," the cuckoo "mocks" and "sings" a "word" of fear, the shepherds "pipe" their pastoral flutes, and the maidens "bleach" their smocks. The last may need some explanation. The "lady-smocks" (l. 885) are "silver-white"; painted by nature, these flowers help paint the meadows. In the second stanza of Spring, the human equivalent to Nature's creation is found in the "maidens," the ladies who "bleach" their "smocks" white, a human painting. Reminding us of the ar-tifice in this natural scene, these words point to the resolu-tion of the Art-Nature problem, for imagination here is simply not distinguished from the world at large but is a breathing part of it. Yet it is not just the theme of the songs, telling us the way to this resolution, which most awes us, but the achievement of it, the embodiment of that resolution in the art that fashioned them. Consider, for example, the relation between the painting metaphor, discussed in the previous chapter, and the opening section of Spring:

> When daisies pied and violets blue
>> And lady-smocks all silver-white
> And cuckoo-buds of yellow hue
>> Do paint the meadows with delight, . . .

The very names of the flowers are revelatory of the power of art, from "daisies" to "lady-smocks," from a dead metaphor to a live one. A daisy is, according to the etymology, a "day's eye," and a "lady-smock" is an outer dress. These names, moreover, blend together the animal, vegetable, and human into a reciprocal harmony. Thus a flower is linked to both a "lady-smock" and a "cuckoo," the bird which appears in the refrain; a dove is known as a "turtle"; and a fruit is a "crab."

The songs throughout embody the fusion of Art and Nature in a perfect whole. The names suggest the interrelatedness of every level of Nature, and the multiple personifications—the cuckoo "mocks," the larks are "merry," the owl "stares" and "sings"—demonstrate the ubiquitous force of imagination, giving names and local habitations. The flowers are said to "paint the meadows with delight," but the "delight" belongs to both the flowers and the meadows, to the painters and that which is painted. The art itself, as Polixenes would say, is nature. Or in Yeats' terms, "labour," with implications of work and birth, is "blossoming or dancing." Of the latter activity Yeats asks: "O body swayed to music, O brightening glance, / How can we know the dancer from the dance?" We witness the same conjunction of being and becoming, of cause and effect, of agent and audience, in the songs in Love's Labour's Lost, where all Nature seems to be blossoming, where Nature paints with Art's techniques. It is also significant that Shakespeare gives us in each case the name of the flower first, and then an adjective of color. He seems to call attention to the inverted word order, for nowhere else in the songs, not even in the second stanza of Spring, is such a word order used. The point of this detail is, I think, that Shakespeare is showing us how to "paint" properly. The object is summoned by its name, itself metaphorical, and then given a "color" both literal and rhetorical. Normal word order is restored in the rest of the songs once the initial painting is completed. The artifice of the inverted word order, and the fusion of description and action of the thing described matches, indeed embodies and illustrates, the artifice implied by "paint . . . with delight."

It is not in the least surprising to learn, as J. W. Lever tells us,[5] that Shakespeare apparently got the names of the flowers, not from a close observation of nature, but from a book—Gerard's *Herball*. But this fact is often used against Spring's song, supposedly making it more "artificial" whereas Winter's song is more "realistic." Winter does present the rougher edges of pastoral—a harder life, the penalty of Adam felt more strongly. And the people in Winter are given names, making them apparently more concrete and less idealized than the figures of Spring. But their names are more generic than particular, and hence a rustic equivalent of the flowers' names. "Dick," for example, is often a contemptuous term, as in Berowne's description of Boyet as "Some mumble-news, some trencher-knight, some Dick" (V.ii.464). We have already examined the connotations of "Joan." "Marian," too, was often a generic term for a loose, or at least a low woman, especially when referred to as "Maid Marian."[6] And when Hal, in *I Henry IV*, claims to be a "sworn brother to a leash of drawers," he "can call them all by their christen names, as Tom, Dick, and Francis" (II.iv.6–8). Such names are clearly meant as types. Winter's descriptions, though more concrete than Spring's, are no less artificial. Winter's vision is finally as typical and general as Spring's, but in a different mode.

Puttenham said that the poet's power, rightly used, is "even as nature her selfe working by her owne peculiar vertue and proper instinct" (p. 307). That same concord reverberates in the songs, whose apparent simplicity masks the most cunning complexities. We have already seen how "lady-smocks" become ladies' mocks. It is a short but dramatic step to unpack the latent metaphor in "daisies pied" to hear "day's eye spied." Coupled with "blue" as "blew" (the actual spelling of the Quarto), or past tense of "blow" ("to blossom"), the first line of Spring yields another version of the same event in the past tense: When day's eye spied and violets bloomed. . . . If this seems fanciful, there are more obvious instances of a kind of double grammar that works elsewhere in the songs. "Paint . . . with delight" is one example, and there may be another in the line "When blood is nipp'd, and ways be foul." The parallel syntax supports "be foul" as a copulative, but one hears it also as "befoul," in the sense that the external world acts on man, driving him indoors in winter.[7] When "the wind doth blow," in another cause and effect relation, Dick the shepherd "blows his nail," the same verb governing nature's action on man and man's reaction to it. There is also a cause-and-effect cycle at work between the two songs, one season leading into and implying the other. The flowers of Spring have bloomed and fallen, leaving behind in Winter only the fruit, the "crab," which will nourish man through the season until the following spring. The cuckoo sang "on every tree" in Spring, but some of those trees which blossomed are now used to warm the hall, into which "Tom bears logs." The white lady-smocks and summer smocks of Spring are matched by the "frozen" white of milk in pails and icicles. If procreation has occurred in Spring, if turtles, rooks, daws, and, by the ambiguous conjunctive grammar, maidens have been treading, then Winter shows the result of that action, the nurturing of offspring as "birds sit brooding in the snow." The "merry note" of the owl in Winter urges men to go "to it," to release and gratify the sexual impulse. But it is the very ambiguity of the direction—"to who"?—that can lead, in Spring, to the "word of fear" which heralds the cuckold, victim of the sexual instinct gone uncontrolled. The apparently opposed seasons are continually bound together by theme and image, therefore, and also by the loose syntax. Each of the four stanzas is structured by a "when . . . then" syllogism, a valid and natural seasonal logic which contrasts with the sophistical logic the men have used earlier. Everything is placed in its natural time and order. Moreover, everything is effortlessly merged by the recurring conjunctives. Ten of the thirty-six lines of the songs begin with "and," leading us from flower to man to animal. There is not a single disjunctive in the songs, which seems to me exactly the point; for the songs bridge all the dualisms and oppositions, sweeping aside artificial distinctions affirmed in the rest of the play with an ease that takes the breath away.

As a grand coda to the play, the songs are incomplete only to the extent that the court life which dominates the play seems to have disappeared. The lords and ladies have turned into ploughmen, maidens, and Joans. We find ourselves in field and forest and the great "hall" rather than in the court of Navarre or the park outside it. An overtly "French" play turns suddenly to native English scenery for its conclusion. Human voices have given way to those of animals. None of the linguistic styles heard earlier finds an echo here either. Berowne's verbal slumming, with "wench," was self-conscious, but the low style is embodied in the songs without any conspicuous change in diction. There are few latinate words in the songs, and no word longer than three syllables. In their seemingly effortless grace, their sensitive and sophisticated art, the songs seem to have absorbed and re-created everything in the play. We have seen that "art" has to do with "feigning," not simply with the choice of high or low style, not with inkhorn terms or self-conscious diction. In their easy resolution of the conflict that vexes the rest of the play, the songs depict a world where art is nature and nature art, where both man and nature sing and pipe and paint. They are inimitable.

Some readers of the play persist, with Ralph Berry, in the idea that "Winter is second, and final" (Berry, p. 76). Joseph Westlund says of Winter's song, "this is the 'real' world: the world of milk and blood, of coughing and red noses and cold hands."[8] Winter is indeed second, but it is not final, nor "superior" to Spring's song. That Westlund resorts to quotation marks around the word "real"[9] implies an important qualification. Winter's song is no more the "real" world than

Spring's. They are simply two aspects of one world, as are "Il Penseroso" and "L'Allegro." Neither is complete in itself, because each is defined by its opposite. "Young blood doth not obey an old decree" (IV.iii.214) Berowne tells us with assurance. But he fails, for once, to complete the obvious chiasmus, to note that old blood does not obey young decrees either. The proper relationship between young and old, Spring and Winter, has yet to be arrived at. If we are going to call any world "real," it ought to consist of both.

Moreover, Shakespeare has made the songs marvellously complex by obscuring the usual clear-cut distinctions between the seasons and all that is associated with them. Spring is not just unalloyed joy and fertility, but it also "mocks" and contains a "word of fear"; the sexuality of Spring is ubiquitous and vital, but it is not free from unpleasantness. Winter, conversely, is not simply a world of death and darkness; it cannot be totally identified with the world so dramatically announced by Marcade. It has, paradoxically, a "merry note" in it. That world has been transformed, as has Spring, into something less absolute, something more complex and enduring. There is life and fertility in both. Even in Winter, birds brood, the fire warms, things move. C. L. Barber eloquently sums up, from his point of view, the effect of these songs on us: "Each centers on vitality, and moves from nature to man. . . . In the winter song, the center of vitality is the fire. . . . Even the kitchen wench, greasy Joan, keeling the pot to keep it from boiling over, is one of us, a figure of affection. The songs evoke the daily enjoyments and the daily community out of which special festive occasions were shaped up. And so they provide for the conclusion of the comedy what marriage usually provides: an expression of the going-on power of life."[10] We choose, not one season over the other, but both. There is no other possibility.

Berowne's comment, "That's too long for a play," calls attention to the breach in decorum represented by the unconventional ending of the comedy, the "form confounded."

It also reminds us of the play's special concern with time, dramatic as well as seasonal. And yet it is still all part of the play, it isn't too "long" after all. Since the figurative marriages have just occurred before us, the literal marriages can readily be imagined. The delicate artifice of the play is strengthened by the acknowledgement of its limitations. It can be argued, in fact, that Marcade's entry finally *saves* the play's artifice, by seeming at first to destroy it. We have been brought to a confrontation with death, acknowledged it, and thankfully seen it transformed by the imagination of the dramatist into something more bearable. We have not forgotten mutability, but it has been placed in perspective, against the cycle of fertility-decay-rebirth on into eternity. The "disgrace of death" finally yields to the "grace" which only the imagination can give it, a grace within the reach of art.[11] Ultimately the play transcends the literal time-boundaries which contain it, by referring ahead to its own "sequel," when the traditional plot will be completed by a round of marriages and *Love's Labour's Lost* will become a traditional comedy, *Love's Labour's Won.* The play has been greatly concerned with its own antecedents, and appropriately turns at the end to its descendants. Like Spring and Winter, Art and Nature, it includes both extremes of time in a single moment.

In the final action of the play, we are given one last metaphor of the theater. Armado is the stage-manager, the low characters split into two groups to sing the songs, the characters from the court form an audience, and we look on as still another audience—one final pattern of concentric circles. But this time the play-within-the-play and the play itself are the same, an instance of further reconciliation. The end of the songs concludes not a single theatrical unit, but the entire play. Armado's final words, "The words of Mercury are harsh after the songs of Apollo," apply to every-one—Worthies, court characters, audience. The false eloquence of the men has been transmuted, "words" have been forged into "songs," and there is nothing more to be debated[12] The "dialogue" becomes one voice. As the god of poetry triumphs, so, vicariously, do we. The final line in the Folio text, spoken by the "Brag," or Armado, is a stage-direction: "You that way: we this way." It refers both to the stage-actors, who exit in two groups, Spring and Winter, and to the audience. The remarkable imaginative event that has involved actors and audience in a common world comes to an end, and we are returned, somewhat abruptly, "that way," to the world we ordinarily inhabit, while the actors disappear "this way," into the playhouse, yet continue to live in our imaginations. We realize at last that drama, with its "living" actors and mimed "art," its easy marriage of Art and Nature, of illusion and reality, is itself the best, the most convincing form of "living art."[13]

APPENDICES

Appendix A

THE NINE WORTHIES

It is unnecessary to give a complete history of the Nine Worthies here, for several scholars have already traced their course in some detail.[1] Their studies have not, however, adequately described the tone and context in which *Love's Labour's Lost* refers to the Worthies. A brief sketch of their background will help clarify this question.

The first recorded appearance of the Nine Worthies is apparently c. 1312, in Jacques de Longuyon's "Les Voeux du Paon." His list became the traditional grouping. Three pagans: Hector, Alexander, and Caesar. Three Jews: Joshua, David, and Judas Maccabaeus. Three Christians: Arthur, Charlemagne, and Godfrey of Bouillon. The Worthies thereafter began to appear quite frequently: in *The Parlement of the Thre Ages* (c. 1352–70), in Gower's "In Praise of Peace" (c. 1390–1400), and in Lydgate's "The Assembly of Gods" (c. 1420), among others. Caxton's preface to "Kyng Arthur" (1485) claims that "it is notoyrly knowen thorugh the unyversal world that there been ix worthy."[2] This seems to be but a slight exaggeration, given the large number of references to them throughout the fifteenth and sixteenth centuries.

The lives of the Worthies were exemplary. They were paragons of the heroic life. "Who would not rather be one of the Nine Worthyes," Gabriel Harvey asked confidently, "than one of the Seaven Wise masters?"[3] They are heroes of chivalry, especially, and, as Harvey's question suggests, often models of the active life, as against the contemplative. In *Love's Labour's Lost*, the soldier Armado describes Hector as a "war-man" (V.ii.651); Holofernes, like the other scholars, is an "arts-man" (V.i.76). Navarre attempts to create an academy based solely on the retired life, "still and contemplative in living art" (I.i.14). The introduction of the Worthies, then, can be seen as an attempt to counter this impulse with its polar opposite, a reminder of the active life. One way to view the play, as I have argued, is to see it as an attempt to reconcile contending impulses. A premonition of this union is found in Longaville, who is described at one point as "well fitted in arts, glorious in arms" (II.i.45), but we know that neither he nor his friends has yet achieved a mature balance in life. The structural movement of the play, as we saw in the fifth chapter, leads steadily away from the safe enclosure of the court.

If the lives of the Nine Worthies meant so much to the Renaissance, their deaths were even more portentous. In earlier representations, the Worthies usually served as illustration for an *ubi sunt* or *contemptus mundi* theme, as in Gower's poem:

> See Alisandre, Ector and Julius,
> See Machabeu, David and Josue,
> See Charlemeine, Godefroi, Arthus,
> Fulfild of werre and of mortalite.
> Here fame abit, bot al is vanite;
> For deth, which hath the werres under fote,
> Hath mad an ende of which there is no bote.[4]

In Lydgate's "The Assembly of Gods," Atropos boasts of her power over life:

> Ector of Troy, for all hys chyvalry,
>   Alexaunder, the grete & myghty conquerour,
> Iulius Cesar, with all hys company,
>   David, nor Iosue, nor worthy Artour,
>   Charles the noble, that was so gret of honour,
>   Nor Iudas Machabee for all hys trew hert,
>   Nor Godfrey of Boleyn cowde me nat astert.

All great men, she continues, "at the last I sesyd hem with my mace. / Thus hav I brought every creature / To an ende."[5] As reminders of worldly vanity, then, the Worthies are antidotes to the lords who believe that they will escape the onslaught of time, be graced in "the disgrace of death."

The only relief to be found from oblivion was "fame" (l. 1). The feats of the Worthies had, after all, survived, and they were often introduced by the allegorical figure Fame. In Hawes' *The Pastime of Pleasure* (pr. 1509, repr. 1554–5), for example, Dame Fame, covered "with brennynge tongues," promises Grand Amour that she will spread his fame after he is dead. It is her duty, she says, to spread "by hy auctoryte / The noble dedes of many a champyon / As they are worthy in myne opynyon." The Nine Worthies then appear, each characterized briefly by Dame Fame. But the figures of Time and then of Eternity enter, and we are reminded that they are superior forces.[6] Fame was similarly superseded in Petrarch's *Triumphs*.

Gradually, however, the superiority of time and eternity was forgotten, especially in pageants and Lord Mayor's Shows, where the solemn homiletic *contemptus mundi* tradition had less force. The Worthies now become exemplars of the power of fame, and especially of verse: "Not marble, nor the gilded monuments / Of princes, shall outlive this pow'rful rhyme" (Sonnet 55). As John Taylor reminded us, "Forgot had bin the thrice three worthies names, / If thrice three Muses had not writ their fames."[7] In *Love's Labour's Lost*, as in all such pageants, the Worthies did "live" again, animated by the poet's power, addressing the audience from the undiscovered country beyond the bourn.

The Worthies were not always linked exclusively with the active life, either, but became known for their "arts" as well. As in Taylor's epigram, the Worthies began to be associated with the power of the poet. In Middleton's masque *The World Tost at Tennis* (1620), for example, Jupiter orders Pallas to use "white art" to "summon back to life" the "thrice-three Worthies." The Soldier and Scholar who have engaged in a discussion of the relative merits of the active and contemplative life look on. Jupiter tells Pallas,

> There let 'em [the Soldier and Scholar] see what arts
>   and arms commixt—
> For they [the Worthies] had both—did in the world's
>   broad face;
> Those that did propagate and beget their fames,
> And for posterity left lasting names.
>
> (ll. 258–66)

At this point, a stage direction announces music and song, and the Nine Muses "are discovered, with the Nine Worthies, on the upper-stage; toward the conclusion they descend, each Worthy led by a Muse, the most proper and pertinent to the person of the Worthy, as Terpsichore with David, Urania with Joshua, &c." The song which follows names each of the Muses and bids them each choose one of the Heroes: "We call them Worthies, 'tis their due, / Though long time dead, still live by you." After the Worthies and Muses enter together, exhibit themselves, and leave, the audience within the masque comments on what has just been seen:

> *Jupiter.* Were not these precedents for all future ages?
> *Scholar.* But none attains their glories, king of stars;
>   These are the fames are follow'd and pursu'd,
>   But never overtaken.
>
> (ll. 164–7)

Jupiter goes on to lament the decline of the current age, complaining that in these days "Learnings and arts are theories, no practiques, / To understand is all they study to; / Men strive to know too much, too little do."[8]

After so exalted a resurrection as Middleton performs, it seems almost petty to point out that the Worthies had been ridiculed for at least a quarter of a century and more when he was writing. There was an early tendency to substitute a local favorite as a ninth Worthy, almost always for God-

frey of Bouillon, or even to add a tenth Worthy. Guy of
Warwick[9] and Frederick Barbarossa[10] were understandable
favorite ninths, but Bertrand du Guesclin[11] as a tenth was
less worthy of the honor. Nashe mentions "Salomon" and
"Gedeon" (Nashe, II, 253) and Greene "Scipio" (Greene,
IX, 49) as alternates. Henry VIII[12] and even Henry VI[13]
had been lionized by others. This practice led quickly to
bathos, the substitution of increasingly minor officials, as
in Richard Johnson's poem of 1592, "The Nine Worthies of
London." As described by Venezky, it "depicted the allegorical figures of Fame and Clio calling upon the deceased
ancient worthies of the city to rise from an Elysian bank,
where they rested arm-in-arm, to stand forth, identify themselves, and deliver their stories in verse. Johnson included
Walworth as a representative of the Fishmongers' guild,
while other worthies represented the Grocers, Vintners,
Merchant Taylors, Mercers and Silk Weavers."[14] By 1592,
Johnson's poem seems the rule rather than the exception.
Huizinga describes an early manifestation of a conceit that
became all too common: "At the funeral service of Charles
the Bold at Nancy, his conqueror, the young duke of Lor-
raine, came to honour the corpse of his enemy, dressed 'in
antique style,' that is to say, wearing a long golden beard
which reached to his girdle. Thus got up to represent one of
the Nine Worthies, he prayed for a quarter of an hour."
Parody is another sure sign of debasement, and Molinet is
reported to have composed an early parody, "the nine
worthies of gluttony."[15] Shakespeare gives us the nine
wordies of language.

To invoke the Nine Worthies as praise came to have little
effect. In *Pierce Penilesse* (1592), Nashe complained of a
decline in the observation of honor, noting that "men of
great calling . . . have their names eternizde by Poets; &
whatsoever pamphlet or dedication encounters them, they
put it up in their sleeves, and scarce give him thanks that
presents it." Little good comes to those "golden pens" who
"raise such ungratfull Peasants from the Dung-hil of ob-

scuritie, and make them equal in fame to the Worthies of olde" (Nashe, I, 159). And in *The Unfortunate Traveller* (1594), the orator of the university at Wittenberg makes a long Ciceronian speech, designed to illustrate his learning but exposing his pomposity. The speech is, like those of Holofernes, larded with Latin: "a thousand *quemadmodums* and *quapropters* he came over him with; every sentence he concluded with *Esse posse videatur*: through all the nine worthies he ran with praising and comparing him" (Nashe, II, 246–7). In *The Anatomy of Melancholy* (1621), under the heading of "Pride and Vain-Glory," Burton complains that man is subject to a continual barrage of flattery and immoderate praise—"bombast epithets, glozing titles, false elogiums." No man can resist such hyperbolic compliments: "Let him be what he will, those Parasites will overturn him: if he be a King, he is one of the Nine Worthies, more than a man, a God forthwith" (Burton, p. 257). In the same year in which Middleton exalted the Worthies, Beaumont and Fletcher included this disparaging reference in *The Double Marriage* (1620):[16]

> *Martia.* Thou despis'd fool,
> Thou only sign of man, how I contemn thee!
> Thou woven Worthy in a piece of arras,
> Fit only to enjoy a wall!

Because of the abuse of hyperbolic praise and the attendant decline of the ideal represented by the Worthies, to invoke their name in the 1590s would undoubtedly have produced a laugh in a sophisticated audience. By 1605, one year after the performance of *Love's Labour's Lost* for Queen Anne, the complex irony of Don Quixote's oath is possible: " 'I know who I am,' replied Don Quixote, 'and I know, too, that I am capable of being not only the characters I have named, but all the Twelve Peers of France and all the Nine Worthies as well, for my exploits are far greater than all the deeds they have done, all together and each by himself.' "[17] The shambling condition in which we find them in

Love's Labour's Lost poses the problem of the validity of such ideals—whether it is possible any longer to merge the active and contemplative lives. There must be, and in *Love's Labour's Lost* there is, a thorough re-definition of the idea of worthiness.

Appendix B

Hercules is mentioned in *Love's Labour's Lost* more often than any other mythological figure except Cupid.[1] He is held "worthy" enough by Holofernes to become one of the Nine Worthies in the Pageant. I have been unable to find any other instance in which Hercules is one of the Nine Worthies, but we have seen that there were occasional substitutions for the last of the traditional Nine Worthies, and Shakespeare includes Pompey as well as Hercules here. The Labors of Hercules, however, were often dramatized by *commedia dell'arte* troupes, as K. M. Lea has shown. Such troupes had performed the Labors, and possibly even the Nine Worthies, before English and French audiences on the Continent, and possibly even in England, though there is no record of it. English comedians had performed both subjects on the Continent.[2] Shakespeare's audience would not have been surprised to see a *commedia* troupe present the Worthies and the Labors, though intermingling them seems original with Shakespeare.

Hercules' inclusion in the Pageant seems quite appropriate, whatever the tradition, for the record of his life was for the Elizabethans the image of a lifelong strenuous moral striving. He represented above all the virtues of the active life.[3] In the Choice of Hercules between virtue and pleasure the Renaissance saw a model for all human behavior. It is usually Hercules' energy, his strength and purpose, which are singled out for praise, and eventually allegorized. Like the Nine Worthies, then, the mention of Hercules would weigh against Navarre's plan for an academy in the play's debate between the active and contemplative lives. But the comic reality is that Hercules is "in minority" in *Love's Labour's Lost*.

And yet Hercules, like the Worthies who became associated with "arts," began to represent aspects of the intellectual life as well. The so-called Gallic Hercules was known specifically for his eloquence.[4] As Thomas Wilson put it, "the Poetes do feyne that Hercules being a man of greate wisdome, had all men lincked together by the eares in a chaine, to draw them and leade them even as he lusted. For his witte was so greate, his tongue so eloquente, & his experience suche, that no one man was able to withstand his reason, but everye one was rather driven to do that whiche he woulde, and to wil that whiche he did, agreing to his advise both in word & worke, in all that ever they were able."[5] Puttenham tells the same myth (p. 142). The irony of Moth's silence in the Pageant is all the more pointed, given this tradition.

Hercules could be an exemplar even of wisdom and knowledge. In some accounts, his knowledge was specifically astronomical.[6] In *The Brazen Age*, Heywood's Homer, referring to the story that Hercules took the earth from Atlas' shoulders, asserts "That hee supported heaven, doth well expresse / His Astronomicke skill, knowledge in starres; / They that such practise know, what do they lesse / Then beare heavens weight."[7] In Jonson's *Pleasure Reconciled to Virtue*, Mercury addresses Hercules in a similar way: "My grandsire *Atlas* . . . taught thee all the learning of the Sphere" (Jonson, VII, 485). Hercules is therefore virtually kin to those "earthly godfathers of heaven's lights" that Berowne describes in the first scene.

While the Choice of Hercules was a popular subject with painters[8] and other artists, the Labors had perhaps the greatest dramatic potential. The player in Greene's *Groatsworth of Wit* (1592) brags that "the twelve labors of *Hercules*

237

have I terribly thundred on the stage" (Greene, XII, 131). In *An Apology for Actors* (1612), Thomas Heywood waxed ecstatic over the stage's potential: "To see as I have seene, Hercules, in his owne shape, hunting the boare, knocking downe the bull, taming the hart, fighting with Hydra, murdering Geryon, slaughtering Diomed, wounding the Stymphalides, killing the Centaurs, pashing the lion, squeezing the dragon, dragging Cerberus in chaynes, and lastly, on his high pyramides writing *Nil ultra*, Oh, these were sights to make an Alexander!"[9] There were various ways of allegorizing and interpreting the Labors, but at the least they were understood as models of virtuous action, an image of man conquering his own passions. As Thomas Wilson put it: "What other thyng are the wonderfull labours of Hercules, but that reason shoulde withstande affection, and the spirite for ever should fight, against the fleshe?"[10] The Labors of Hercules are fully appropriate in this play (in which one labor—the labor of love—is lost), for the lords are called by Navarre "brave conquerors . . . That war against your own affections / And the huge army of the world's desires" (I.i.8–10). Yet even Hercules was conquered by his affections, falling in love and becoming a comic figure (cf. Sidney quotation in chapter four [Smith, I, 200]).

At least three of the Labors are referred to in *Love's Labour's Lost*. The first, conquering the Nemean lion, is alluded to in Armado's letter to Jaquenetta (IV.i.87–92). The twelfth Labor, killing the hellhound Cerberus, forms part of Holofernes' Pageant: "Great Hercules is presented by this imp, / Whose club kill'd Cerberus, that three-headed canus" (V.ii.581–2). The story in which Hercules, as a child, strangles the serpents sent by Hera is referred to twice (V.i.130; V.ii.583–4), and his famous club twice (I.ii.166; V.ii.582).

One of the most interesting allusions in the play is to the eleventh Labor, in which, according to the standard version, Hercules was sent to bring back the Golden Apples of the Hesperides, took the burden of Atlas (supporting the earth) while he went to retrieve them, and then tricked Atlas into taking the burden back. In another version, Hercules went to the Garden himself and conquered the dragon guarding the apples. When Cominius warns Menenius that the angry Coriolanus will shake Rome down about his ears, he replies, "As Hercules / Did shake down mellow fruit" (*Cor.*, IV.vi.100–1). In *Love's Labour's Lost*, Berowne refers to the valiant Cupid as "a Hercules, / Still climbing trees in the Hesperides" (IV.iii.337–8). Shakespeare understands Hesperides to refer to the island, or at least the garden, rather than to the daughters of Hesperus who guarded the apples. The implications of this allusion should be examined briefly.

The eleventh Labor of Hercules apparently held great fascination for the Elizabethans. When Friar Bungay chooses an illusion with which to impress Vandermast in Greene's *Friar Bacon and Friar Bungay*, he produces first the tree "with the dragon shooting fire," then Hercules himself (that is, a fiend taking his shape) "in his Lions skin," conveniently speaking Latin. Vandermast commands him to "Pull off the sprigs from the Hesperian tree, / As once thou didst to win the golden fruit," and then the figure "begins to breake the branches" (Greene, XIII, 59–60). In another reference, Antiochus warns Pericles away from his daughter by alluding to the danger involved in the Labor: "Before thee stands this fair Hesperides, / With golden fruit, but dangerous to be touched; / For deathlike dragons here affright thee hard" (*Per.*, I.i.28–30).

The "golden fruit" was variously interpreted. One tradition had it that there was no fruit at all: Diodorus Siculus explained that "Atlas . . . possessed flocks of sheep which excelled in beauty and were in colour of a golden yellow, this being the reason why poets, in speaking of these sheep as *mela* [sheep], called them golden *mela* [apples]."[11] In Spenser's Garden of Proserpina grow "golden apples glistring bright," and among them are those "which Hercules with conquest bold / Got from great Atlas daughters . . .

suggested, as the context of the Promethean Fire speech indicates, simply a quest for beauty and, more indirectly, a poetic quest—Cupid in the next line is "as sweet and musical / As bright Apollo's lute" (IV.iii.339), and the figure of Hercules on his eleventh Labor was the sign of the theater in which the play was (at least once) performed.[14]

List of Works Cited

Abrams, M. H. *The Mirror and the Lamp*. New York: Norton, 1958.

Adams, Joseph Quincy, ed. *Chief Pre-Shakespearean Dramas*. Boston: Houghton Mifflin Co., 1924.

Agnew, Gates K. "Berowne and the Progress of Love's Labour's Lost." *ShakS*, IV (1968), 40–72.

Allen, D. C. "Some Theories of the Growth and Origin of Language in Milton's Age." *PQ*, XXVIII (1949), 5–16.

Atkins, J.W.H., ed. *The Owl and the Nightingale*. Cambridge: Cambridge Univ. Press, 1922.

Bacon, Francis. *Works*. Ed. James Spedding, Robert Ellis, Douglas Heath. London: Longmans, 1857–74.

Baldwin, T. W. *William Shakspere's Small Latine & Lesse Greeke*. Urbana, Ill.: Univ. of Illinois Press, 1944.

Barber, C. L. *Shakespeare's Festive Comedy*. Princeton: Princeton Univ. Press, 1959.

Barish, Jonas A. *Ben Jonson and the Language of Prose Comedy*. Cambridge, Mass.: Harvard Univ. Press, 1960.

———. "The Prose Style of John Lyly." *ELH*, 23 (1956), 14–35.

Beaumont, Francis, and Fletcher, John. *The Works of Francis Beaumont and John Fletcher*. Ed. A. R. Waller. Cambridge: Cambridge Univ. Press, 1905–12.

Berry, Ralph. "The Words of Mercury." *ShS 22* (1969), 69–77.

Borges, Jorge Luis. *Labyrinths*. New York: New Directions, 1964.

Bradbrook, Muriel C. *The School of Night. A Study in the Literary Relationships of Sir Walter Raleigh*. Cambridge: Cambridge Univ. Press, 1936.

Brereton, J. Le Gay. *Writings on Elizabethan Drama*. Melbourne: Melbourne Univ. Press, 1948.

Bullough, Geoffrey, ed. *Narrative and Dramatic Sources of Shakespeare*. New York: Columbia Univ. Press, 1957–66.

Bundy, Murray W. "Fracastoro and the Imagination." *PQ*, XX (1941), 236–49.

――――. " 'Invention' and 'Imagination' in the Renaissance." *JEGP*, XXIX (1930), 535–45.

Burckhardt, Sigurd. *The Drama of Language: Essays on Goethe and Kleist*. Baltimore: Johns Hopkins Press, 1970.

――――. *Shakespearean Meanings*. Princeton: Princeton Univ. Press, 1968.

Burton, Robert. *The Anatomy of Melancholy*. Ed. Floyd Dell and Paul Jordan-Smith. New York: Tudor Publishing Co., 1927.

Calderwood, James L. "*Love's Labour's Lost*: A Wantoning with Words." *SEL*, V (1965), 317–32. Rpt. in *Shakespearean Metadrama*. Minneapolis: Univ. of Minnesota Press, 1971.

Campbell, O. J. "*Love's Labour's Lost* Re-Studied." *Studies in Shakespeare, Milton and Donne by Members of the English Department of the University of Michigan*. New York: The Macmillan Co., 1925.

Cassirer, Ernst. *Language and Myth*. New York: Dover Publications, 1946.

Caxton, William. *The Prologues and Epilogues of William Caxton*. Ed. W.J.B. Crotch. London: Oxford Univ. Press, 1928.

Cervantes, Miguel de. *The Adventures of Don Quixote*. Trans. J. M. Cohen. Baltimore: Penguin Books, 1967.

Chambers, E. K. *William Shakespeare. A Study of Facts and Problems*. Oxford: Clarendon Press, 1930.

Chapman, George. *Bussy D'Ambois*. Ed. Nicholas Brooke. Cambridge, Mass.: Harvard Univ. Press, 1964.

Charlton, H. B. *Shakespearian Comedy*. London: Methuen, 1938.

Clark, Eva Turner. *The Satirical Comedy Love's Labour's Lost*. New York: William Farquhar Payson, 1933.

Cody, Richard. *The Landscape of the Mind*. Oxford: Clarendon Press, 1969.

Cole, Howard. *A Quest of Inquirie*. New York: Bobbs-Merrill, 1973.

Coleridge, S. T. *Biographia Literaria*. Ed. J. Shawcross. Oxford: Oxford Univ. Press, 1907.

———. *Shakespearean Criticism*. Ed. T. M. Raysor. 2nd ed. London: J. M. Dent & Sons, 1960.

Crawley, Thomas F. "*Love's Labour's Lost* and the Pageant of The Nine Worthies: A Thematic and Structural Analysis." Diss. Univ. of Nebraska, 1969.

Curtius, Ernst. *European Literature and the Latin Middle Ages*. New York: Pantheon Books, 1953.

Daniel, Samuel. *The Complete Works*. Ed. Alexander B. Grosart. London: Hazell, Watson and Viney, 1885–96.

Davies, John. "Nosce Teipsum." *Silver Poets of the Sixteenth Century*. Ed. Gerald Bullet. London: J. M. Dent & Sons, 1947.

Day, Angel. *The English Secretorie 1586*. Menston, England: Scolar Press, 1967.

Donne, John. *Complete Poetry*. Ed. John T. Shawcross. Garden City, N.Y.: Anchor Books, 1967.

Doran, Madeleine. *Endeavors of Art: A Study of Form in Elizabethan Drama*. Madison: Univ. of Wisconsin Press, 1954.

Dryden, John. *The Poetical Works of Dryden*. Ed. George R. Noyes. Cambridge, Mass.: Houghton Mifflin Co., 1950.

Edwards, Philip. *Shakespeare and the Confines of Art*. London: Methuen, 1968.

Ellis, Herbert A. *Shakespeare's Lusty Punning in Love's Labour's Lost*. The Hague: Mouton, 1973.

Evans, Bertrand. *Shakespeare's Comedies*. Oxford: Clarendon Press, 1960.

Evans, Malcolm. "Mercury Versus Apollo: A Reading of *Love's Labor's Lost*." SQ, XXVI (1975), 113–27.

Fraunce, Abraham. *The Arcadian Rhetoric (1588)*. Menston, Eng.: Scolar Press, 1969.

Frazer, J. G. *The Golden Bough*. New York: Macmillan, 1948.

Frye, Northrop. "Shakespeare's Experimental Comedy." *Stratford Papers on Shakespeare 1961*. Ed. B. W. Jackson. Toronto: 1962.

Galinsky, G. Karl. *The Herakles Theme: The Adaptations of the Hero in Literature from Homer to the Twentieth Century*. Oxford: Basil Blackwell, 1972.

Goldstien, Neal L. "*Love's Labour's Lost* and the Renaissance Vision of Love." *SQ*, XXV (1974), 335–50.

Gollancz, Israel, ed. *The Parlement of the Thre Ages*. London: Nichols & Sons, 1897.

Gosson, Stephen. *The School of Abuse*. London: Shakespeare Society Reprint, 1841.

Gower, John. *The English Works of John Gower*. Ed. G. C. Macaulay. London: K. Paul, Trench, Trubner & Co., 1900–01.

Granville-Barker, Harley. *Prefaces to Shakespeare*. Princeton: Princeton Univ. Press, 1947.

Gray, Henry David. *The Original Version of "Love's Labour's Lost."* Stanford: Stanford Univ. Press, 1918.

Green, William. "Humours, Characters, and Attributive Names in Shakespeare's Plays." *Names*, 20, 157–65.

Greene, Robert. *The Life and Complete Works in Prose and Verse of Robert Greene*. Ed. A. B. Grosart. London: 1881–6.

Greene, Thomas M. "*Love's Labour's Lost*: The Grace of Society." *SQ*, XXII (1971), 315–28.

Hagstrum, Jean. *The Sister Arts*. Chicago: Univ. of Chicago Press, 1958.

Halliwell, J. O., ed. *The Debate and Stryfe Betwene Somer and Wynter*. London: 1860.

Hamilton, A. C. *The Early Shakespeare*. San Marino, Calif.: The Huntington Library, 1967.

Harbage, Alfred. "*Love's Labor's Lost* and The Early

Shakespeare." *Stratford Papers on Shakespeare 1961*. Ed. B. W. Jackson. Toronto: 1962. Rpt. from *PQ*, XLI (1962), 18–36.

Hawes, Stephen. *The Pastime of Pleasure*. Ed. William E. Mead. London: Early English Text Society, 1928.

Hawkes, Terence. "Shakespeare's Talking Animals." *ShS 24* (1971), 47–54.

Haydn, Hiram. *The Counter-Renaissance*. New York: Scribner's Sons, 1950.

Heninger, S. K., Jr. "The Pattern of *Love's Labour's Lost*." *ShakS*, VII (1974), 25–53.

Heywood, Thomas. *An Apology for Actors*. London: Shakespeare Society Reprint, 1841.

———. *Dramatic Works*. New York: Russell & Russell, 1964.

Hibbard, G. R. *Thomas Nashe. A Critical Introduction*. Cambridge, Mass.: Harvard Univ. Press, 1962.

Hoskins, John. *Directions for Speech and Style*. Ed. Hoyt H. Hudson. Princeton: Princeton Univ. Press, 1935.

Howell, A. C. "*Res et Verba*: Words and Things." *ELH*, 13 (1946), 131–42. Rpt. in *Seventeenth Century Prose: Modern Essays in Criticism*. Ed. Stanley E. Fish. New York: Oxford Univ. Press, 1971.

Huizinga, Johan. *The Waning of the Middle Ages*. London: Edward Arnold Ltd., 1955.

Hunt, John D. "Grace, Art and the Neglect of Time in *Love's Labour's Lost*." *Shakespearian Comedy*. Stratford-upon-Avon Studies 14, 1972.

Hunter, G. K. *John Lyly: The Humanist as Courtier*. Cambridge, Mass.: Harvard Univ. Press, 1962.

Hunter, Robert G. "The Function of the Songs at the End of *Love's Labour's Lost*." *ShakS*, VII (1974), 55–64.

Johnson, Samuel. *Johnson on Shakespeare*. Ed. Walter Raleigh. London: Oxford Univ. Press, 1908.

Jones, R. F. "Science and Language in England of the Mid-Seventeenth Century." *JEGP*, XXXI (1932), 315–31. Rpt. in *Seventeenth Century Prose: Modern Essays in*

Criticism. Ed. Stanley E. Fish. New York: Oxford Univ. Press, 1971.

Jonson, Ben. *Ben Jonson: The Complete Masques.* Ed. Stephen Orgel. New Haven: Yale Univ. Press, 1969.

————. *Works.* Ed. C. H. Herford and Percy Simpson. Oxford: Clarendon Press, 1925–47.

King, Arthur H. *The Language of Satirized Characters in Poetaster.* Lund Studies in English, X (1941). Lund: 1941.

Knowles, Richard. "Myth and Type in *As You Like It.*" *ELH,* 33 (1966), 1–22.

Kökeritz, Helge. *Shakespeare's Pronunciation.* New Haven: Yale Univ. Press, 1953.

Lea, K. M. *Italian Popular Comedy.* New York: Russell & Russell, 1962.

Lefranc, Abel. *Sous le Masque de "William Shakespeare."* Paris: Payot, 1918–19.

Leishman, J. B., ed. *The Three Parnassus Plays.* London: Nicholson & Watson, 1949.

Lennam, Trevor. " 'The ventricle of memory': Wit and Wisdom in *Love's Labour's Lost.*" *SQ,* XXIV (1973), 54–60.

Lever, J. W. *The Elizabethan Love Sonnet.* London: Methuen, 1956.

————. "Three Notes on Shakespeare's Plants." *RES,* n.s. III (1952), 117–20.

Levin, Harry. "Shakespeare's Nomenclature." *Essays on Shakespeare.* Ed. Gerald W. Chapman. Princeton: Princeton Univ. Press, 1965.

Lydgate, John. *The Assembly of Gods.* Ed. O. L. Triggs. Chicago: Early English Text Society, 1895.

Mack, Maynard. "Engagement and Detachment in Shakespeare's Plays." *Essays on Shakespeare and Elizabethan Drama in Honor of Hardin Craig.* Ed. Richard Hosley. Columbia, Mo.: Univ. of Missouri Press, 1962.

McLay, Catherine M. "The Dialogues of Spring and Winter: A Key to the Unity of *Love's Labour's Lost.*" *SQ,* XVIII (1967), 119–27.

Mahood, M. M. *Shakespeare's Wordplay*. London: Methuen, 1957.

Marston, John. *Plays*. Ed. H. H. Wood. Edinburgh: Oliver and Boyd, 1934–9.

Matthews, William. "Language in 'Love's Labour's Lost.'" *Essays and Studies*, 1964, 1–11.

McKee, Kenneth. *Scenarios of the Commedia dell'Arte*. Trans. Henry F. Salerno. New York: New York Univ. Press, 1967.

Middleton, Thomas. *Works*. Ed. A. H. Bullen. London: J. C. Nimmo, 1885–6.

Milton, John. *Complete Poems and Major Prose*. Ed. Merritt Y. Hughes. New York: Odyssey Press, 1957.

Mulcaster, Richard. *The First Part of the Elementary 1582*. Menston, Eng.: Scolar Press, 1970.

Nashe, Thomas. *The Works of Thomas Nashe*. Ed. R. B. McKerrow, rev. F. P. Wilson. Oxford: Basil Blackwell, 1958.

Nevinson, John L. "A Show of the Nine Worthies." *SQ*, XIV (1963), 103–7.

Nichols, John G., ed. *The Chronicle of Queen Jane and of Two Years of Queen Mary*. London: Camden Society, No. 48, 1850.

Oakeshott, Walter. *The Queen and the Poet*. London: Faber and Faber, 1960.

Ogden, C. K. "The Magic of Words." *Psyche*, XIV (1943), 9–87.

Panofsky, Erwin. *Hercules am Scheidewege. Studien der Bibliothex Warburg 18*. Leipzig: 1930.

———. *Studies in Iconology*. New York: Harper & Row, 1967.

Parsons, Philip. "Shakespeare and the Mask." *ShS 16* (1963), 121–31.

Peacham, Henry. *The Garden of Eloquence*. Gainesville, Fla.: Scholars' Facsimiles & Reprints, 1954.

Piaget, Jean. *The Child's Conception of the World*. Totowa, N.J.: Littlefield, Adams & Co., 1972.

Plato, *Cratylus*. Trans. H. N. Fowler. Cambridge, Mass.: Harvard Univ. Press, 1953.

Puttenham, George. *The Arte of English Poesie*. Ed. Gladys D. Willcock and Alice Walker. Cambridge: Cambridge Univ. Press, 1936.

Ralegh, Sir Walter. *Works*. New York: Burt Franklin, orig. pub. 1829.

Roberts, John H. "The Nine Worthies." *MP*, XIX (1921), 297–305.

Roberts, Michael A. "Marlowe's *Tamburlaine*: A Study of Verbalism in the Drama." Diss. Yale Univ., 1969.

Roesen, Bobbyann. "*Love's Labour's Lost*." *SQ*, IV (1953), 411–26.

Schrickx, W. *Shakespeare's Early Contemporaries. The Background of the Harvey-Nashe Polemic and Love's Labour's Lost*. Antwerp: Nederlandsche Boekhandel, 1956.

Shakespeare, William. *Love's Labour's Lost*. Ed. Richard David. Fifth edn. London: Methuen, 1956.

———. *Love's Labour's Lost*. Ed. H. H. Furness. New York: Dover Publications, 1964 (rpt. of 1904 third edition).

———. *Love's Labour's Lost*. Ed. John Dover Wilson. Second edn. Cambridge: Cambridge Univ. Press, 1962.

Smith, G. C. Moore, ed. *Gabriel Harvey's Marginalia*. Stratford-upon-Avon: Shakespeare Head Press, 1913.

Smith, G. Gregory, ed. *Elizabethan Critical Essays*. Oxford: Oxford Univ. Press, 1904.

Smith, Hallett. "Leontes' Affectio." *SQ*, XIV (1963), 163–6.

Soellner, Rolf. "The Madness of Herakles and the Elizabethans." *Comp. Lit.*, 10 (1958), 309–24.

Stratton, L. D. "The Nine Worthies." *Ashland Studies in Shakespeare*, 1956, 67–97.

Swift, Jonathan. *Gulliver's Travels*. Ed. Herbert Davis. Oxford: Basil Blackwell, 1959.

———. *A Proposal for Correcting the English Tongue*. Ed.

Herbert Davis with Louis Landa. Oxford: Basil Blackwell, 1957.

Sylvester, Joshua. *Works*. Ed. A. B. Grosart. New York: AMS Press, 1967.

Tayler, Edward W. *Nature and Art in Renaissance Literature*. New York: Columbia Univ. Press, 1964.

Taylor, Rupert. *The Date of Love's Labour's Lost*. New York: Columbia Univ. Press, 1932.

Thomson, J.A.K. *Shakespeare and the Classics*. London: George Allen & Unwin Ltd., 1952.

Tufte, Virginia. *Grammar as Style*. New York: Holt, Rinehart and Winston, 1971.

Tuve, Rosemond. *Elizabethan and Metaphysical Imagery*. Chicago: Univ. of Chicago Press, 1947.

Venezky, Alice S. *Pageantry on the Shakespearean Stage*. New York: Twayne Publishers, 1951.

Waith, E. M. *The Herculean Hero*. New York: Columbia Univ. Press, 1962.

Wells, John E., ed. *The Owl and the Nightingale*. Boston: D. C. Heath and Co., 1907.

Westlund, Joseph. "Fancy and Achievement in *Love's Labour's Lost*." *SQ*, XVIII (1967), 37–46.

White, Harold O. *Plagiarism and Imitation During the English Renaissance*. Cambridge, Mass.: Harvard Univ. Press, 1935.

Wilkinson, L. P. *Ovid Recalled*. Cambridge: Cambridge Univ. Press, 1955.

Wilson, Thomas. *The Arte of Rhetorique*. Gainesville, Fla.: Scholars' Facsimiles & Reprints, 1962.

Yates, Frances A. *The French Academies of the Sixteenth Century*. London: The Warburg Institute, 1947.

———. *A Study of Love's Labour's Lost*. Cambridge: Cambridge Univ. Press, 1936.

Young, David P. *Something of Great Constancy: The Art of "A Midsummer Night's Dream."* New Haven: Yale Univ. Press, 1966.

Related Works

Anderson, J. J. "The Morality of 'Love's Labour's Lost.'" *ShS 24* (1971), 55–62.

Boughner, Daniel C. *The Braggart in Renaissance Comedy.* Minneapolis: Univ. of Minnesota Press, 1954.

Bradbrook, Muriel C. "Fifty Years of the Criticism of Shakespeare's Style: A Retrospect." *ShS 7* (1954), 1–11.

———. *The Growth and Structure of Elizabethan Comedy.* London: Chatto & Windus, 1955.

———. *Shakespeare and Elizabethan Poetry.* London: Penguin Books, 1964.

Bronson, Bertrand. "Daisies Pied and Icicles." *MLN*, LXIII (1948), 35–8.

Brown, John Russell. "The Interpretation of Shakespeare's Comedies: 1900–1953." *ShS 8* (1955), 1–13.

———. *Shakespeare and His Comedies.* 2nd edn. London: Methuen, 1962.

Champion, Larry S. *The Evolution of Shakespeare's Comedy.* Cambridge, Mass.: Harvard Univ. Press, 1970.

Charlton, H. B. "The Date of *Love's Labour's Lost.*" *MLR*, XIII (1918), 257–66, 387–400.

———. "A Textual Note on *Love's Labour's Lost.*" *The Library*, 8 (1917), 355.

Colie, Rosalie. *Shakespeare's Living Art.* Princeton: Princeton Univ. Press, 1974.

Craig, Hardin, ed. *Two Coventry Corpus Christi Plays.* 2nd edn. London: Oxford Univ. Press, 1957.

Croft-Murray, Edward. "Lambert Barnard: An English Early Renaissance Painter." *Archaeological Journal*, CXIII (1956), 108–25.

Cunningham, J. V. " 'With That Facility': False Starts and Revisions in *Love's Labour's Lost.*" *Essays on Shakespeare.* Ed. Gerald W. Chapman. Princeton: Princeton Univ. Press, 1965.

Evans, B. Ifor. *The Language of Shakespeare's Plays.* 2nd edn. London: Methuen, 1959.

Furnivall, F. J. "The Nine Worthies and the Heraldic Arms They Bore." *N&Q*, 7th ser., VIII (1889), 22–3.

Godshalk, William L. "Pattern in *Love's Labour's Lost.*" *Renaissance Papers 1968*, 41–8.

Gray, Austin K. "The Secret of *Love's Labour's Lost.*" *PMLA*, XXXIX (1924), 581–611.

Hill, R. F. "Delight and Laughter: Some Aspects of Shakespeare's Early Verbal Comedy." *ShStud*, 3 (1964), 1–21.

Howard-Hill, Dr. T. H., ed. *Love's Labour's Lost. A Concordance to the Text of the First Quarto of 1598.* Oxford: Clarendon Press, 1970.

Hoy, Cyrus. "*Love's Labour's Lost* and the Nature of Comedy." *SQ*, XIII (1962), 31–40.

Hulme, Hilda M. *Explorations in Shakespeare's Language.* London: Longmans, Green & Co., 1962.

Joseph, Sister Miriam. *Shakespeare's Use of the Arts of Language.* New York: Columbia Univ. Press, 1947.

Lawrence, Natalie Grimes. "A Study of Taffeta Phrases and Honest Kershey Noes." *Sweet Smoke of Rhetoric.* Ed. Natalie Grimes Lawrence and J. A. Reynolds. Univ. of Miami Publications in English and American Literature, VII (1964), 93–107.

Loomis, R. S. "Verses on the Nine Worthies." *MP*, XV (1917), 211–19.

McFarland, Thomas. *Shakespeare's Pastoral Comedy.* Chapel Hill: Univ. of North Carolina Press, 1972.

Phialas, Peter G. *Shakespeare's Romantic Comedies.* Chapel Hill: Univ. of North Carolina Press, 1966.

Reader, Francis W. "Tudor Mural Paintings in the Lesser Houses in Bucks." *Archaeological Journal*, LXXXIX (1932), 116–73.

Reid, J. S. "Shakespeare's 'Living Art'." *PQ*, I (1922), 226–7.

Righter, Anne. *Shakespeare and The Idea of The Play*. London: Chatto & Windus, 1962.

Shakespeare, William. *Love's Labour's Lost 1598*. *Shakespeare Quarto Facsimiles No. 10*. Ed. W. W. Greg. Oxford: Clarendon Press, 1957.

Sorenssen, Fred. "The Masque of Muscovites in *Love's Labour's Lost*." *MLN*, I (1935), 499–501.

Stevenson, David L. *The Love-Game Comedy*. New York: Columbia Univ. Press, 1946.

Talbert, Ernest W. *Elizabethan Drama and Shakespeare's Early Plays*. Chapel Hill: Univ. of North Carolina Press, 1963.

Tillyard, E.M.W. *Shakespeare's Early Comedies*. London: Chatto & Windus, 1965.

Vyvyan, John. *Shakespeare and Platonic Beauty*. New York: Barnes & Noble, 1961.

———. *Shakespeare and the Rose of Love*. New York: Barnes & Noble, 1960.

Willcock, Gladys D. "Shakespeare and Elizabethan English." *ShS* 7 (1954), 12–24.

———. "Shakespeare and Rhetoric." *Essays and Studies*, 1943, 50–61.

———. *Shakespeare as Critic of Language*. The Shakespeare Association, vol. 18, 1934.

Wilson, John Dover. *Shakespeare's Happy Comedies*. Evanston: Northwestern Univ. Press, 1962.

Withington, Robert. *English Pageantry*. Cambridge, Mass.: Harvard Univ. Press, 1918–20.

Notes

Introduction

¹ M. C. Bradbrook, *The School of Night. A Study in the Literary Relationships of Sir Walter Raleigh* (Cambridge: Cambridge Univ. Press, 1936); Eva Turner Clark, *The Satirical Comedy Love's Labour's Lost* (New York: William Farquhar Payson, 1933); Thomas F. Crawley, "*Love's Labour's Lost* and the Pageant of the Nine Worthies: A Thematic and Structural Analysis," Diss. Nebraska, 1969; Herbert A. Ellis, *Shakespeare's Lusty Punning in Love's Labour's Lost* (The Hague: Mouton, 1973); Henry D. Gray, *The Original Version of "Love's Labour's Lost" With a Conjecture as to "Love's Labour's Won"* (Stanford: Stanford Univ. Press, 1918); Abel Lefranc, *Sous le Masque de "William Shakespeare"* (Paris: Payot, 1918–19); Walter Oakeshott, *The Queen and the Poet* (London: Faber & Faber, 1960); W. Schrickx, *Shakespeare's Early Contemporaries. The Background of the Harvey-Nashe Polemic and Love's Labour's Lost* (Antwerp: Nederlandsche Boekhandel, 1956); Rupert Taylor, *The Date of Love's Labour's Lost* (New York: Columbia Univ. Press, 1932); Frances A. Yates, *A Study of Love's Labour's Lost* (Cambridge: Cambridge Univ. Press, 1936).

² Attributed to Dryden in *The Poetical Works of Dryden*, ed. George R. Noyes (Cambridge, Mass.: Houghton Mifflin, 1950), p. 912.

³ A. C. Hamilton, *The Early Shakespeare* (San Marino, Calif.: The Huntington Library, 1967), p. 5.

⁴ See the *Arden* discussion, pp. xxxii–xxxv.

⁵ Thus Holofernes is taken as an anagram for "Iohnesfloreo" (John Florio), or else he may represent Harriot, Chapman, even Bruno. Armado usually equals Ralegh, Lyly, or Gabriel Harvey. Moth is definitely Nashe, if not a French ambassador named La Mothe-Fenelon, and the four lords are said to suggest

Ralegh or Southampton and their circle. The most elaborate and reasonable exposition of topical allegory is found in Miss Yates' book.

⁶ E. K. Chambers, *William Shakespeare. A Study of Facts and Problems* (Oxford: Clarendon Press, 1930), II, 332.

⁷ Walter Raleigh, ed., *Johnson on Shakespeare* (London: Oxford Univ. Press, 1965), p. 89.

⁸ S. T. Coleridge, *Shakespearean Criticism*, ed. T. M. Raysor (London: J. M. Dent & Sons, 1960), I, 83.

⁹ Taylor, p. 70.

¹⁰ H. B. Charlton, *Shakespearian Comedy* (London: Methuen, 1938), p. 270.

¹¹ James L. Calderwood, "*Love's Labour's Lost:* A Wantoning with Words," *SEL*, V (1965), p. 329.

¹² Harley Granville-Barker, *Prefaces to Shakespeare* (Princeton: Princeton Univ. Press, 1947), II, 423.

¹³ Geoffrey Bullough, *Narrative and Dramatic Sources of Shakespeare* (New York: Columbia Univ. Press, 1961), I, 427.

¹⁴ Bobbyann Roesen, "*Love's Labour's Lost*," *SQ*, IV (1953), 411–26.

¹⁵ The term is David Young's, *Something of Great Constancy: The Art of "A Midsummer Night's Dream"* (New Haven: Yale Univ. Press, 1966), pp. 91–4.

¹⁶ I have assumed a date of composition for the play between 1593 and 1597, probably 1594—see the discussions in the *Arden* (pp. xxxi–xxxii) and *Cambridge* (pp. xxi–xxii, 124–9) editions. In "*Love's Labor's Lost* and The Early Shakespeare," *Stratford Papers on Shakespeare 1961* (Toronto: 1962), however, Alfred Harbage has strongly argued the belief that the play was written about 1588–89 and revised about 1596–97 (p. 119), and that it may have been written for one of the boys' companies. I have also assumed that *The Comedy of Errors, The Two Gentlemen of Verona*, and *The Taming of the Shrew* were written before *Love's Labour's Lost*, and that *A Midsummer Night's Dream* came after it.

CHAPTER ONE

¹ Ernst Cassirer, *Language and Myth* (New York: Dover Publications, 1946), pp. 84, 97. For the history of this idea, see

also the discussions in C. K. Ogden, "The Magic of Words," *Psyche*, XIV (1943), 9–87; D. C. Allen, "Some Theories of the Growth and Origin of Language in Milton's Age," *PQ*, XXVIII (1949), 5–16; and the excellent summary in the final chapter of M. M. Mahood's *Shakespeare's Wordplay* (London: Methuen, 1968). For another perspective see the second chapter of Jean Piaget's *The Child's Conception of the World* (Totowa, N.J.: Littlefield, Adams & Co., 1972). I owe a large general debt to Mahood's fine study, although I disagree with her belief that the ending of the play suggests the conclusion that "there is no substance in speech" (p. 176). I have also found the fine article by James L. Calderwood, *"Love's Labour's Lost:* A Wantoning with Words," *SEL*, V (1965), 317–32, to be of great interest, although his sense of the women's importance as linguistic reforming agents differs somewhat from my emphasis on the songs' similar role.

[2] Plato, *Cratylus*, trans. H. N. Fowler (Cambridge: Harvard Univ. Press, 1953), p. 183.

[3] Richard Mulcaster, *The First Part of the Elementary 1582* (Menston, England: Scolar Press, 1970), p. 167.

[4] Mulcaster, p. 167.

[5] Joshua Sylvester, *Works*, ed. A. B. Grosart (New York: AMS Press, 1967), p. 140 (ll. 263, 283–6, 407–9).

[6] Quoted in Michael A. Roberts, "Marlowe's *Tamburlaine:* A Study of Verbalism in the Drama," Diss. Yale 1969, p. 103.

[7] Sylvester, p. 140 (ll. 272–9).

[8] The entire section on rhetoric in Canto I (ll. 81–118) seems to describe Holofernes.

[9] John Milton, *Complete Poems and Major Prose*, ed. M. Y. Hughes (New York: Odyssey Press, 1957), p. 631.

[10] Mahood, p. 170.

[11] Sigurd Burckhardt, *The Drama of Language: Essays on Goethe and Kleist* (Baltimore: Johns Hopkins Press, 1970), p. 3.

[12] In a fascinating article entitled "Shakespeare's Nomenclature," in *Essays on Shakespeare*, ed. Gerald W. Chapman (Princeton: Princeton Univ. Press, 1965), Harry Levin explains the "psychological onomatopoeia" of many of the names of Shakespeare's characters. William Green does something similar in "Humours, Characters, and Attributive Names in Shakespeare's Plays," *Names*, 20, 157–65.

¹³ Thomas Wilson, *The Arte of Rhetorique* (Gainesville, Fla.: Scholars' Facsimiles & Reprints, 1962), pp. 192, 193; Abraham Fraunce, *The Arcadian Rhetoric* (*1588*) (Menston, Eng.: Scolar Press, 1969), Sig. A3ᵛ.

¹⁴ S. T. Coleridge, *Biographia Literaria*, ed. J. Shawcross (Oxford: Oxford Univ. Press, 1907), I, 61.

¹⁵ See Frances A. Yates, *The French Academies of the Sixteenth Century* (London: The Warburg Institute, 1947), for the widespread currency of the idea.

¹⁶ Terence Hawkes, "Shakespeare's Talking Animals," *ShS 24* (1971), p. 51.

¹⁷ Malcolm Evans, "Mercury Versus Apollo: A Reading of *Love's Labor's Lost,*" *SQ*, XXVI (1975), p. 122.

¹⁸ "Euphuism" is a term often too loosely used with reference to the parody in this play. For a very specific imitation of euphuism, see Falstaff in *1H4*, II.iv.380–4.

¹⁹ Cf. the same pun in *Much Ado About Nothing*, V.ii.3–6.

²⁰ Sigurd Burckhardt, *Shakespearean Meanings* (Princeton: Princeton Univ. Press, 1968), pp. 24–5.

²¹ Kenneth McKee, *Scenarios of the Commedia dell'Arte*, trans. Henry F. Salerno (New York: New York Univ. Press, 1967), p. xv.

²² It is at least twice spelled by one Elizabethan writer as the "ix wordes"—*The Diary of Henry Machyn, Citizen and Merchant-Taylor of London* (*1550–1563*), ed. J. G. Nichols (London, 1848), pp. 47–8; quoted in Howard Cole, *A Quest of Inquirie* (New York: Bobbs-Merrill, 1973), p. 390.

²³ David, in the *Arden* edition, silently alters the "vnderstoode" of the Quarto to "understand."

²⁴ O. J. Campbell, "*Love's Labour's Lost* Re-Studied," in *Studies in Shakespeare, Milton and Donne by Members of the English Department of the University of Michigan* (New York: Macmillan, 1925), pp. 42–3.

²⁵ J. Le Gay Brereton, *Writings on Elizabethan Drama* (Melbourne: Melbourne Univ. Press, 1948), p. 91.

²⁶ Henry Peacham, *The Garden of Eloquence* (Gainesville, Fla.: Scholars' Facsimiles & Reprints, 1954), p. 27; see also Puttenham, p. 188.

²⁷ Herbert A. Ellis, *Shakespeare's Lusty Punning in Love's Labour's Lost* (The Hague: Mouton, 1973), pp. 58–9.

[28] Pointed out by Northrop Frye, "Shakespeare's Experimental Comedy," *Stratford Papers on Shakespeare 1961* (Toronto, 1962), p. 12.

[29] Angel Day, *The English Secretorie 1586* (Menston, England: Scolar Press, 1967), p. 43.

[30] Jonathan Swift, *Gulliver's Travels*, ed. Herbert Davis (Oxford: Basil Blackwell, 1959), pp. 185–6.

[31] O. J. Campbell, p. 34.

[32] Hawkes, p. 51.

[33] Walter Raleigh, ed., *Johnson on Shakespeare* (London: Oxford Univ. Press, 1908), p. 88.

[34] Samuel Daniel, *Complete Works*, ed. A. B. Grosart (London: Hazell, Watson and Viney, 1885–96), I, 255–6.

[35] Helge Kökeritz, *Shakespeare's Pronunciation* (New Haven: Yale Univ. Press, 1953), pp. 296–7. For more on this subject, see G. D. Willcock, *Shakespeare as Critic of Language*, The Shakespeare Association, Vol. 18 (1934); William Matthews, "Language in 'Love's Labour's Lost,'" *Essays and Studies* (1964), 1–11; and Baldwin.

[36] Jonathan Swift, *A Proposal for Correcting the English Tongue*, ed. Herbert Davis with Louis Landa (Oxford: Basil Blackwell, 1957), p. 14.

[37] J.A.K. Thomson, *Shakespeare and the Classics* (London: George Allen & Unwin, 1952), p. 68.

[38] Quoted in Virginia Tufte, *Grammar as Style* (New York: Holt, Rinehart and Winston, 1971), p. 41.

[39] Holofernes' poem may have reminded the audience of another infamously bad rhyming poem, *Pugna Porcorum per P. Porcium Poetam*, by a friar, Joannes Leo Placentius. It was published c. 1530 (Hoskins, p. 69) and kept in print throughout the sixteenth century. Every word of the 250 lines began with the letter P. Hoskins' term for the poem was—naturally—"swinish."

[40] Cf. Touchstone's parody of the figure in *AYL*, V.i.46–52.

[41] Hoskins (pp. 30–1), Peacham (pp. 130–1), and Fraunce (Sig. A8ʳ) all give "let pass" as examples.

[42] Kökeritz, p. 320.

[43] See *Variorum* note, p. 5; *Arden* note at IV.iii.149; and *MND*, V.i.307–11. The pun is also pointed out in G. K. Hunter, *John Lyly* (Cambridge, Mass.: Harvard Univ. Press, 1962), p. 366.

[44] G. R. Hibbard, *Thomas Nashe* (Cambridge, Mass.: Harvard Univ. Press, 1962), p. 121. But see also the *Arden* discussion, pp. xxxix–xliv.

[45] Arthur H. King, *The Language of Satirized Characters in Poetaster* (Lund: Lund Studies in English, 1941), p. xxxiii.

[46] See A. C. Howell, "*Res et Verba:* Words and Things," in *Seventeenth Century Prose: Modern Essays in Criticism*, ed. Stanley E. Fish (New York: Oxford Univ. Press, 1971), pp. 187–99; rpt. from *ELH*, 13 (1946), 131–42.

[47] R. F. Jones, "Science and Language in England of the Mid-Seventeenth Century," in *Seventeenth Century Prose*, p. 104; rpt. from *JEGP*, XXXI (1932), 315–31.

CHAPTER TWO

[1] The terms are those of Maynard Mack, "Engagement and Detachment in Shakespeare's Plays," *Essays on Shakespeare and Elizabethan Drama in Honor of Hardin Craig*, ed. Richard Hosley (Columbia, Mo.: Univ. of Missouri Press, 1962), pp. 275–96.

[2] Or he may have climbed to an upper stage. See Dover Wilson's note to IV.iii.19 (*Cam.*, p. 163).

[3] Cf. a similar scene in *Troilus and Cressida* (V.ii). Bertrand Evans briefly describes the sonnet-reading scene and the Masque of Muscovites in similar terms in *Shakespeare's Comedies* (Oxford: Clarendon Press, 1960), pp. 19–24.

[4] Mack, p. 289.

[5] In " 'The ventricle of memory': Wit and Wisdom in *Love's Labour's Lost*," *SQ*, XXIV (1973), 54–60, Trevor Lennam suggests that the moral pattern of the Wit moralities, such as John Redford's *Wit and Science*, stands behind the play. He does not mention Berowne's speech in IV.iii, however. Cf. also Armado's mention of an "evil angel" (I.ii.162). In "Berowne and the Progress of *Love's Labour's Lost*," *ShakS*, IV (1968), Gates K. Agnew also notices this echo of the Morality tradition, and he points to Neither-Lover-Nor-Loved in John Heywood's *Play of Love* (pp. 68–9, n. 10) as possibly one of Berowne's ancestors.

[6] This is still far from the gracious sympathy Theseus displays to the mechanicals (*MND*, V.i.81–3).

[7] See the *Arden* discussion, pp. xxx–xxxi, of possible sources.

[8] In "*Love's Labour's Lost* and the Renaissance Vision of

Love," *SQ*, XXV (1974), Neal Goldstien argues that the entire Masque "is a sensually-based parody of the Petrarchan-Neoplatonic vision of love" (p. 344).

⁹ For background of the Worthies, see the Appendix.

¹⁰ See David Young's discussion in *Something of Great Constancy: The Art of "A Midsummer Night's Dream"* (New Haven: Yale Univ. Press, 1966), pp. 32–59.

¹¹ In "A Show of the Nine Worthies," *SQ*, XIV (1963), 103–107, John L. Nevinson explains a part of the joke through reference to contemporary illustrations of Alexander.

¹² See Appendix.

¹³ E. M. Waith, *The Herculean Hero* (New York: Columbia Univ. Press, 1962), p. 65. On "Ercles' vein," see Young, pp. 34–41.

¹⁴ John Donne, *Complete Poetry*, ed. John T. Shawcross (Garden City, N.Y.: Anchor Books, 1967), p. 286.

CHAPTER THREE

¹ George Chapman, *Bussy D'Ambois*, ed. Nicholas Brooke (Cambridge, Mass.: Harvard Univ. Press, 1964), II.ii.186–8. Cf. Shylock in *The Merchant of Venice*: "for affection, / Master of passion, sways it to the mood / Of what it likes or loathes" (IV.i.50–2).

² Quoted in Madeleine Doran, *Endeavors of Art* (Madison: Univ. of Wisconsin Press, 1954), p. 219. Cf. John Davies, "Nosce teipsum," pp. 376–8, in *Silver Poets of the Sixteenth Century*, ed. Gerald Bullet (New York: Dutton, 1947).

³ See the discussions of this passage in the *Arden* (pp. 165–7) and *Variorum* (pp. 27–31) editions of *The Winter's Tale*, as well as Hallet Smith's "Leontes' *Affectio*," *SQ*, XIV (1963), 163–6.

⁴ Quoted by Rosemond Tuve, *Elizabethan and Metaphysical Imagery* (Chicago: Univ. of Chicago Press, 1947), p. 182, from the 1577 edition of *The Garden of Eloquence*.

⁵ Stephen Gosson, *The School of Abuse* (London: Shakespeare Society Reprint, 1841), p. 22.

⁶ Language does not, however, similarly reveal the women in this play. The word "affection" is never used by or about the ladies, indicating perhaps that in them the affections are securely

balanced by cool reason. The women are clearly the moral center of the play, the "teachers" of the immature academics. For a dissenting viewpoint, see Philip Edwards, *Shakespeare and the Confines of Art* (London: Methuen, 1968), p. 45.

[7] J. W. Lever, *The Elizabethan Love Sonnet* (London: Methuen, 1956), p. 92.

[8] Lever, p. 143.

[9] A list of the other authors included in *England's Helicon*—Sidney, Spenser, Drayton, Greene, Lodge, Breton, Peele, Surrey, Dyer, Marlowe—suggests that the editor looked chiefly to the earlier generation of Elizabethan lyricists. In a recent article, "*Love's Labour's Lost* and the Renaissance Vision of Love," *SQ*, XXV (1974), Neal Goldstien outlines the extensive background of Florentine Neoplatonism and Petrarchanism against which much of the play, and especially the lords' poems, is directed. He sees the play as firmly iconoclastic: it "seems in its entirety a vehicle for the discarding of the higher ideals of another age" (p. 339), and he argues that the lords' poems represent in context a "veiled attack . . . upon the central principle of Renaissance love theory" (p. 344). I agree with Goldstien here, and will try to extend his argument to include Renaissance poetic theory as well.

[10] See the discussion of this trope by Curtius, pp. 302–47.

[11] There is some dispute whether Holofernes is correct here; see the *Arden* note at IV.ii.117.

[12] Cf. Longaville's comment when he observes Berowne's recognition of his own mis-delivered sonnet: "It did move him to passion, and therefore let's hear it" (IV.iii.200).

[13] Goldstien, p. 347.

[14] In *Shakespeare and the Classics* (London: George Allen & Unwin, 1952), however, J.A.K. Thomson holds that the verses "are in fact distinctly Ovidian—or let us say Neo-Ovidian, Renaissance-Ovidian. Holofernes is such an ass that he does not recognize the Ovidian qualities when he meets them" (p. 187). But Goldstien describes the lords' sonnets, including Berowne's, as by and large "conventional Petrarchan complaints" (p. 344).

[15] L. P. Wilkinson, *Ovid Recalled* (Cambridge: Cambridge Univ. Press, 1955), p. 412.

[16] This point has recently received a concise but thorough discussion by Howard Cole, *A Quest of Inquirie* (New York:

Bobbs–Merrill, 1973), pp. 216–26. See also his material on the background of Holofernes' other pronouncements, pp. 208–16. Also helpful is Harold O. White, *Plagiarism and Imitation During the English Renaissance* (Cambridge, Mass.: Harvard Univ. Press, 1935).

[17] *Arte*, p. 3. Cf. Sidney in Smith, I, 158; and Ben Jonson's *Timber*: "The third requisite in our *Poet*, or Maker, is *Imitation*, to bee able to convert the substance, or Riches of an other *Poet*, to his owne use" (VIII, 638).

[18] T. W. Baldwin cites Quintilian (II, 234). But see Cole, pp. 216–26.

[19] Cf. Jonson's poem, "On Poet-Ape" (VIII, 44).

[20] For a discussion of the troublesome "fox, ape, and humble-bee" riddle (III.i.82–96), see the *Arden* edition, pp. xlii–xliii, and *Cambridge* edition, p. xxxvii.

[21] White, p. 18.

[22] Thomson, p. 155.

[23] J. B. Leishman, ed., *The Three Parnassus Plays* (London: Nicholson & Watson, 1949), p. 192 (ll. 1191–7).

[24] This aspect of the play is discussed at length by Gates K. Agnew, "Berowne and the Progress of Love's Labour's Lost," *ShakS*, IV (1968), 40–72.

[25] Cf. the same pun in *Twelfth Night*, I.v.185–6.

[26] Jorge Luis Borges, *Labyrinths* (New York: New Directions, 1964), pp. 36–44.

[27] The parallels, both thematic and stylistic, between *Love's Labour's Lost* and the sonnets have often been noted. Sonnet 127, for example, contains several echoes of Berowne's declaration that "black is fair." Three of the lords' sonnets, moreover, were included in the same collection, *The Passionate Pilgrim* (1599), as were sonnets 138 and 144. But the lords' sonnets would have suffered considerably by contrast had they been in the same collection as, say, sonnets 73, 94, or 129.

Chapter Four

[1] Murray W. Bundy, "Fracastoro and the Imagination," *PQ*, XX (1941), pp. 238–9.

[2] John Davies, "Nosce teipsum," *Silver Poets of the Sixteenth Century*, ed. Gerald Bullet (New York: Dutton, 1947), p. 377.

Bacon develops the same image in the *Advancement of Learning*: "God hath framed the mind of man as a mirror or glass etc." (III, 265).

[3] Cf. for example Puttenham's *Arte*, p. 15. And Jonson: Shakespeare "had an excellent *Phantsie* . . . wherein hee flow'd with that facility, that sometime it was necessary he should be stop'd" (VIII, 584), but Jonson said of himself that he was "oppressed with fantasie, which hath ever mastered his reason, a generall disease in many poets" (I, 151). Cf. also the speech of Quadratus in Marston's *What You Will* (*Plays*, ed. H. H. Wood [Edinburgh: Oliver and Boyd, 1934–9], II, 250), his "Most Phantasticall protection of Phantasticknesse," in which he argues that

> *Phantasticknesse,*
> That which the naturall *Sophysters* tearme
> *Phantusia incomplexa*, is a function
> Even of the bright immortal part of man.
> It is the common passe, the sacred dore,
> Unto the prive chamber of the soule:
> . . .
> By it we shape a new creation,
> Of things as yet unborne, by it wee feede
> Our ravenous memory, our intention feast:
> Slid he thats not Phantasticall's a beast.

[4] Bundy, p. 239. See also his " 'Invention' and 'Imagination' in the Renaissance," *JEGP*, XXIX (1930), 535–45.

[5] Earlier, Moth invokes "My father's wit and my mother's tongue assist me!" (I.ii.90). Rosaline says of Berowne, "His eye begets occasion for his wit" (II.i.69).

[6] Bundy, " 'Invention,' " p. 537.

[7] Davies, p. 377.

[8] Cf. Dante, *Inferno*, XX, 124–6; and *Paradiso*, II, 49–51. Also *MND*, III.i.51–3, and *Tmp*, II.ii.133–7.

[9] James L. Calderwood, "*Love's Labour's Lost*: A Wantoning with Words," *SEL*, V (1965), p. 327.

[10] Cf. *Two Gentlemen*: "I have a sonnet that will serve the turn / To give the onset to thy good advice" (*TGV*, III.ii.92–3). The "trick" here is to see the anagrammatic "turn" in "sonnet" to "onset." Abraham Fraunce, incidentally, declared that "Braverie of speach consisteth in Tropes, or turnings; and in Figures or fashionings"—*The Arcadian Rhetoric* (*1588*) (Menston, Eng.:

Scolar Press, 1969), sig. A3ᵛ. "A Trope or turning," he argued, "is when a word is turned from his naturall signification, to some other."

¹¹ Cf. *Romeo and Juliet*, II.iv.33-4.

¹² Northrop Frye, "Shakespeare's Experimental Comedy," *Stratford Papers on Shakespeare 1961* (Toronto, 1962), p. 7, makes a similar point.

¹³ See the *Arden* note to III.i.16 for other references. The famous Lothian portrait shows Donne in a similar pose.

¹⁴ "Love" or "loves" occurs 115 times; "lover" or "lovers" 12 times; other variants 14 times.

¹⁵ See Erwin Panofsky's discussion of the iconology of "Blind Cupid" in *Studies in Iconology* (New York: Harper & Row, 1967), pp. 95-128.

Chapter Five

¹ In *The Landscape of the Mind* (Oxford: Clarendon Press, 1969), however, Richard Cody has convincingly argued against such interpretations as Berry's, noting that "if a study of pastoralism can do anything, it can correct the view that for the Renaissance artist nature and art are merely opposites. They are rather the opposites which he undertakes to reconcile by imposing the unity of an art that goes beyond art" (p. 122). This chapter attempts to prove the same thing but from a different point of view; my sixth chapter argues that the reconciliation is found in the final songs.

² There is a fine description of this moment in Bobbyann Roesen's "*Love's Labour's Lost*," *SQ*, IV (1953), p. 424.

³ G. K. Hunter, *John Lyly* (Cambridge, Mass.: Harvard Univ. Press, 1962), p. 339. See Hunter's entire discussion of *Love's Labour's Lost*, pp. 330-42.

⁴ Madeleine Doran, *Endeavors of Art* (Madison: Univ. of Wisconsin Press, 1954), p. 311. See also the discussions of the debate form in *The Owl and the Nightingale*, ed. John E. Wells (Boston: D. C. Heath, 1907), pp. liii-lxiv; in *The Owl and the Nightingale*, ed. J.W.H. Atkins (Cambridge: Cambridge Univ. Press, 1922), pp. xlvii-lv; and in Hunter, pp. 118-23.

⁵ *The Debate and Stryfe Betwene Somer and Wynter*, ed. J. O. Halliwell (London, 1860), pp. 16-7.

6 Catherine M. McLay, "The Dialogues of Spring and Winter: A Key to the Unity of *Love's Labour's Lost*," *SQ*, XVIII (1967), p. 121.

7 J. G. Frazer, *The Golden Bough* (New York: Macmillan, 1948), pp. 315–6.

8 See Hiram Haydn, *The Counter-Renaissance* (New York: Scribner's, 1950); Edward Tayler, *Nature and Art in Renaissance Literature* (New York: Columbia Univ. Press, 1964); Doran, pp. 54–70; and Rosemond Tuve, *Elizabethan and Metaphysical Imagery* (Chicago: Univ. of Chicago Press, 1947), passim.

9 Jonas Barish, "The Prose Style of John Lyly," *ELH*, 23 (1956), p. 22.

10 Marvell's "The Garden" is undoubtedly the best-known example of this *topos*.

11 See Appendix on Hercules.

12 Cf. Cervantes in *The Adventures of Don Quixote*, trans. J. M. Cohen (Baltimore: Penguin Books, 1967): "art is not better than nature, but perfects her. So nature combined with art, and art with nature, will produce a perfect poet" (p. 569).

13 See Tuve's chapter, pp. 61–78.

14 Philip Parsons, "Shakespeare and the Mask," *ShS 16* (1963), p. 122.

15 Cf. the same distinction between kersey and velvet in *Measure for Measure*, I.ii.31–4.

16 Cf. Tayler: "the greater number of Elizabethans viewed the Savage Man with contempt and distaste. Far from placing him in the golden world, most Elizabethan accounts of the Savage Man emphasized his brutishness, irrationality, excess, and lack of true religion" (p. 84).

17 Harley Granville-Barker, *Prefaces to Shakespeare Volume II* (Princeton: Princeton Univ. Press, 1947), pp. 425–7.

18 Stephen Gosson, *The School of Abuse* (London: Shakespeare Society Reprint, 1841), p. 10.

19 See Tuve's chapter, pp. 50–60; and Jean Hagstrum's *The Sister Arts* (Chicago: Univ. of Chicago Press, 1958), especially pp. 57–92.

20 Cf. Tayler, pp. 14–5.

21 Cf. *Two Noble Kinsmen*: "O vouchsafe / With that thy rare green eye, which never yet / Beheld thing maculate, look on thy virgin" (V.i.143–5).

[22] See the discussion of this famous problem in the *Arden* edition, pp. xliv–xlvi, and the *Cambridge* edition, pp. xlvii–li.

[23] Cf. *Romeo and Juliet*: "These happy masks that kiss fair ladies' brows, / Being black puts us in mind they hide the fair" (I.i.228–9).

[24] Sigurd Burckhardt, *Shakespearean Meanings* (Princeton: (Princeton Univ. Press, 1968), pp. 22–3.

[25] Quoted in M. H. Abrams, *The Mirror and the Lamp* (New York: Norton, 1958), p. 291.

[26] J. Q. Adams, ed., *Chief Pre-Shakespearean Dramas* (Boston: Houghton Mifflin, 1924), p. 572.

[27] Tuve, pp. 230–1. See her entire discussion, pp. 192–247; and also Doran, pp. 77–9; and Cole, passim.

[28] The "arts and arms" combination occurs frequently in Shakespeare: *Per*, II.iii.83; *2H4*, IV.v.73; *Tro*, IV.iv.77; and *PP*, 15.13. See the Appendix for more on the active/contemplative split.

[29] See the *Arden* note to I.i.14 on the relation between "living art" and the Stoic concept of *ars vivendi*.

[30] Philip Edwards' doubt, in *Shakespeare and the Confines of Art* (London: Methuen, 1968), that "there *may* be weddings at the end of a year" (p. 48), is a lonely exception.

[31] Thomas M. Greene, "*Love's Labour's Lost*: The Grace of Society," *SQ*, XXII (1971), p. 318.

[32] David P. Young, *Something of Great Constancy: The Art of "A Midsummer Night's Dream"* (New Haven: Yale Univ. Press, 1966), p. 147. Several scholars have speculated that this was the end of the original, "unrevised" play.

Chapter Six

[1] The *Cambridge* edition adds an extra "Tu-who" in each stanza of Winter's song to correspond with the "Cuckoo" in ll. 890 and 899 (p. 189).

[2] Thomas M. Greene, "*Love's Labour's Lost*: The Grace of Society," *SQ*, XXII (1971), p. 325.

[3] Richard Cody, *The Landscape of the Mind* (Oxford: Clarendon Press, 1969), p. 121, points out the pun. Some other readers see a link with Mercury (as "Mercade," the French version of Marcade), the messenger of the gods, whose name is invoked at the end of the play.

[4] Catherine M. McLay, "The Dialogues of Spring and Winter: A Key to the Unity of *Love's Labour's Lost*," *SQ*, XVIII (1967), 119–27.

[5] J. W. Lever, "Three Notes on Shakespeare's Plants," *RES*, n.s. III (1952), 117–20.

[6] Cf. *Err*, III.i.31; *Shr*, Ind., ii, 20; *1H4*, III.iii.109; *Tmp*, II.ii.47.

[7] The Quarto reading, however, is "ways be fall." The Heber and Devonshire copies read "be full."

[8] Joseph Westlund, "Fancy and Achievement in *Love's Labour's Lost*," *SQ*, XVIII (1967), p. 45.

[9] "One of the few words which mean nothing without quotes," Vladimir Nabokov, *Lolita* (New York: G. P. Putnam's Sons, 1955), p. 314.

[10] P. 118. Arguing specifically against the passage by Barber quoted in the text, Neal Goldstien ("*Love's Labour's Lost* and the Renaissance Vision of Love," *SQ*, XXV [1974]) finds that the "total view" of the songs, on the contrary, "is one of cynical, and questioning, detachment." He suggests that "they are a cynical look at the sensuality to which the rest of the play has directed itself" (p. 349). I cannot agree with Goldstien here, for I think he has missed the tone, and the thematic significance, of the songs completely.

[11] See the articles dealing with "grace" in its various connotations by Thomas M. Greene and by John D. Hunt, "Grace, Art and the Neglect of Time in *Love's Labour's Lost*," *Shakespearian Comedy* (Stratford-upon-Avon Studies 14, 1972).

[12] Along with most readers of the play, I understand Mercury as the god of eloquence or "words," and Apollo as the god of poetry or "song." Jonson makes the same distinction in his elegy on Shakespeare: "When like *Apollo* he came forth to warme / Our eares, or like a *Mercury* to charme!" (Jonson, VIII, 392). In "Mercury Versus Apollo: A Reading of *Love's Labor's Lost*," *SQ*, XXVI (1975), Malcolm Evans attempts to explain the famous line by tracing the Renaissance tradition of these two mythological figures, and he shows how each stands for a dominant theme in the play. Oddly enough, however, Evans only briefly considers the final songs, which are surely the "songs of Apollo" (though the phrase has a much broader reference as well).

[13] Two important new articles on the play were published in

Shakespeare Studies, VII (1974) as I completed my own study. Each makes suggestive comments about the songs. In "The Pattern of *Love's Labour's Lost*" (pp. 25–53), S. K. Heninger, Jr. observes that in the final song "all pairs of extremes are reconciled in unified nature. When seen in this largest possible frame, the song presents the totality of human life, bringing together the two extremes of optimism and despair. This reconciliation of opposites is the condition necessary for stability, for order despite mutability" (p. 33). Heninger also notices the frequent use of the figure of antithesis in the play (p. 46). In "The Function of the Songs at the End of *Love's Labour's Lost*" (pp. 55–64), Robert G. Hunter describes two opposed ideas of time which correspond with the division I make in this chapter. Hunter calls them "Lenten," or "rectilinear," and "Carnival," or "circular" (p. 57). He interprets the entire play in terms of these concepts, arguing that at the end of the play "The young men's Carnival love must prove itself capable of eternity by enduring for a bit in Lenten time" (p. 61). Hunter concludes, like Heninger, that the final songs assert a balance: "The dialogue of the owl and the cuckoo does not deny the truth of this apprehension of [Lenten] time. It does deny, by its existence, that the Lenten view is the whole truth. . . . The resolution which Shakespeare is attempting to engineer for the conflict in *Love's Labour's Lost* is not a victory for one side or the other. Rather he is trying to create an alliance that will combine the seemingly irreconcilable strengths of both" (p. 63). Although I disagree with both Heninger and Hunter in interpreting various details, their basic view of the songs as reconciling opposites is the same as mine. I find Hunter's summary especially convincing.

APPENDIX A

[1] For background on the Worthies, see *The Parlement of the Thre Ages*, ed. Israel Gollancz (London: Nichols & Sons, 1897); J. H. Roberts, "The Nine Worthies," *MP*, XIX (1921–2), 297–305; Thomas F. Crawley, "*Love's Labour's Lost* and the Pageant of the Nine Worthies," Diss. Nebraska 1969; L. D. Stratton, "The Nine Worthies," *Ashland Studies in Shakespeare* (Ashland, Ore.: Institute of Renaissance Studies, 1956), 67–97; the *Arden* note at V.i.113; and the *Variorum* notes, pp. 282–4.

² William Caxton, *The Prologues and Epilogues of William Caxton*, ed. W.J.B. Crotch (London: Early English Text Society, 1928), p. 92.

³ G. C. Moore Smith, ed., *Gabriel Harvey's Marginalia* (Stratford-upon-Avon: Shakespeare Head Press, 1913), p. 151.

⁴ John Gower, *The English Works of John Gower*, ed. G. C. Macaulay (London: Early English Text Society, 1900–01), II, 489.

⁵ John Lydgate, *The Assembly of Gods*, ed. O. L. Triggs (Chicago: Early English Text Society, 1895), ll. 463–78 (p. 15).

⁶ Stephen Hawes, *The Pastime of Pleasure*, ed. William E. Mead (London: Early English Text Society, 1928), ll. 5505–6.

⁷ Quoted in Stratton, p. 90.

⁸ Thomas Middleton, *Works*, ed. A. H. Bullen (London: J. C. Nimmo, 1885–6), VII, 164–9.

⁹ The *Arden* editor errs in his note at V.i.113 when he says that Guy was the standard ninth Worthy, rather than Godfrey.

¹⁰ Stratton, p. 70.

¹¹ Johan Huizinga, *The Waning of the Middle Ages* (London: Edward Arnold, 1955), p. 61.

¹² John G. Nichols, ed., *The Chronicle of Queen Jane and of Two Years of Queen Mary* (London: Camden Society, 1850), p. 79.

¹³ Alice S. Venezky, *Pageantry on the Shakespearean Stage* (New York: Twayne Publishers, 1951), p. 108.

¹⁴ Venezky, pp. 104–5.

¹⁵ Huizinga, pp. 301, 61.

¹⁶ Beaumont and Fletcher, *Works*, ed. A. R. Waller (Cambridge: Cambridge Univ. Press, 1905–12), VI, 384. Cf. also the allusions in *The Prophetess*, V, 369, and in *Thierry and Theodoret*, X, 29.

¹⁷ Miguel de Cervantes, *The Adventures of Don Quixote*, trans. J. M. Cohen (Baltimore: Penguin Books, 1967), I, v. Cf. also I, xx.

Appendix B

¹ For general background on Hercules, see G. Karl Galinsky, *The Herakles Theme: The Adaptation of the Hero in Literature from Homer to the Twentieth Century* (Oxford: Basil Black-

well, 1972); E. M. Waith, *The Herculean Hero* (New York: Columbia Univ. Press, 1962); Richard Knowles, "Myth and Type in *As You Like It*," *ELH*, 33 (1966), 1–22; Erwin Panofsky, *Hercules am Scheidewege, Studien der Bibliothex Warburg 18* (Leipzig, 1930); Rolf Soellner, "The Madness of Herakles and the Elizabethans," *Comp. Lit.*, 10 (1958), 309–24; and in *The Landscape of the Mind* (Oxford: Clarendon Press, 1969), Richard Cody includes a discussion of Hercules in his chapter on *Love's Labour's Lost*. Cody concludes: "To an audience aware that a court pastoral is in progress, Ferdinand's opening speech plainly rehearses the pose of Hercules *in bivio*. And plainly his one-sided version of it will never do. No self-respecting prince, no Platonizing academic, could regard the claims of books and ladies' eyes as alternate ways to 'living art,' the *ars vivendi* of the Stoics. The only royal way to the good life is to have it all ways" (p. 108).

² K. M. Lea, *Italian Popular Comedy* (New York: Russell & Russell, 1962), II, 406–7. See also E. K. Chambers, *William Shakespeare. A Study of Facts and Problems* (Oxford: Clarendon Press, 1930), II, 90 and I, 152.

³ Galinsky, pp. 201–212; Waith, pp. 40–51.

⁴ Galinsky, pp. 222–4; Waith, p. 65. Cf. Jonson's reference to the "French Hercules" in *Volpone*, IV.iv.22 (Jonson, V, 98).

⁵ Thomas Wilson, *The Arte of Rhetorique (1553)* (Gainesville, Fla.: Scholars' Facsimiles & Reprints, 1962), pp. 10–11.

⁶ Galinsky, p. 193; Waith, p. 212, n. 11.

⁷ Thomas Heywood, *Dramatic Works* (New York: Russell & Russell, 1964), III, 183.

⁸ See especially Panofsky's study.

⁹ Thomas Heywood, *An Apology for Actors* (London: Shakespeare Society Reprint, 1841), p. 21.

¹⁰ Wilson, p. 221.

¹¹ Quoted in *Ben Jonson: The Complete Masques*, ed. Stephen Orgel (New Haven: Yale Univ. Press, 1969), p. 490.

¹² Sir Walter Ralegh, *Works* (New York: Burt Franklin, orig. pub. 1829), II, 167.

¹³ Waith, p. 40.

¹⁴ Also cf. Kitely in *Every Man In His Humour*: "Againe, what earthie spirit but will attempt / To taste the fruit of beauties golden tree, / When leaden sleepe seales up the Dragons eyes?" (Jonson, III, 346).

Index

Characters, scenes, and speeches from the play are listed under *Love's Labour's Lost*; figures of speech are listed under Stylistic Devices.

Horace, 122
Hoskins, John, 21, 43, 48, 58, 259n.
Huizinga, Johan, 233
Hunter, G. K., 170
Hunter, Robert G., 269n.

Imitation, 215; discussion, 121–131

Johnson, Richard, 233
Johnson, Samuel, 6, 39
Jones, R. F., 62
Jonson, Ben, 37, 41, 42, 103, 123, 183, 237, 263n., 264n., 268n., 271n.
Juvenal, 18, 55

King, Arthur H., 61

Language, discussion, 11–64; as substitute for plot, 7; central concern of play, 11, 22; Hebrew as original language, 24; antithetical structures, 59–60, 169; eloquence, 40, 92–93, 177, 237; liberation vs. judgment, 28, 57, 63–64, 72; euphuism, 25, 60, 258n.; garment of style, 176–182, 188–189; *ut pictura poesis*, 182–189; instability of, 27, 155; creation *ex nihilo*, 35–36, 95, 159; oral vs. written speech, 23–24; link with masks, 79; schemes vs. tropes, 57–58, 60–61; signs and referents, 75–76, 80; solipsism, 24, 27, 44, 51, 125, 142; words and things (*res et verba*), 36, 61–62. *See also* Decorum, Names and Naming, Stylistic Devices
Lea, K. M., 236
Lennam, Trevor, 260n.
Lever, J. W., 102–103, 221

Levin, Harry, 257n.
"Living art," 199, 204, 226
Longuyon, Jacques de, 229
"Love," 159–165
Love's Labour's Lost: GENERAL
Sources, 5; texts, 5–6; topical allegory, 5; review of criticism, 5–8; traditional objections, 6–7; standard interpretation, 9; structure, 167–174
Love's Labour's Lost: SCENES AND SPEECHES
—Deer-shooting scene (IV.i), discussion, 91–92
—Masque of Muscovites (V.ii), discussion, 72–82; circles of awareness, 74; use of masks, 74–75, 78–79; Boyet as presenter, 79–80
—Pageant of the Nine Worthies (V.ii), 18–19; discussion, 82–88; decorum, 83–85; verisimilitude, 85; no authorial commentator, 87. *See also* Nine Worthies
—Promethean Fire speech (IV.iii), 59–60, 106; discussion, 148–153; Petrarchan elements, 150–151
—Final songs (V.ii), 10, 24, 131, 202, 204; discussion, 205–226; pastoralism, 217–218; names of flowers, 219–220; names of characters, 221; double grammar, 221–222; syntax, 214, 222; debate structure, 170–173
—Self-conscious ending, 202–204, 214, 225–226
—Sonnet-reading scene (IV.iii), discussion, 66–72; verisimilitude, 66; concentric circles, 67–70; Berowne as commentator, 69–72

Library of Congress Cataloging in Publication Data

Carroll, William C. 1945–
    The great feast of language.

    Originally presented as the author's thesis, Yale.
    Includes bibliographies and index.
    1. Shakespeare, William, 1564–1616.   Love's labour's
lost.   I. Title.
PR2822.C3 1976   822.3'3   76-3249
ISBN 0-691-06309-5